RUMORS

AND

RUMOR CONTROL

LEA's Communication Series

Jennings Bryant / Dolf Zillmann, General Editors

For a complete list of titles in LEA's Communication Series, please contact Lawrence Erlbaum Associates, Publishers at www.erlbaum.com

RUMORS

AND

RUMOR CONTROL

A Manager's Guide
to Understanding
and Combatting Rumors

Allan J. Kimmel
ESCP-EAP, European School of Management

LAWRENCE ERLBAUM ASSOCIATES, PUBLISHERS
2004   Mahwah, New Jersey   London

Lawrence Erlbaum Associates, Inc., Publishers
10 Industrial Avenue
Mahwah, New Jersey 07430

Cover design by Sean Sciarrone

Library of Congress Cataloging-in-Publication Data

Kimmel, Allan J.
Rumors and rumor control : a manager's guide to understanding and
combatting rumors / Allan J. Kimmel.
    p. cm.
Includes bibliographical references and index.
ISBN 0-8058-3875-9 (cloth : alk. paper)
ISBN 0-8058-3876-7 (pbk. : alk. paper)
1. Communication in management. 2. Rumor. 3. Crisis management.
    I. Title.
HD30.3.K55   2003
659.2—dc21   2003044095
                                                          CIP

Books published by Lawrence Erlbaum Associates are printed on acid-free
paper, and their bindings are chosen for strength and durability.

Printed in the United States of America
10 9 8 7 6 5 4 3 2 1

This book is dedicated
to my father, Donald Kimmel,
and to the memory
of my mother, Helen Kimmel.

Contents

Preface

Whatever words we utter should be chosen with care for people will hear them and be influenced by them for good or ill.
—Siddhartha Gomo or Buddha

In this new millennium, the expression *information age* has been used so frequently to describe the modern era that to cite it here may be seen as belaboring the obvious. Yet, what better terminology to characterize an era in which newly emergent technologies allow us to communicate with one another with far greater facility than at any other time in history? Unlike previous periods, we are now as likely to exchange information with total strangers as with people we know. The information available to each of us at any particular time has also expanded exponentially over the years. As Richard Saul Wurman (1989) pointedly observed in his book *Information Anxiety,* "a weekday edition of *The New York Times* contains more information than the average person was likely to come across in a lifetime in seventeenth-century England" (p. 32). This is perhaps nowhere more evident than in the business world. If you were to look at a Reuter's financial market screen for 10 minutes, you would see 10 times the information you would ever need.

In this context, with any desired bit of information instantaneously available with a click of a computer mouse, we might expect that rumors, which traditionally have flourished during periods of news blackouts and information famines, would be a thing of the past. Ironically, the opposite seems to be the case. In contemporary society, rumors circulate like the air we breathe; more and more, they seem to arise not from a lack of information, but within a context of information overload. This apparent contradiction can be traced in large part to the public's seemingly insatiable need to know. As demands for greater access to news and instantaneous communication continue to grow, the reliability of any one piece of information has become that much more difficult to assess. Indeed, the veracity of much publicly circulating information has become progressively more suspect as the capacity for its rapid and widespread flow has expanded. In many cases we do not know whether the facts have been verified and often we do not even know where the information originated. Lacking the identity of the true source, we are left with the thorny task of discriminating reality from fiction, truth from nontruth, and fact from rumor.

With respect to the questionable truthfulness of information, the stakes are perhaps nowhere higher than in the contemporary business world. At no other time have rumors represented such an imposing competitor in the marketplace of information exchange. Rumors can tear at the heart and soul of a business and the fight to control them ultimately engages most managers at one time or another. Given that there are alternative explanations for the evolution and spread of rumors, in addition to the complex dynamics of the rumor process, it would be naive to expect that one approach to rumor control would be feasible in all situations. In fact, most rumor specialists advocate the use of multiple rumor control tactics within any business setting to optimize the chances that rumors will be identified and addressed early, before they manage to wreak much damage.

Although it is essential that each company formulate an approach for dealing with the rumor problem, there is no foolproof plan for preventing or neutralizing rumors that can guarantee success for different kinds of companies or varying circumstances. Although the stakes clearly are on a smaller scale, the fight against commercial rumors shares much in common with the ongoing international war against terrorism. In both cases, the specific enemy and timing of the strike are not known until it is too late to avoid potentially dire consequences. Even the strongest prevention efforts cannot successfully ward off every single blow. Yet there are measures that can be taken to reduce the likelihood of attack and the severity of damage inflicted once the battle has been joined.

When I first set out to write this book, I had two objectives in mind: (a) to shed light on the often perplexing phenomenon of rumor by integrating disparate approaches from the behavioral sciences, marketing, and communication fields; and (b) to offer something of a blueprint for going about the formidable tasks of attempting to prevent and neutralize rumors in business contexts. In essence, these objectives reflect the two faces of this book, one of which is theoretical and the other applied. Social psychologist William McGuire (1965) once adroitly commented that application without regard to theory is "as inelegant and inefficient as trying to push a piece of cooked spaghetti across the table from the back end" (p. 139). Similarly, we can say that efforts to cope with the rumor problem in the marketplace and workplace without an appreciation of what has been learned to date about the multifaceted and elusive nature of hearsay are ultimately doomed to failure. With these dual goals in mind (one theoretical, the other applied), I am hoping that this book will be of equal interest to academics and managers in a wide range of professional contexts.

The world is a much different place now than it was when this book was first conceived. Events such as the September 11 terrorist attacks in the United States and the collapse of Enron have done little to deflate the problem of marketplace rumors. On the contrary, by raising public anxieties, uncertainty, and skepticism, these events have served to exacerbate the very forces that underlie the generation and spread of rumors. The challenges for product and brand managers, public relations specialists, employers, and behavioral scientists have never been greater. Companies must be prepared to ward off competing campaigns of misinformation by revealing rather than concealing the truth, reducing uncertainties, and proactively establishing and maintaining trust among their various publics. It is hoped that this book can serve as one tool toward achieving such daunting tasks.

My interest in the psychology of hearsay dates back to my early days as a graduate student at Temple University. It was there that I met and began to work with one of the key crusaders in the investigation of rumor, Ralph Rosnow, who one September afternoon in 1976 invited me to contribute an article about gossip for a special issue of the *Journal of Communication* he was editing. Little did I realize at that early stage in my professional career (my first month in graduate school!) that I was about to embark on a fascinating journey that would culminate in the writing of this book. It now has been more than 25 years since that article (coauthored with Jack Levin) was published and I have remained actively engaged in the study of rumor ever since.

—*Allan J. Kimmel*
Paris, France

ACKNOWLEDGMENTS

In one way or another, the ideas and views presented in this volume were strongly influenced by several colleagues with whom I have crossed paths over the years as we mutually pursued the elusive truths about rumors, marketplace communication, and consumer behavior. Foremost among these individuals are Fredrick Koenig (Tulane University), Jack Levin (Northeastern University), Elyette Roux (ESSEC), Michael Koller (Phillips University Marburg), Robert Keefer (Mount Saint Mary's College), Elisabeth Tissier-Desbordes (ESCP-EAP), and, especially, Ralph L. Rosnow (Temple University). I also am indebted to the LEA editorial staff for their faith in this project and their painstaking efforts to bring the book to fruition. Most importantly, I thank my wife, Marie-Ange, for her continued patience, unflagging support, and divine inspiration.

Part I

Understanding Rumors and Rumor Transmission

Rumour is a pipe
Blown by surmises, jealousies, conjectures
And of so easy and so plain a stop
That the blunt monster with uncounted heads,
The still-discordant wavering multitude,
Can play upon it ....

—William Shakespeare, *Henry IV*

CHAPTER ONE

Introduction:
Identifying Rumors and Related
Forms of Communication

Rumor. Think about this word. Say it out loud. Rumor. It has such ugly connotations, doesn't it? A statement that cannot be proved or disproved. Rumor. Rhymes with tumor.

—La Monica (1999a)

Whether one chooses to equate it with a malignant growth, a poisonous vapor, or an information virus, the underlying message is clear: Rumor spreads rapidly, is difficult to control, is invisible yet nearly impossible to ignore, and can have damaging and perhaps even deadly consequences. We know it is probably bad for us, and we know it can hurt those around us, but we often find it hard to resist becoming active participants in the rumor-spreading process.

Rumors have been a basic element of human interaction for as long as people have had questions about their social environment. Yet, despite its obvious negative connotations, a rumor has the capacity to satisfy certain fundamental personal and social needs, and in this sense can be beneficial to those who participate in its transmission. To a great extent, rumors are communicated as an effort after meaning; in other words, they help people make sense of what is going on around them. Rumormongering is a way of trying to explain what is happening and why—whether it be a crime in the neighborhood, a political crisis, or a change in a company's management. Spreading rumors becomes a means by which people try to get the facts, to obtain enough information so that it reduces their psychological discomfort and relieves their fears.

RUMORS IN THE MARKETPLACE

Despite the positive aspects of rumors, in the business environment, unfounded assertions and speculation can be especially potent and undeniably

3

dangerous. In fact, for many contemporary managers, rumors often represent an imposing competitor in the marketplace of information exchange. Virtually every type of company is plagued from time to time by the spread of unverified stories and questionable information about its operations. Most of these stories are relatively harmless, drawing little serious attention and quickly fading away before developing into something more formidable. However, sometimes the situation festers and takes on a life of its own, and what may have started out as a seemingly innocuous assertion about some aspect of the company's activities evolves into a full-blown whispering campaign that spreads quickly and uncontrollably throughout the company's various publics. In such cases, rumors can strike at the very heart and soul of a business. They can severely damage company and brand images, undermine corporate credibility, stimulate consumer boycotts, adversely affect employee job performance and satisfaction, and have far-reaching effects on financial markets. Although most rumors have a discernible life cycle, contemporary communication media have the potential to speed up the process dramatically—in fact, some rumors cause damage overnight and disappear immediately; others are more persistent and can have insidious effects over the long term, appearing and reappearing along with changes in the social or psychological climate.

Many managers have learned the hard way that a failure to react quickly and effectively to false rumors can have devastating consequences. This is something that the corporate executives and brand managers at Procter & Gamble (P&G), one of the world's most successful consumer goods manufacturers, are all too well aware of. P&G has been the target of negative rumor campaigns off and on over the past two decades, and there is little reason to expect that the trouble will not reemerge again in the future. The P&G case represents one of the longest, most widely publicized, and most expensive confrontations with rumor in the consumer marketplace. Accordingly, it can serve as a useful starting point in efforts to fulfill the basic objectives of this volume: to dissect the nature of rumor, understand its dynamics, and develop strategies for coping with it. Following a detailed description of the P&G story and some related examples, the remainder of this introductory chapter tackles the thorny and often elusive issue of what a rumor is, identifying its characteristics and properties, and distinguishing the concept from related forms of communication with which it is often confused.

Procter & Gamble and the Man in the Moon

The beginning of trouble for P&G has been traced back to early 1979, when rumors began to circulate that the company was secretly controlled by the Reverend Sun Myung Moon's Unification Church (so-called Moonies). As we consider in greater detail later, it typically is very difficult to pinpoint the exact origins of a rumor and the P&G case is no exception. Nonetheless, it has been suggested that the onset of the Moonies rumors could have had something to do with the Unification Church's purchase of property in Florida (Koenig, 1985). This action caused a general sense of uneasiness in the local population that may have been transferred back to the American Midwest by tourists who spent their winter holidays in the South. The strange image of the man in the moon in P&G's logotype, which appeared on more than 70 household products at the time, may have served to link the company and the church for anxious consumers (see Fig. 1.1).

The Moonie rumors first became apparent to P&G officials when the company's Public Affairs Division received inquiries from a handful of reporters and consumers in Florida about ownership by the Unification Church (Koenig, 1985). Shortly thereafter, telephone calls from around the country began to trickle in to the Consumer Services Department, whose toll-free telephone number was printed on every product package. In each case, the callers said that they had heard that the company had been acquired by the followers of the Reverend Sun Myung Moon. By the end of 1980, hundreds of telephone calls, cards, and letters were arriving each month, compelling the company to deny the allegations by writing to news organizations in the states that apparently were most affected. Eventually, however, many of the inquiries began to focus on P&G's involvement with witchcraft and the devil, with a growing number alleging that the company's century-old trademark, a circle with a design depicting the man in the moon and 13 stars representing the original American colonies, was a symbol of Satanism. The situation appeared to have died down following P&G's unequivocal denials, until late 1981 when a deluge of Satanic-related queries suddenly beset the company. During December 1981 alone, 1,152 inquiries were received, mainly from the West Coast (Salmans, 1982). At that time, the Moonie ownership rumors appeared to fade away as the Satanism rumors became more specific and elaborate,

FIG. 1.1. Procter & Gamble's moon and stars logo. Reprinted with permission of The Procter & Gamble Company.

quickly spreading across the country. Many callers reported hearing that a company executive (often identified as the "owner") had appeared on a nationally popular television program and admitted a Faustian pact with the devil to gain success for the company. Interestingly, a nearly identical story had circulated about the McDonald's Corporation a few years earlier.

It was now becoming apparent that what had started out as a more or less localized story about company ownership was rapidly evolving into a national crisis situation for P&G. This case predates the Internet, but a formidable word-of-mouth network was constructed through the use of more traditional media, including newsletters, circulars, and face-to-face interactions. Anonymous fliers, usually misspelling the company's name, began to appear at supermarkets, alleging that the company was donating 10% of its earnings to the Church of Satan and urging shoppers to boycott P&G products. For example, in one anonymous flier, the call to boycott took the following form: "Do you realize, that if all the Christians in the World would stop buying Proctor and Gamble [sic] Products this Company would soon be out of business?" (Such urgings for consumers to boycott a company at the center of a rumor-generated controversy are frequent; see Box 1.1). There were reports that the ministers of some small fundamentalist churches were also attacking the company and urging parishioners to boycott its products. Church newsletters distributed throughout the Southeast Bible Belt, Texas, and Oklahoma reiterated the Satanism claims, detailing the alleged television program and eventually adding a new twist regarding the P&G logo. The fliers described how the logo included the figure "666"—the sign of the Beast according to the Book of Revelation. This additional indication of devil worship was apparent when the 13 stars were connected and also could be seen in the curls of the man in the moon's beard when the logo was held up to a mirror (see Fig. 1.2). By the spring of 1982, P&G was receiving 12,000 queries monthly about the devil rumors and there was little to encourage the company that the rumors would soon go away on their own.

Coping: Procter & Gamble Fights Back

In an attempt to cope with a growing crisis that threatened the company's strong leadership position in several product categories, P&G officials initially feared that going public to fight the rumors would add fuel to the fire and bring the stories to the attention of people who were not already aware of them. There is nothing unusual about this concern—it is a typical reaction of many companies that are put in the position of dealing with hearsay about their operations or marketplace offerings. After a second mailing to news organizations on the West Coast had little apparent impact, and as there was little to suggest that the Satanism rumors would die a natural death, P&G's president enlisted the cooperation of conservative religious leaders, including

---

Box 1.1.   Marketplace Rumors and Consumer Boycotts:
From "Xeroxlore" to "Cyberlore"

A number of commercial rumors that have plagued well-known consumer products companies have been accompanied by calls for a consumer protest or boycott of products and brands (cf. Friedman, 1999). Such demands typically are targeted at companies that raise concerns or fears within certain groups about unethical business practices or unsafe product offerings (so-called conspiracy or contamination rumors; see chap. 2), and traditionally have been spread through the use of anonymous, printed leaflets and fliers. In the past, such media represented one of the most efficient mechanisms for conveying a lot of information. For example, in the case of the P&G rumors, leaflets and fliers were required to list all of the company's many products and brands so that they could be boycotted (Kapferer, 1990). Further, in contrast to rumors that are transmitted orally through word-of-mouth, those that appear in printed form often seem more authoritative and credible, especially when they are accompanied by the signatures of influential people. According to Kapferer (1990), the tendency for the individuals involved in the rumor-spreading process to simply photocopy and distribute large numbers of leaflets in mailboxes or public settings has led to the emergence of a category of rumors called "Xeroxlore."

In recent years, with the emergence of the Internet, a new form of Xeroxlore has begun to take shape in cyberspace. Rather than engaging in the tedious task of physically providing hundreds of consumers with photocopied rumor leaflets, a word-processed version of the flier can now be sent out to thousands of e-mail boxes within a few minutes. Given the steady rise of spam (or electronic junk mail) in cyberspace, it remains to be seen whether "e-mail lore" or "cyberlore" will turn out to be as persuasive as the more traditional fliers and leaflets in adding fuel to the rumor-spreading process. A recent example of false rumors about Nike and Coca Cola and accompanying calls to boycott the companies turned up in the e-mail in-box of one of my students. Excerpts of the crudely written message appear here, with the accompanying photos:

My Dear Muslim this is Symbol Qyamat (Dooms Day). Wakeup my dear (Iyman waloo). Go through the mention below message and photograph.
BOYCOTT COCA COLA

Attention all Muslim Media's and Muslims of the World!!!!

Last year famous jew's shoe making company "NIKE" designed shoes with written ALLAH using the art of Calligraphy. Now once again they are back by using the art of calligraphy but with very internationally well known beverage product Coca Cola. In normal we read Coca Cola but actually its reversed calligraphy art and if u read it, it means "NO MOHAMMAD NO MAKKHA".

... please ask Muslim Ummah to Boycott drinking Coca Cola and should ask Company official to immediately change their monogram ...

(continued)

DO NOT DRINK !

The word Coca Cola:

If you read it from left to right (mirror orientation)
it clearly says: "NO MOHAMMAD NO MEKKAH"
in arabic letters ➔ (لا محمد لا مكة)

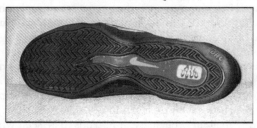

".. rank hatred has already appeared from their mouths: What
their hearts conceal is far worse .." ➔ Quran

Jerry Falwell and Billy Graham, who prepared letters strongly avowing that the company was not associated in any way with Satanism or devil worship. The letters were mailed to 48,000 Southern churches, but appeared to have little effect in killing off the rumors. By June 1982 more than 15,000 monthly queries were reaching the company about the trademark (Salmans, 1982).

On July 1 P&G executives decided to fight fire with fire by publicly attacking the rumors with an all-out crisis management offensive. The company's

Rumored symbolism

Connected to one another, the stars form the number 666, a symbol of the Antichrist. Curls in the "sorcerer's" beard also form 666 when the logo is held up to a mirror.

P&G's explanation

The man-in-the-moon was "a popular decorative fancy" adopted in an early version of the logo in 1859. The 13 stars represent the original United States colonies.

FIG. 1.2. Alleged references to Satan in the P&G logo. Source: *Rumor in the Marketplace,* Fredrick Koenig. Copyright © 1985 by Auburn House Publishing Company. Reproduced with permission of Greenwood Publishing Group, Inc., Westport, CT.

public relations department, advised to forget earlier cautions, mounted a three-pronged attack consisting of mass mailings to churches, denials to the media, and lawsuits against persons known to be spreading the rumors. The litigation was intended as a forceful means of generating publicity (Salmans, 1982). Underlying this offensive were the goals of reaching as many people as possible with the antirumor campaign as many times as possible (called *reach and frequency* in the advertising trade). It was believed that this approach would curtail the spread of the false, malicious rumors and forestall their future reappearance. As with most public relations campaigns, P&G also hoped to influence public opinion to accomplish the broader objective of protecting the company's reputation and that of its many products (see Box 1.2).

As a result of this aggressive strategy, calls about the rumors quickly fell off by half and it appeared that the rumors were on the way to being successfully quashed. The lawsuits filed against seven individuals believed to have spread the rumors were especially effective in generating a flurry of publicity and calling attention to the company's seriousness in combatting the whispering campaign. The initial lawsuits, which were filed against distributors of competing household products and a lay minister, all were resolved out of court when the defendants publicly apologized and stated that the rumors were untrue.

By the spring of 1983, the situation seemed to have calmed down, but as P&G soon learned, its battle against rumors was hardly over. As this case illus-

Box 1.2. The Public Relations Transfer Process

As the term suggests, *public relations* (PR) is a mass-promotion technique that involves a company's attempts to develop good relations with its various publics by obtaining favorable publicity, building a good corporate image, and managing any unfavorable events or crises that threaten its reputation or corporate earnings (Kotler, Armstrong, Saunders, & Wong, 1999). When unfounded, negative rumors about a company's operations, products, or services begin to receive widespread attention, the situation can become a PR nightmare that threatens to rapidly spiral out of control. The negative publicity generated by increasing media attention to the story typically requires some sort of carefully managed response by the company concerned.

PR experts Jefkins and Yadin (1998) developed a simple conceptualization of the PR process that is quite useful to our understanding of the important tasks at hand when a firm is confronted by rumors and forced to respond to them. In their *public relations transfer process*, Jefkins and Yadin suggested that the classic PR situation requires the conversion of four negative states into four positive ones. The basic aim of this transfer process—in fact, the principal aim of PR—is the creation of understanding, which comes about from knowledge provided through the company's PR efforts. In short, a company or its specific marketplace offerings (e.g., a brand, an advertising campaign, a sales promotion, a trademark design, a retail outlet) may be subject to one or more of the negative states depicted in the left box of the model.

Negative   Positive

Hostility	Sympathy
Prejudice	Acceptance
Apathy	Interest
Ignorance	Knowledge

The PR transfer process: Knowledge leads to understanding (Jefkins & Yadin, 1998; Reprinted with permission of Pearson Education Limited).

For example, we might imagine that members of certain religious groups, on hearing of P&G's alleged relationship with Satan, would be outraged by the company's practices. This hostility, which might be accompanied by some of the other negative attitudes in the box (e.g., prejudice and ignorance), could be expected to lead to a variety of actions that would be potentially harmful to the company, such as the boycotting of its products, vandalism toward the firm, and the repetition of malicious rumors. P&G's PR challenge would be to launch a communication campaign to successfully convert the hostility into sympathy, such as by convincing consumers that the company is the innocent victim of clearly false and unfair rumors. (See chaps. 5 and 6 for more details about how this conversion could be accomplished.)

trates, some rumors never die, and instead periodically return to do further damage. This is precisely what happened with the Satan rumors, which reappeared with rejuvenated force in late October 1984. At that time there was a network radio news report that the company was again being victimized, and the problem was reiterated the next day in the *Wall Street Journal*. According to a front-page story in that week's *Advertising Age*, queries about the Satan connection had increased to about 3,000 in October. Although the problem did not appear to be as widespread as it had been 2 years earlier, this time a different network of rumor transmitters seemed to be involved. P&G responded locally to outbreaks of the rumor in areas of the country where Catholic nuns and priests were putting notices in newsletters and church bulletins urging people to boycott the company's products. Apparently, these members of the Catholic clergy had not been reached by the national media campaign that had been launched 1 year earlier.

Following another serious flare-up of the Satan rumor across several mid-Atlantic states in early 1985, P&G announced that it would be removing the moon-and-stars trademark from its product packages as each package underwent routine redesign. It was believed that the removal of the trademark, in use since 1850, would help counter the belief that it represented a symbol of Satanism. At the time of the announcement, a company spokesperson explained, "The bottom line is the move is being made because there appears to be little advantage to having the trademark on product packages. At the same time, it will remove one part of those false and malicious stories" ("P.&G. Drops Logo," 1985, p. D1).

During previous outbreaks of the Satanism and Moonie rumors, P&G had firmly rejected suggestions that it simply remove the controversial symbol from its packages. This decision was a contentious one, perhaps bolstering the suspicions of some consumers. However, internal company research had revealed that customers generally did not notice the trademark on product packages and assigned little meaning to it ("P.&G. Drops Logo," 1985). Indeed, on some products, the trademark had been reduced for design purposes to only one-eighth of an inch in diameter. Also, one must bear in mind that the moon-and-stars symbol was a readily identifiable company logo that had been associated with P&G's numerous products for more than 100 years (see Fig. 1.3), including such well-known brands as Crest toothpaste, Tide laundry detergent, Ivory soap, and Pampers disposable diapers. At the time of its adoption, the man in the moon profile was a fad, much like the happy face of more contemporary times, and the company founders took a liking to it. In retrospect, although it can be argued that the removal of the logotype should have been accomplished much earlier, this represented a tough decision for the company. Ultimately, the company settled for a compromise, eliminating the logo from its product packages while maintaining its use on corporate letterheads and publications (Wilcox, Ault, & Agee, 1989).

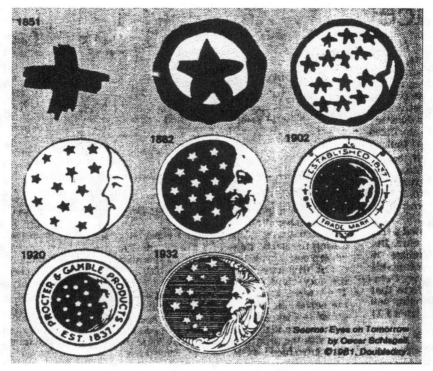

FIG. 1.3. Evolution of the Procter & Gamble logo. Reprinted with permission of the Procter & Gamble Company.

For the next 10 years, the combination of antirumor strategies implemented by P&G appeared finally to succeed in pushing the rumors that plagued the company for so long into the background, although not killing them entirely. During that time, there apparently was a small but persistent group of Americans who still believed that P&G was linked with the devil and who periodically circulated poorly copied fliers. The company continued to receive up to 20 calls per day about the Satanic rumors and initiated additional lawsuits, one against a Kansas couple who worked as distributors for Amway, a P&G competitor, which resulted in a $75,000 judgment ("Trade Mark of the Devil," 2000). In 1991 the elements rumored to represent the Satanic number 666 were removed from the trademark.

The P&G rumors have made more than one major comeback in recent years, most notably in 1994 and 1999. In each case, the stir was precipitated by the recycled tale alleging that the company president had announced on a popular television program that he was a Satanist and his company associated with the Church of Satan. One added twist to the 1994 version was the assertion that a Satanic ram's horn symbol would start appearing on the company's products, bearing the number 666 ("Trade Mark of the Devil," 2000). Over the course of its rumor troubles, P&G has filed 15 lawsuits against individuals identified as making false and defamatory statements linking the company to Satanism, 6 of which have been initiated against Amway distributors. Try as they might to kill the rumors, they invariably spring to life again.

The Consequences: Tallying the Damages

Just who was responsible for the P&G rumors? Although it might be suspected that rival companies were behind the rumor campaigns launched against P&G, no evidence has ever emerged suggesting that competitors pushed their circulation or that the campaigns were economically inspired (Salmans, 1982; "Trade Mark of the Devil," 2000). Despite the involvement of some overexuberant Amway distributors in the rekindling and spreading of the rumors, much of the problem appears to have come from the activities of religious groups unhappy about P&G's sponsorship of controversial television programs. In fact, an Amway spokesperson emphasized that his company had "bent over backwards to help Procter & Gamble stop this rumor," and added that P&G had handled the problem badly from the start from a public relations perspective, allowing the Satanism rumors to spread far and wide (Franks, 1999). In Chapter 2 we consider some other plausible explanations for the rumors and why they have been so difficult to eliminate completely. However, before leaving the P&G case, it is instructive to consider the extent of the impact of the rumors on the company.

As is often the case, the costs and effects of a rumor on a business enterprise are difficult to gauge accurately. It goes without saying that unfounded rumors have been a major source of irritation for P&G officials and have entailed considerable unanticipated expenses. By the time the decision was made to remove the trademark from product packages, a company spokesperson estimated that $100,000 had been spent fighting the Satanism rumors ("P.&G. Drops Logo," 1985). Resources were diverted in various ways to deal with the problem, including the hiring of additional staff to respond to consumer letters and telephone calls. The lawsuits, which represented an additional expense in terms of time and money, also posed a significant risk, because a lost case would considerably damage the image of the company. Finally, it is impossible to assess to what extent P&G sales were affected by consumers who heeded the various calls to boycott its products. However, one estimate of the impact on purchasing was obtained during an early point in the crisis by the SRI Research Center, which was commissioned by the publication *Advertising Age* to conduct a nationwide survey ("Procter & Gamble Rumor," 1982). SRI obtained the responses of more than 1,200 American adults during the summer of 1982 and found that of those who believed the Satanism rumors or were unsure about their veracity, 17% said they were reducing their purchases of P&G products. Of those who were aware of the rumors, only 5% (or 1.6% of all respondents) claimed to be buying fewer products, and 1% said they were buying more. The authors of the survey concluded that the rumors did not seem to be having much of an adverse impact on sales, a point further supported by the finding that 79% of the people surveyed could not identify any of P&G's products. Of course, for company officials, any loss of sales attributed to factors outside the spheres of economic influences or product integrity was no doubt a matter of serious concern.

Marketplace Rumors: Some Additional Examples

Like P&G, numerous other corporations have had to fight unfounded rumors in the consumer marketplace. In fact, the major corporation that has not been targeted by external rumors of one sort or another is clearly an exception in the contemporary business environment. As mentioned earlier, the McDonald's restaurant chain also had to fight off a rumored link to the Church of Satan a few years before P&G was victimized by the very same rumor. Some of the same elements were apparent in the McDonald's case: the reported television appearance by the company owner to publicly admit his pact with the devil, the involvement of some members of the clergy in the perpetuation of the rumor, and the numerous inquiries to the company from concerned or angry consumers. Briefly, the general strategy of McDonald's was to respond to each flare-up of the rumor locally by enlisting the support of ministers and television producers of the programs on which the company's owner actually had appeared. These respected individuals prepared letters attesting to the falsity of the rumor and to the Christian integrity of the company's owner, and verbatim transcripts of the television appearances were made available. Each time this approach was effective in putting out the fire in one part of the country, the rumor quickly reappeared elsewhere. Eventually, the story was picked up by the mass media and rapidly spread across the nation 1 year after its initial onset. However, just as the P&G Moonie accusations quickly faded when another rumor appeared, the Satanic rumor ended suddenly for McDonald's with the emergence of a potentially more damaging whispering campaign. This time the rumors concerned the contents of McDonald's hamburgers, which allegedly contained red worms to boost their protein levels.

Like the Satanic rumor, the worm allegation is another example of a false story that had been around for a while, most notably targeting Wendy's, another American hamburger chain, before moving on in 1978 to cause substantial damage for McDonald's. Company officials at McDonald's were wary of the worm rumor even before it affected their company, but were too distracted at the time fighting the Satanic rumors to take preventive action (Koenig, 1985). The specific details of the McDonald's response to the worm rumor are described in Chapter 6, but in brief the company went on the offensive immediately, issuing denials, sending out letters, and distributing press kits to franchise owners attesting to the high quality of their hamburgers' ingredients. Before long, however, the rumor had spread like wildfire across the country, with many consumers reporting that they had heard it and believed it. The McDonald's Corporation quickly began to suffer substantial losses, seriously affecting sales in certain areas that represented hotbeds of activity for the worm rumor (Esposito & Rosnow, 1983). Toward the end of the year, company officials held a national press conference during which they emphatically denied the rumor about "protein additives," and a follow-up advertising campaign reiterated the facts. Shortly thereafter, the McDonald's rumor was beaten (only to be briefly revived once again in the Philippines in 1996).

The P&G and McDonald's rumors represent two of the most noteworthy examples in the annals of commercial rumors. Both cases involved the spontaneous emergence of ultimately damaging falsehoods, although the nature and alacrity of response taken by the companies differed, with varying consequences. Although commercial rumors have been around since the turn of the 20th century, only in recent decades have they become one of the most prominent forms of rumor in circulation. A quick search of the World Wide Web typically reveals numerous marketplace rumors in circulation at any given time (see Box 1.3).

ORGANIZATIONAL GRAPEVINE RUMORS

To this point, our focus has been limited to rumors that appear in the consumer marketplace. By their very nature, such rumors represent a very public form of hearsay, whereby various mass-mediated communication channels may or may not be intentionally complicit in the transmission of an unverified story. Marketplace rumors are passed along through interpersonal and electronic networks that function outside the companies that are targeted and may be of interest even to people who are not current customers of the companies involved. By contrast, within organizations, rumors represent an everyday aspect of corporate life that is much more private in nature and far less likely to interest persons who are not members (or their friends and relatives) of the organizations themselves. Such rumors spread through a discernible communication chain known as the *grapevine*, the informal information system that flourishes in every company.

Perhaps the key aspect of the organizational grapevine is its informal nature. Unlike the formal network of communication within an organization, which involves the more structured transmission of information through channels such as memos, company newsletters, official notices and reports, and staff meetings and conferences, grapevine interactions may consist of casual conversations that take place in lunchrooms, carpools, around water coolers, through e-mail

Box 1.3. Commercial Rumors and the World Wide Web

The Internet and other emerging communication technologies are particularly well suited to serve as conduits for the spread of marketplace rumors, providing for the instantaneous transmission of unverified information to a global audience. In many cases, what often starts as a localized whispering campaign quickly expands into a nationwide (and, at times, international) spread of falsehoods as the unfounded hearsay provides the grist for Internet chat groups, discussion forums, and message board postings.

The following sampling of false rumors, which were reported on The San Fernando Valley Folklore Society's Current Urban Legends and Netlore (www.snopes.com) site during April 2000, are representative of the sorts of stories regularly circulating in cyberspace:

- The energy drink Red Bull contains a dangerous stimulant originally created by the U.S. government to keep soldiers motivated in Vietnam.
- Pantene shampoo contains an additive that, when injected, will get the user high.
- A mixture of Enfalac baby formula and dog food causes a baby's stomach to explode.
- Flesh-eating bacteria on Costa Rican bananas will ultimately kill 15,000 Americans, an "acceptable number" according to the Food and Drug Administration.
- Kentucky Fried Chicken became KFC after the government ruled that the genetically altered poultry KFC uses could no longer be called "chicken."
- The U.S. Congress or Canadian government is to impose a 5-cent surcharge per e-mail.

A comprehensive listing of links to current netlore are available on the urbanlegends.com Web site. The following marketplace-related examples were included in the listing during May 2001:

- EMI/Time Warner Merger Giveaway
- GeoCities Is Closing Down!
- Gerber Savings Bond Giveaway
- "Good Samaritan" Killer at the Mall
- Harry Potter Turns Kids to Satanism
- HIV Needles on Gas Pumps (variations include needles in movie theater seats, pay phone coin slots, and vending machines)
- Honda Car Giveaway
- KFC Uses Mutant Chickens
- McDonald's Donations to Palestinians Injured in Uprising
- Microwaved Water Explodes in Man's Face
- "Progesterex"—New Date Rape Drug
- Rat Urine on Soda Pop Cans Is Lethal

- Shampoo Cancer Warning
- Snakes Kill Child in Burger King Ball Pit
- Tommy Hilfiger Made Racist Statements on Oprah
- Toxic Sponges From P&G

messages and phone conversations, and the like (see Box 1.4). Because of its informal nature, the information that is transmitted through the grapevine tends to be undocumented and thereby susceptible to variation and interpretation. Further, there is the potential for communication among all participants in an organization and information tends to flow rapidly through the grapevine. Be-

---

Box 1.4. A Universal Water Cooler?

We have described how the Internet has become a growing force as a conduit for the emergence and spread of marketplace rumors. Now we find that much the same can be said with regard to this medium's role in the transmission and sharing of organizational grapevine content. Enter the Electronic Watercooler (www.vaultreports.com), an online network of uncensored bulletin boards for more than 800 American companies that displays office rumors, complaints about work hours and pay, and responses to job applicants' queries about salary and work life. The site, created in March 2001 by the New York employment service Vault Reports, is intended to expand globally on the age-old natural tendency for employees to engage in informal small talk about their jobs at the proverbial water cooler (Rosenberg, 1999).

During its initial period on the Internet, the Watercooler site was attracting more than 1,000 postings per week from employees of such companies as Andersen Consulting, Morgan Stanley, Dean Witter, Merrill Lynch & Co., Microsoft Corp., and P&G. Of course, transferring the company water cooler to the Internet in the form of (typically) anonymous message postings poses some potential risks to both employees and job applicants. Because of the anonymity it provides, there is nothing to prevent the posting of a misleading or outright fictional message from someone posing as a company employee or competitor. Additionally, if employers are able to determine which of their employees are conveying damaging messages, there is not much that could be done to stop the company from taking action.

According to one employment expert, the electronic version of the organizational grapevine is an imperfect equivalent that probably should not be taken too seriously. Like the bar across street from the workplace, it involves not only current company employees, but also former employees and total strangers, and there is no way to verify that the discussants have the insider information that they claim to have. Nonetheless, the concept represents a potentially useful tool for employees and job seekers with information needs that cannot be satisfied through more formal channels.

cause of these characteristics, the organizational grapevine represents a fertile breeding and testing ground for rumors.

When rumors are spread through a company's informal communication networks, their content tends to involve topics that deeply affect employees, such as job status and organizational change. Typical forms of organizational rumors are those involving turnover (e.g., a top-level manager will leave the company to join a competitor), management–union relations (e.g., employees are considering a strike action; contract talks are underway), hierarchical status (e.g., a colleague is maneuvering to win the promotion promised to someone else), job security or job quality (e.g., a production plant will close, resulting in massive layoffs; employees can expect a large end-of-year bonus), organizational change (e.g., a major restructuring), and costly errors or safety conditions (e.g., a faulty computer software program resulted in the loss of an important account; Davis, 1953, 1969; Esposito & Rosnow, 1983). Such rumors may serve a variety of functions, such as to fill information gaps, to influence decisions, to vent feelings, or to signal status or power.

Because it operates as an informal network for interpersonal speculation, the grapevine is also a conduit for the spread of more titillating organizational hearsay, such as speculation about the sexual exploits or predilections of an employee or the assertion that two coworkers are romantically involved. In this case, the hearsay is more likely to be labeled as gossip, although the distinction between rumor and gossip is often a difficult one to make, particularly when the communication spreads through the office grapevine. In one highly publicized example, the former chief executive officer (CEO) of the Bendix Corporation was said to be having an affair with the company's vice president of strategic planning. Their repeated denials only seemed to fuel the scandal, which ultimately led to the resignation of the vice president. Despite the denials, the two were married less than 2 years after the story first broke (Cole, 1985).

As suggested by the Bendix case, much hearsay information transmitted through the grapevine ultimately turns out to be true. This statement might seem somewhat surprising at first glance, given the informal nature and accelerated speed by which information flows through grapevine pathways. These characteristics of information transmission would suggest that messages become increasingly inaccurate as they are transmitted from person to person, given the lack of time any one individual may have to critically assess the message content. However, it turns out that much of the information transmitted through the grapevine ultimately turns out to be accurate. In one study of a particular company's grapevine efficiency, Walton (1961) reported that 82% of the information communicated on a single occasion was accurate. According to other estimates, more than 80% of the specific "bits" of a rumor that work their way through an organization's grapevine prove to be accurate (Arnold, 1983; Davis, 1969).

An overabundance of grapevine rumors undoubtedly can be taken as a sign of organizational disfunctioning, reflecting a loss of confidence in the company's hierarchy, excessive secrecy and fear, and political problems within the company (Kapferer, 1990). Nevertheless, as a source of highly sought information that is not forthcoming through more formal channels of communication (e.g., during closed negotiation sessions), the grapevine can actually be seen as a healthy sign that people within the organization are talking to each other. Thus, it rarely is in the best interest of company officials to attempt to completely shut down the company's internal grapevine. However, it is no less important than in the case of public marketplace rumors for companies to adopt mechanisms for managing the spread of information through organizational networks, to whatever extent possible. In the corporate setting, this is especially important during times of organizational change, when uncertainties and fears among company personnel are likely to be most acute.

Grapevine Rumors and Organizational Change

Some companies take great pains to assure that the communication of organizational change is carried out as timely and efficiently as possible to offset the emergence of potentially destructive hearsay. The importance of doing so was highlighted by a study of change in 43 organizations, which revealed that when a change effort resulted in failure, it was likely to have been caused by one of the following three reasons (Semeltzer, 1991): (a) the presence of inaccurate and negative rumors, (b) the fact that employees learned of the company's plans through outsiders, and (c) management's reliance on impersonal communication channels (e.g., memos) rather than face-to-face interactions with employees. These findings point to the fact that it is of primary importance for management to communicate effectively with its employees during times of change, rather than placing greater priority on informing the public and stockholders of its plans.

Various strategies that can be taken to effectively communicate organizational change are described in Chapter 7, along with recommendations for managing the grapevine to minimize the potential damaging effects of false rumors and misinformation. However, at this point, a brief description of the communication techniques employed by Delta Airlines during a major restructuring can serve as a useful example of how a company can offset the emergence of harmful hearsay during transitional periods.

The Delta restructuring effort, known as Leadership 7.5, began in 1994 to improve the company's standing in a rapidly changing and increasingly competitive industry. Almost from the outset, it was evident that Delta, which previously had a strong reputation for retaining its workers, would have to lay off several thousand employees. As we will see in subsequent chapters, this is just the sort of situation that fosters the emergence of organizational rumors due to the high levels of anxiety and uncertainty it entails. To counter the enormous amount of fear likely to be generated by the planned program and to establish a sense of security within its workforce, Delta's management created a detailed communication plan (Richardson & Denton, 1996). At the outset, they put into place a toll-free telephone hotline to provide current updates on the change effort and respond to employee comments and questions. Linked to the in-house company newsletter, *The Delta Newsline*, more than 6,000 calls were received on the day news of the restructuring program was presented to the employees; by the end of the week, that number had risen to more than 14,000. Further, to respond to information requests from managers and supervisors, a special communication center was established.

Another strategy employed by Delta was for management representatives to maintain direct personal contact with the company's workforce to convey the perception of openness and to further reduce any sense of insecurity. This was done by having a senior manager appear in an airplane hangar within hours of the initial restructuring announcement to provide detailed information and respond to questions in an open forum, and by arranging periodic visits by senior management at various Delta facilities around the country during the ensuing weeks. Another important aspect of the communication program was a systemwide management conference, held on the day after the announcement, during which the restructuring and related program were fully explained. A video presentation of the conference was then distributed to all personnel (Delta Air Lines, 1994).

The two elements of Delta's communication program that stand out as particularly key to its ultimate success were speed and accuracy. That is, senior company officials appeared eager to provide the workforce with as much information as possible, in the most prompt and accurate fashion possible. In situations in which employees are confronted by the possibility of a major change in their employment situation, this approach goes a long way toward restoring confidence, reducing anxiety, and maintaining trust. It also represents an effective strategy for reducing the flow of misinformation throughout the company grapevine.

DEFINING RUMOR

The foregoing discussion was intended to provide the reader with some preliminary insight into the nature of rumors and some of the various kinds of rumors that might emerge in business settings. One point that should be clear from the examples is that whether a rumor pertains to events unfolding in the marketplace or within an organization, it tends to have something to do with the need for people to know what is happening and why in situations in which they are implicated. Before we can shed greater light on the psychological and social dynamics of rumor generation and transmission, it is essential that we have a clearer understanding of what a rumor is—its characteristics and properties—and how it differs from related forms of interpersonal communication, such as gossip and news.

There is general agreement that a *rumor* is a story or statement in general circulation without confirmation or certainty as to facts (Box 1.5). Rumors are public communications, usually embellished by allegations or attributions based on circumstantial, unverified evidence, that reflect people's assumptions or suspicions about how the world works. Historically, the understanding was that rumors circulate as a function of what has been referred to as the "talk factor," or everyday word-of-mouth conversations (Wilson, 1994), as reflected by the phrase "passed along from person to person, usually by word-of-mouth" from Allport and Postman's (1947) classic early definition. Of course, now it is clear that many rumors are either given birth or reinforced by print and electronic media, including the Internet. Although they have not supplanted the importance of word-of-mouth communication in the rumor transmission process, the mass media represent a direct source of rumor content and a formidable intermediary in the spread of rumors (Rosnow, 2001; Zerner, 1946).

A critical element of rumor is that there is a lack of certainty as to the validity of its message; that is, it is an unconfirmed proposition. The fact that there exists some degree of uncertainty regarding the truthfulness of a rumor is not

---

Box 1.5. Defining Rumor

Although there are differences in the precise terminology used, there tends to be general agreement among rumor experts as to the sorts of communications that can be classified as rumor. Some representative definitions, dating back to the 1940s, include the following:

1. A proposition for belief of topical reference disseminated without official verification (Knapp, 1944).
2. A specific (or topical) proposition for belief, passed along from person to person, usually by word-of-mouth, without secure standards of evidence being present (Allport & Postman, 1947).
3. An unverified account or explanation of events circulating from person to person and pertaining to an object, event, or issue of public concern (Peterson & Gist, 1951).
4. A proposition that is unverified and in general circulation (Rosnow & Fine, 1976).
5. The emergence and circulation in society of information that is either not yet publicly confirmed by official sources or denied by them (Kapferer, 1990).
6. An unverified proposition for belief that bears topical relevance for persons actively involved in its dissemination (Rosnow & Kimmel, 2000).

meant to imply that all rumors are untrue. The key is that the rumor may eventually turn out to be true or false, but until that time, the communication is subject to the dynamics of rumor. A story in widespread circulation that has been officially verified as false may nevertheless be considered a rumor, so long as there is a suspension of disbelief in the story's content. Should the rumor turn out to be true (or verified), its content then becomes subject to the limitations presented by the facts at hand.

To clarify these distinctions, consider the following example. Let us say that one day I overhear a couple of English-speaking tourists on the Paris metro discussing how the British retail chain Marks & Spencer is about to announce the closure of all of its stores in continental Europe, including those in France. As a loyal Marks & Spencer shopper, I may find this story difficult to believe (let's say because I recently read that the French stores are very profitable and every time I shop in the Paris outlets they seem to be doing a very brisk business), but unsettling nonetheless because it could be true. Perhaps the people I overheard had some inside information; maybe they were friends or relatives of company officials—whatever the reason, they apparently had heard something that I had not. Because in my mind there was some doubt about the credibility of the story I overheard, it would constitute a rumor whether I was aware of that fact or not (e.g., I may simply consider it as a piece of unconfirmed news). Should I repeat what I had heard to the friend I was meeting in a café later that day, I would have become an active participant in the rumor transmission process.

As it turns out, Marks & Spencer did publicly announce on March 30, 2001 that it would be shutting down its operations in a number of overseas settings, including France, to cope with declining profits (Cowell, 2001). Once the announcement was reported by a number of news outlets, the story was converted from a rumor (assuming that there previously had been speculation about store closures) to news. Had I read about the company's decision in the *Wall Street Journal Europe* shortly after it was announced, or learned about it through some other credible news source, my fears would have been confirmed and the story I overheard in the metro would no longer constitute a rumor (for me, at least). My friend from the café, however, might not have been keeping up with the news around that time and, as a result, she might have continued to consult others about a rumor she had heard. In short, a communication can be classified as a rumor when it is in widespread circulation, it is unverified, and it bears topical relevance for persons actively involved in its dissemination.

Rumor Versus News

As the preceding example shows, rumor and news are two forms of communication that are closely related, but distinguished on the basis of the presence or absence of secure standards of evidence. Unlike news, which is presumed to be based on fact, rumor is always unconfirmed. The recognition that rumor might be thought of as unconfirmed news moved sociologist Tamotsu Shibutani (1966) to refer to it as "improvised news." Thus, it is not surprising that the line between rumor and news often blurs. This might explain in part why much rumor-related content often is not directly identified as such. Because of the rush to "scoop" competitors at a time in which many news stories are reported instantaneously, with minimal prior fact checking, we now find that more and more unconfirmed stories are reported as if they were verified—that is, as news. The fact that rumors have increasingly begun to resemble (or be mistaken for) news also can be attributed to some extent to the new technologies that exist for the transmission of interpersonal messages. Once limited to localized discussions with people they know, consumers now can broadcast information to total strangers around the world through Internet discussion groups, personal or company Web sites, and the like (Rosen, 2000).

Because of the frequently negative connotation of rumors, people often are reluctant to acknowledge that a communication is, in fact, a rumor. Such acknowledgment highlights the possibility that the transmitted information could be false and that the bearer is irresponsibly communicating misinformation (Kamins, Folkes, & Perner, 1997; Rosnow, 1991). Moreover, as communication technologies have accelerated the pace by which news and information are transmitted to the public, there is an increasing tendency for communications to be based on unverified content, although they may readily be accepted as verified news by a public craving clarification regarding matters of current or local concern. Perhaps nowhere is this tendency more pronounced than in the financial marketplace.

One recent example of how an unconfirmed story can be reported as news involved a false report that was intentionally planted about the financial standing of Emulex, the California computer networking equipment manufacturer. On August 25, 2000 a bogus press release appeared on Internet Wire, a Web-based news dissemination service, and was immediately picked up and transmitted by leading financial news wires, including Bloomberg News and Dow Jones Newswires, as well as the cable news channel CNBC and numerous Web sites (Goldstein & Carrel, 2000). The original press release reported that Emulex was under federal investigation by the Securities and Exchange Commission (SEC), that it was revising its quarterly earnings to show a loss, and that its CEO had resigned. The story about the SEC investigation, in particular, spread like wildfire on online message boards and, not surprisingly, the false reports had a devastating impact on Emulex's stock, causing it to plummet as soon as markets opened. The impact of the unconfirmed news was swift—Emulex stock plunged more than 50% within 15 minutes of the story hitting wider distribution. Specifically, the company's shares fell as much as $68, or 61%, which represented a loss of $2.45 billion in market value (see Fig. 1.4). By afternoon, trading was halted once news of the hoax was discovered

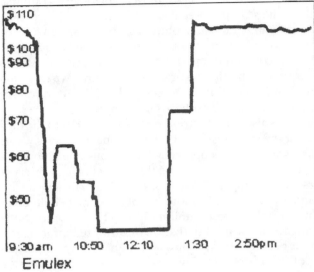

Emulex share price on Aug. 25

FIG. 1.4. The impact of the Emulex hoax in the financial marketplace. From Goldstein & Carrel (2000). Reprinted with permission of SmartMoney, 2000.

and the company mounted a public relations campaign and issued denials in a desperate attempt at damage control. Although the stock recovered much of its losses by day's end as exposure of the fraud received widespread media coverage, Emulex shares nonetheless had fallen 6.5% on Friday (the day the hoax appeared) and another 5.9% on Monday ("Echoes of a Hoax," 2000).

The origins of the Emulex hoax were traced to Mark Jakob, a 23-year-old American college student who previously had been an employee of Internet Wire. The hoax was initiated by an e-mail message he forwarded to Internet Wire containing a release from a fake public relations company describing Emulex's supposed difficulties. The e-mail included phrases commonly used by the wire service suggesting that the contents of the story had been verified earlier and, as a result, the Internet Wire staff did not feel it was necessary to further check the story's accuracy. Apparently motivated by a desire to recoup money he had lost after suffering major losses trading Emulex stock and at the same time attain some measure of revenge on the company, Jakob earned close to $250,000 in profit on the day of the hoax, but he was arrested the following week by the Federal Bureau of Investigation (FBI) and charged with securities and wire fraud (Becton & O'Harrow, 2000). Such a crime in the United States could result in a prison sentence of up to 15 years.

Ironically, some financial analysts concluded that Emulex was not substantially harmed by the hoax and actually may have benefited from it as a result of the national exposure the company received in its aftermath. However, this case highlights the growing influence of information technologies and the competitive nature of public relations and news wire services. Despite controls, in their rush to beat the competition with apparent breaking news, the financial information services in this case failed to verify the accuracy of the false news release. Unlike the P&G rumors, which were generated largely through the distribution of crudely prepared fliers distributed by religious groups, the bogus press release about Emulex's market difficulties was instigated by a single individual, but spread instantaneously through the Internet and other electronic media. The stark differences in the life cycles of these two cases reflects the rapidly changing nature of communication in business and financial contexts.

According to one assessment, the Emulex story "underscores the high stakes and potential dangers of real-time financial journalism, in which unconfirmed reports can blow a large hole in a company's stock before the truth catches up" ("Echoes of a Hoax," 2000, p. 17). In fact, the Emulex hoax was not an isolated case; there have been several similar incidents in which fake press releases were posted directly to online message boards (Goldstein & Carrel, 2000). One year earlier, PairGain Technologies was subject to a fake Internet news story developed by a disgruntled former employee suggesting that the company was about to be taken over ("Hoax Sends," 2000). In this case, PairGain's stock jumped more than 30%, demonstrating how false rumors of this sort can cause stocks to soar. The fact that this does not happen more frequently has to do with the controls that are used by established news wire services. We cover more about these controls and additional steps that can be taken to regulate and prevent the spread of unconfirmed news reports in later chapters.

A fair question that can be asked with regard to the sorts of Internet hoaxes described here is whether or not they actually constitute examples of rumors. Because these stories spread and had their effects prior to official verification, this would suggest that they do fit the definition of rumor presented here. However, unlike more traditional rumors, which have a clearly defined life cycle (see chap. 2), Internet rumors often come and go with amazing alacrity. In fact, the Internet has begun to spawn its own hearsay terminology, providing somewhat varying interpretations of what constitutes a rumor in cyberspace. For example, David Emery's "Urban Legends and Folklore" Internet site distinguishes between rumor ("anecdotal claims; may be true, false, or in-between") and three related categories of Web-based messages: hoax ("false, deliberately deceptive information"), urban legend ("a popularly believed narrative, typically false"), and junk ("flotsam and jetsam of the Net"). Collectively, the four message forms are referred to as *netlore*.

Rumor Versus Gossip

Now that we have considered some of the differences that exist between rumor and the sort of significant (and confirmed) information content that constitutes news, we next turn our attention to the other end of the spectrum to consider how rumor can be distinguished from nonessential small talk, or gossip. Informal talk about people is often speculative and, as a result, the line between content that may be considered either rumor or gossip often is a fuzzy one. This was suggested earlier when we pointed out that some of the interpersonal exchanges that flow through the organizational grapevine can more accurately be referred to as gossip than as rumor, such as when it pertains to the romantic comportment of employees.

The terms rumor and gossip are often used interchangeably, yet there are clear differences between them, often based on the situation in which the communication occurs (Hannerz, 1967). Gossip invariably pertains to people, whereas this is not an essential characteristic of rumor. Further, unlike rumor (which is never verified) or news (which is confirmed), gossip might or might not be supported by facts. Once described as "intellectual chewing gum" (Lumley, 1925), in common parlance, gossip refers to idle or apparently trivial conversation about the private, personal qualities or behaviors of others (see Box 1.6).

Box 1.6. The Cardinal Rules of Gossip

Much of the informal information system that flourishes in organizations consists of small talk about the personal and professional characteristics of coworkers and employers. Popular psychologist Perry Buffington suggested that the sort of gossip that flows through the company grapevine can be typified by 10 predictable characteristics and principles, which he summarized in his so-called "cardinal rules of gossip." Although some of his points have yet to be empirically validated, most are consistent with everyday observations of human exchange.

1. Everyone gossips. Even if you've just stood around listening, it's tantamount to gossiping.
2. No one ever asks if the information is true. Everyone assumes that it is.
3. The greater the potential damage, the faster the gossip travels.
4. The more you try to tell people that the gossip is not true, the more they will believe it is.
5. Major decisions have been based on gossip. When the decision turns out to be bad, gossipy rumors arise to explain the bad decision.
6. Of all forms of communication, gossip is the most easily distorted.
7. Men gossip just as much as women, and gossip is filtered through socioeconomic strata by both genders.
8. People gossip to protect their own reputations. When the focus is on someone else, one receives a momentary reprieve.
9. The more demeaning or hurtful the gossip, the longer it takes for the victim to hear about it.
10. Gossip thrives in an atmosphere of secrecy and competition. It tends to thrive most where there is too much secrecy and where advancement is based on overcompetition. (Cole, 1985, p. 13)

A more studied consideration of the nature of gossip suggests that it represents a form of interpersonal communication that is more amorphous and superfluous than rumor and, in many ways, more directly identified by the context in which it occurs. Gossip typically takes the form of conversational content that emerges spontaneously in informal social situations. Although it is likely to be treated with apparent indifference (or even disdain) by the parties involved in the discussion, its purpose or ulterior motive may be substantial (Rosnow, 2001).

As an example, let us assume that rather than overhearing a couple of tourists on the Paris metro (as described in a previous example), I instead was privy to a discussion involving two businesspeople, apparently associates at the same company, who were on their way back to work following their lunch break. Imagine that they were casually discussing a mutual acquaintance, such as a client, in rather unflattering terms. Maybe it was a function of the wine from lunch or the opportunity to unwind following a stressful morning, but they seemed very relaxed and none too concerned about the implications of what they were discussing. The conversation proceeded the way many of our everyday exchanges with close friends or colleagues might, with a lot of jumping around from one topic or anecdote to another and with accompanying nonverbal behaviors, such as chuckles, groans, and outright guffaws. Apparently, the recently divorced client who was the focus of much of this interaction had been seen at a local nightclub, where he drew attention to himself by telling off-color jokes and making inappropriate passes at some single women. He also appeared to have a rather odd sense of color coordination when it came to his selection of clothing. Of course, there was no way of knowing whether any of these points were true, but as they did not concern me, I did not really care one way or the other. In my view, this was just idle chatter between two colleagues. Although it appeared nonessential in the context in which it was taking place, it clearly was not neutral, but rather had a distinctly evaluative—in this case, negative—orientation and tone. It suggested certain behaviors or personal quirks that were considered to be morally wrong or assessed as illegitimate in the social context and inappropriate conduct for an important business professional. Additionally, putting down a business associate in this way perhaps enabled the two discussants to bolster their own self-image while tightening the bond they shared with each other.

In this example, the key defining characteristics of gossip should be clear: Gossip typically is packaged as idle talk, but it has a normative or evaluative essence that serves particular social and psychological functions. Gossip may be positive in nature, but it usually bears a pejorative connotation and is more likely to involve negative references to an absent third party. As suggested, it also is determined by the context in which it appears. If a conversation had come up about the client's inappropriate professional conduct during an in-house meeting with the company director, it surely would not be viewed as gossip—even though the target of the discussion was absent—but rather as a legitimate element of a business discussion, perhaps influencing decision making regarding whether or not the company should drop undesirable and potentially unprofitable clients. This "legitimacy factor" represents a key way that gossip diverges from rumor. According to Rosnow (2001), "what counts is not simply that the message is of a personal nature—many rumors also focus on personal affairs—but that the news is 'nonessential' in the context of the exchange" (p. 211). Rumor, on the other hand, pertains to message content that is significant to the parties involved in its transmission.

To say that gossip is nonessential is somewhat misleading when one recognizes its potential for either direct or indirect consequences in organizational contexts and the consumer marketplace. Clearly, whether gossiping about a colleague on a subway train, in a washroom in the workplace, or during an executive board meeting, word inevitably could get out across the grapevine and irreversibly harm an individual's chances for a promotion or pay raise. Numerous other examples no doubt come to mind when one considers the potential for idle talk to harm careers, relationships, and social status. Now that "happy talk" about the successes and foibles of well-known persons, including business personalities, has become a mainstay of mass media reporting, much gossiping is transformed from a private form of admonishment to a public one, so its potential consequences can be even more severe and immediate than in the past.

Less obvious are the consequences of gossip in the consumer marketplace. After all, one could hardly gossip about a laundry detergent or DVD player. Nonetheless, in a fascinating recent book about marketplace "buzz"—that is, the totality of comments or word-of-mouth that is exchanged among people at any given time about a certain brand or product—Emanuel Rosen (2000) suggested that gossip may be inextricably linked with consumer products and services offerings. This becomes clear when we recognize that our everyday conversations about products and services often focus on the people we associate with them. For example, word-of-mouth about restaurants often focuses on the people who eat or work there; book buzz often consists of talk about the characters; and movie or TV buzz tends to involve talk about the actors, the filmmaker, and the persons we shared the viewing experience with. In this vein, Rosen suggested that the enormous popularity of the American cable television series *The Sopranos* could be attributed to the buzz generated by an intelligently written program about colorful and unusual characters (New Jersey mobsters and their relations). Similarly, one might imagine that small talk about a retail shop's salespersons, neighbors who recently purchased a product, and celebrities or characters who promote certain brands can be seen as an indirect form of marketing buzz relating to a company. It is no wonder that some businesses, such as the clothing retailers Benneton and Kookäi, actively attempt to stimulate buzz about their product offerings through the development of controversial promotional campaigns (see Box 1.7).

Box 1.7. Creating Marketing Buzz Through Controversial Promotional Campaigns

One way for companies to break through the advertising clutter in the contemporary marketplace is to launch controversial campaigns that are sure to capture attention and stimulate consumer discussions. The clothing firm Benetton has been a pioneer in this regard. Oliviero Toscani, the company's creative director from 1981 until recently, created a number of risky Benetton advertisements that appeared in magazines and billboards, including news photos of the blood-soaked Army fatigues of a Croatian soldier killed in Bosnia, a dying AIDS patient, a Catholic nun and priest kissing, buttocks bearing the stamp "H.I.V. positive," and a bloody newborn baby with umbilical cord intact. Although critics of these campaigns arguably outnumber their supporters, one thing is certain: The campaigns successfully created buzz for the firm.

In recent years, more and more companies have followed in the footsteps of Benetton by developing promotional campaigns that have little to say about products and brands, but are primarily intended to get people talking about the company. This was seen in a recent French campaign by Kookäi, a women's clothing firm, which has run attention-getting mass media and outdoor advertisements depicting miniaturized men at the mercy of dominant women.

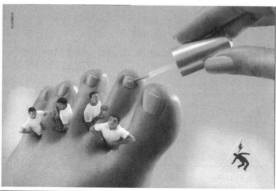

Characteristics of Rumor: Summary

The foregoing discussion indicates that whether or not a communication constitutes a rumor depends on the extent to which it possesses certain identifying
properties, the foremost of which involve (a) the significance or interest of the
message content, and (b) the extent to which the message is supported by evidence. By considering two additional properties—(c) whether the communication deals with people and (d) is positive or negative—it is possible to more
clearly identify rumor and to differentiate it from related forms of communication, such as gossip and news (see Table 1.1).

To summarize, we have found that rumor is significant to message recipients and transmitters, but is never supported by evidence. It might or might
not concern people and might or might not be negative. According to Table
1.1, the basic way that rumor differs from news is in its lack of confirming evidence. By contrast, rumor can be more clearly distinguished from gossip in
that the latter is likely to involve message content that is deemed trivial to the
gossips (although probably not to the gossip target), always pertains to people,
and is more likely than rumor to have a negative connotation. Figure 1.5 uses
Venn diagrams to represent the unique and overlapping properties of these
three forms of communication. The diagrams underscore why rumor, gossip,
and news frequently seem to blend and be confused with one another, yet they
also help us recognize that the three types of exchange clearly are not identical
forms of communication.

The overlap among these various forms of communication is even more
striking when one considers the functions that they serve for their publics. In
one way or another, all three types of communication serve to inform, although here the essential nature of news and rumor stand in contrast to the
typically nonessential content represented by gossip. All three types of messages also may serve to influence, to satisfy social or psychological needs, and
to entertain, although in varying degrees, depending on the circumstances inherent in the social context and the personal characteristics of the individuals
involved in the exchange.

TABLE 1.1

Properties of Rumor, News, and Gossip

Property	Rumor	News	Gossip
Significant	Yes	Yes	No
Evidential basis	No	Yes	Yes or no
People-oriented	Yes or no	Yes or no	Yes
Connotation	– or +	– or +	–

Note. Adapted from Kimmel, Moore, Rind, and Rosnow (1992).

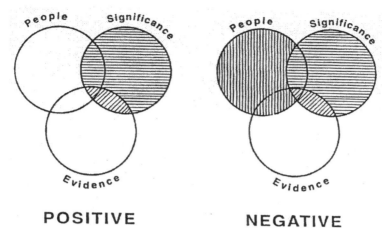

POSITIVE   NEGATIVE

FIG. 1.5.   Venn diagrams illustrate the shared and unique properties of rumor, news, and gossip (as noted in Table 1.1). Rumor is represented by horizontal lines, gossip by vertical lines, and news by diagonal lines. From Kimmel, Moore, Rind, and Rosnow (1992).

CONCLUSION

This overview of rumor has revealed that it is an amorphous and somewhat slippery subject, hard to get hold of because of its seemingly elusive nature. Once pretty much limited to ordinary social conversation, in contemporary societies rumors now proliferate and in many cases are fueled by the media. Additionally, emerging communication technologies such as the Internet have sped up the processes by which rumors are transmitted and have damaging effects on their targets. As we will see in subsequent chapters, these media also represent potential mechanisms by which rumors can be effectively combatted.

In business settings, as our examples revealed, rumors can pertain to a company's personnel or product and service offerings. Whereas some companies, such as Procter & Gamble, have become unfortunate targets for rumor-mongers over a long term, others have been more successful at dodging the rumor bullet through either good fortune or sound management and marketing practices. In later chapters we focus in depth on these practices, by considering the steps that companies can take to control the often unwieldy flow of rumors through consumer word-of-mouth networks, the company grapevine, and the mass media, to limit their negative effects on corporate profits, brand image, employee satisfaction, and the like. First, however, in Chapter 2 we continue with the dissection of the nature of rumors by focusing on the social and psychological dynamics that give rise to rumor generation and spread.

CHAPTER TWO

Understanding Rumor: The Dynamics of Rumor Transmission and Belief

In our highly industrialized, increasingly denatured culture, the indelicate sights and sounds of the slaughterhouse are kept far from the public eye, perpetuating the consumer fantasy of a shrink-wrapped, bar-coded product that was made, not born. The corporatization and globalization of the food industry have alienated us from the meat on the ends of our forks, and there's a creeping unease about the dirty details. Most of us would rather not know how that McDonald's Happy Meal began its life, and what happened to it on the way to our plate.

—Dery (1999, p. 134)

In his book *Rumor in the Marketplace*, social psychologist Frederick Koenig (1985) pondered the reasons why the majority of rumors in contemporary society are related to the marketplace. It is true that one can find examples dating back to the 1930s that bear much resemblance to the sorts of rumors that are now so familiar to us. For example, one cigarette company was rumored to employ a leper in the plant where the brand was packaged, and another was believed to be associated with the Vatican. Soft drinks were occasionally rumored to contain undesirable ingredients. However, without the prominence of electronic journalism and the media sensationalism that characterizes today's reporting of marketplace events, these early rumors tended to be low-key, restricted to local communities, and relatively short-lived. As Koenig observed, it was not until the late 1970s that the commercial rumor emerged as the dominant form of present-day hearsay.

Dery's quote at the beginning of this chapter represents a good starting point for understanding why commercial rumors are so pervasive in modern society, and his comments reflect the conclusions that Koenig (1985) reached in his book. Much of the answer lies in the fact that despite dramatic technological, scientific, and medical advances in recent decades, our modern world has, in many respects, become a scarier and more dangerous place than ever before. It is those very advances that increasingly have given rise to consumer anxieties, including those associated with the mass production of food products, genetically modified fruits and vegetables, cloning, globalization, corporate mergers, and the like. In *The Pyrotechnic Insanitarium: American Culture on the Brink*, Dery (1999) discussed the implications of "anxieties spurred by out-of-control technological change" and the "indeterminate nature of things in postmodern culture, where quotation, hybridization, and mutation are the order of the day" (pp. 134–135). When shared anxieties are coupled with uncertainties and a lack of understanding about how our new world works, the conditions are such that we find a potent combination of ingredients for the onset of rumors. In this chapter, these and other ideas are examined to shed light on the forces that give rise to rumors and stimulate their spread.

The nature of rumor is such that it has drawn the attention of analysts and experts from a wide range of disciplines and professional backgrounds, including the behavioral sciences (psychology, sociology, anthropology), communications theory, political science, psychoanalysis, popular culture and folklore studies, and the mass media. This complicates somewhat our attempt to unravel the dynamics of rumor and rumor transmission, given that a single perspective is likely to be inadequate for fully explicating the processes underlying such an elusive form of interpersonal exchange. With that in mind, although much of the analysis here draws on social-psychological research and theory, my approach has been to attempt to integrate a number of ideas from other sources and fields. At the outset, I provide a description of the various types of rumors that appear in commercial and organizational settings. This identification is essential for establishing a framework by which we can address the question, "Why and under which circumstances do people spread rumors?" This question represents the central focus of concern in this chapter.

RUMOR TYPES

As elaborated in subsequent chapters, success in controlling a rumor, as when one attempts to fight a medical disease or illness, rests in the correct diagnosis of the rumor's nature. A first step in that direction, as Kapferer (1990) noted, is to construct a typology of the possibilities. Several classification schemes have been offered to identify the various types of rumors, reflecting differences in message content, etiology, and underlying motive or purpose.

Pipe Dreams, Bogies, Wedge Drivers, and Homestretchers

One of the earliest and perhaps most widely known classification schemes was suggested by Knapp (1944), based on his work in collaboration with the Massachusetts Committee on Public Safety during World War II. Following an analysis of rumors collected during September 1942 from mass-circulation magazines and the Boston Rumor Clinic, Knapp concluded that rumors can be labeled as either pipe dream (or wish fulfillment) rumors, bogie (or fear) rumors, or wedge driving (or aggression) rumors.

Pipe dream rumors represent the most positive form of rumors in the sense that they reflect public desires and wished-for outcomes (e.g., that Japan's oil reserves during the war were low or that the war was soon to end). By contrast, bogie rumors reflect feared or anxiety-provoking outcomes (e.g., that an enemy surprise attack is imminent). Wedge drivers represent a second form of negative hearsay in that they are intended to divide group loyalties or otherwise undermine interpersonal relations (e.g., that American Catholics were actively seeking to avoid the draft). A fourth category of rumors subsequently was added to Knapp's typology by two of his associates, Gordon Allport and Leo Postman, two social psychologists who eventually emerged as pioneers in the academic study of rumor. According to Allport and Postman (1947), rumors also can take the form of so-called homestretchers, or anticipatory rumors that precede an expected event (e.g., that the U.S. president is about to give a dramatic address to the nation about the war).

In his analysis of more than 1,000 wartime rumors, Knapp (1944) found that negative rumors were more likely to be heard and transmitted than positive ones, with only 2% classified as pipe dreams, compared with 66% as wedge-drivers and 25% as bogies. (An additional 7% were unclassifiable.) In a more recent study, Nkpa (1975) collected rumors in circulation during the Nigerian Civil War of 1967 through 1970 and reported that pipe dream rumors were most common, representing nearly two thirds of the total; conversely, wedge drivers encompassed only 18% of all tales collected. As pointed out by Rosnow and Fine (1976), the disparity in findings between these two studies reflects the important role of motivational and emotional elements in determining the nature and types of rumors that circulate in varying situations. Differences in the methodology used by the researchers also may have determined to some degree the obtained results. In contrast to Knapp's content analysis of rumor-related source material, Nkpa relied on interviews with students and Biafran residents, who may have been concerned about not appearing overly pessimistic or aggressive in front of researchers.

Depending on the specific circumstances, it is easy to imagine that any of the four varieties of rumors could be common at a particular time in marketplace and organizational settings. If it is true that consumer anxieties have grown in recent years, as suggested at the outset of this chapter, it is reasonable to assume that bogie rumors may be particularly prevalent. Indeed, a quick perusal of the marketplace rumors listed in Box 1.3 reveals that a majority are related to fear, such as those pertaining to consumer products rumored to contain harmful ingredients. In organizational settings, especially during difficult economic times, divisive rumors can be expected to have the upper hand, such as when employees are vying against each other to keep their jobs or when corporate takeover battles are raging.

In apparently the only assessment to date of the relative frequency of rumors in the marketplace, Kamins et al. (1997) conducted a field survey of 361 members of a consumer research panel in the state of Arkansas. Consistent with Knapp's (1944) early findings, the consumers studied by Kamins et al. reported that they were exposed to and repeated more negative (wedge driver and dread) rumors than positive (wish) rumors. Of 271 rumors about companies or brands that the respondents recalled hearing during the preceding year, 7.4% were considered wish, 74.9% were classified as dread, and 17.7% were identified as wedge drivers. Unlike Knapp, who revealed that divisive rumors were most prevalent during a wartime situation, the Kamins et al. study demonstrates how fear-related rumors tend to prevail in the context of the contemporary marketplace.

The role of the Internet in the determination of the types of rumors in circulation also must be taken into account. Like rumors that emerge in other contexts, Internet rumors may be positive or negative, invoking hoped-for consequences or forecasting feared or disappointing ones. Many critics have argued that without controls, the Internet provides a ready outlet for hate groups to vent their hostilities in the form of unconfirmed, divisive accusations about disliked others (see Box 2.1). In terms of the marketplace, one interesting development has been the emergence of the "something for nothing" rumor, a variety of wish-fulfillment hearsay that has appeared with increasing frequency in the in-boxes of Internet users (see Box 2.2).

Spontaneous, Premeditated, and Self-Fulfilling Rumors

Another common approach to describing rumor types is found in the distinction between spontaneous and premeditated rumors. The spontaneous (or unintentional) rumor emerges naturally during a crisis or in other situations marked by excesses of stress, mistrust, and confusion about how circumstances will be resolved. Such rumors are apt to thrive until they become irrelevant or the crisis dies down and thus tend to be relatively short-lived. An example is provided by the rumors that grew out of the Three Mile Island nuclear power plant accident that occurred in 1979 near Harrisburg, Pennsylvania (Rosnow & Kimmel, 1979). Three days after the accident, a rumor spread throughout surrounding towns that the plant was about to explode and that harmful radioactivity would blanket a vast area. Despite the fact that there was no imminent threat of an explosion, this and dozens of other rumors spontaneously emerged and rapidly spread across a wide area during the period in which serious dangers remained present.

Premeditated (or intentional) rumors typically are started for a reason, often to serve Machiavellian purposes. Such rumors tend to appear in highly

Box 2.1. Racial Rumors and Tropical Fantasy

Prior to the proliferation of commercial rumors, one of the most dominant forms of hearsay involved wedge driving rumors pertaining to racial conflict. As Koenig (1985) pointed out, the contemporary version of the traditional racial wedge driver is now more often implicitly manifest in rumors targeting companies. Stroh's beer, Church's Fried Chicken, and Domino's Pizza are among the companies that at one time or another have been targeted by rumors reflective of fears that tend to divide American racial groups.

One of the most insidious recent versions of a racial wedge driver to emerge in the consumer marketplace was the one involving the Brooklyn Bottling Company's Tropical Fantasy, a new line of fruit-flavored soft drinks. Tropical Fantasy was introduced into the marketplace in 1991 and was instantly successful, drawing business away from Coca-Cola, Pepsi, and other brands that were sold at a higher price. The new line of soft drinks was marketed to minorities living in poor, inner-city neighborhoods of the American Northeast. After a steady 6-month rise in sales, Tropical Fantasy became the subject of a rumor, allegedly started by a rival, that the drink was manufactured by the Ku Klux Klan (KKK) and contained an ingredient that would make Black men sterile ("A Storm," 1991; Turner, 1993). The rumor initially took off thanks to a mysterious flier addressed to Blacks and other minority groups that began appearing in New York City, as shown here. In support of the rumor, the flier challenged consumers to try to find the soft drink in nonminority areas of the city, claiming that the distribution was limited to Harlem and other minority neighborhoods for a reason. As with many rumors, the credibility of the story was boosted by the false assertion that the story had been reported on a national news program.

ATTENTION!!! ATTENTION!!! ATTENTION!!!
50 CENT SODAS
<u>BLACKS</u> AND <u>MINORITY</u> <u>GROUPS</u>
DID YOU SEE (T.V. SHOW) 20/20???
PLEASE BE ADVISE, "Top Pop" & "Tropical Fantasy" .50 sodas
are being manufactured by the Klu..Klux..Klan.
Sodas contain stimulants to sterilize the black man,
and who knows what else!!!!
They are only put in stores in Harlem and minority areas.
You won't find them down town.... Look around....
YOU HAVE BEEN WARNED
PLEASE SAVE THE CHILDREN
—Source: Ellis (1991)—
(Reprinted with permision of Bill Ellis and FOAFTale News.)

Despite the fact that this outlandish story was patently false and no evidence ever was uncovered that rival soft drink producers were responsible for it, the rumor had a devastating impact on Tropical Fantasy sales, which dropped by 70% (Freedman, 1991). Despite strong denials issued by the spread rapidly to other cities largely through consumer word-of-mouth. As an example of the story's impact on consumer behavior, one reporter described observing a shopper who had approached the supermarket checkout with a bottle of Tropical Fantasy in hand, only to stop and utter, "I forgot … it's made by the KKK to poison Blacks," before turning back to get a Sprite (Freedman, 1991).

Eventually, the Tropical Fantasy rumor was successfully combatted, but only after a concerted campaign was launched by the bottling company, which included the distribution of "truth fliers" by company employees in affected neighborhoods, a statement issued by the New York City Health Department attesting to the safety of the drink, and appearances by city officials, including the Black New York City mayor, who consumed the drink in public.

Tropical Fantasy is one of several product lines that have had to battle racially divisive rumors. Such rumors, also alleging KKK involvement, have swirled around better-known brands and products in recent years, including Jockey underwear (makes Black men sterile), Snapple soft drinks (the letter K on the bottle label stands for the KKK), Domino's Pizza (pizzas contaminated with the AIDS virus by a disgruntled Black kitchen worker), and Marlboro cigarettes (when packages are stacked it is possible to see the letters KKK). Despite much progress in race relations in the United States, a racial divide still exists between Blacks and Whites, and the fears and suspicions that these groups have for each other are revealed in—and justified by—the wedge driving rumors that circulate in the consumer marketplace.

competitive environments and are especially prevalent in the financial marketplace, where rumors about stocks may have a significant impact on trading. In organizations, rumors may be intentionally planted to gain an advantage or satisfy some personal motives, as was the case for one CEO of a major company who admitted to having planted rumors with young executives to test whether they were leakproof (Esposito & Rosnow, 1983). Premeditated rumors in the consumer marketplace often appear in the form of intentional hoaxes perpetrated by angry or dissatisfied consumers or by persons merely craving attention. In one example that occurred during mid-June 1993, newspapers in Seattle and New Orleans carried reports about people who claimed that they had found syringes in Diet Pepsi cans ("The Right Moves," 1993). Within 1 week, more than 50 persons from 20 different states had come forward with similar stories, all of which turned out to be fraudulent. The origin of this potentially disastrous scare was traced to an elderly couple in Tacoma, Washington, who, for some unknown reason, were the first to come forward with the false claim. A U.S. Food and Drug Administration (FDA) investigation concluded that virtually all the other cases were copycat hoaxes; eventually, more than a dozen people were arrested for filing false

---

Box 2.2. Wish Rumors in Cyberspace

An increasingly prevalent addition to the "flotsam and jetsam" of the Internet is the junk mail that accumulates in our e-mail in-boxes with alarming regularity. Such messages often are of dubious origin and veracity; many are filled with misinformation and others are simply outright hoaxes (www.snopes.com). In a recent variation of the more traditional free gift come-ons and chain letters that consumers have grown so familiar with, the "something for nothing" e-mail letter has rapidly become a common feature of the new technological landscape. The typical form of this Internet version of the wish fulfillment rumor involves the promise of some sort of reward (usually either a free product or money) for simply forwarding the e-mail message to others.

In one of the initial versions of this bogus claim, a "something for nothing" message announced that Bill Gates was offering a $1,000 reward to everyone who forwarded his e-mail. This sort of hoax has caught on, with other companies rumored to be engaged in similar giveaway plans, including Disney (free cash or vacations), Honda (free cars), the Gap (free clothes or gift certificates), Nokia (free wireless telephones), Coca-Cola (free Coke), AOL/Netscape (free cash), and Columbia House (free music CDs), among others. Other versions of the "something for nothing" rumors have appeared, including the claim that Yahoo! was planning to start a new site called 21 yahoo.com where it would be giving away free stock; that the Miller Brewing Company planned to give away 2 million cases of free beer to celebrate the year 2000; and that if you sent your old shoes (any brand) to Nike, the company would mail you a free pair. A more complete listing of such rumors is available at the snopes.com "Inboxer Rebellion" link, which is maintained and regularly updated by Barbara and David P. Mikkelson.

The prevalence of the "something for nothing" rumors on the Internet doubtless reflects the public's overly optimistic expectations that accompanied the many exaggerated claims about what the technology of the new millennium can do for us. However, as the Mikkelsons caution on their Web page, "people keep expecting that companies are going to serve up free lunches via the Internet. If they didn't give away free merchandise, cash, and stocks in the real world, they're not about to start doing it in a virtual one."

---

reports. A combination of speedy and intelligent rumor-fighting tactics by Pepsi (further discussed in chap. 6), the assistance of the FDA, and a surveillance video from a Colorado retailer that showed a customer sneaking a syringe into a Diet Pepsi can vindicated the company and enabled it to dodge the rumor bullet (Magiera, 1993).

As illustrated by the Pepsi case, intentional rumors often set off a vicious rumor cycle. This is especially true with regard to product tampering scares, whereby a single report of tampering almost inevitably leads to additional reported incidents. Such was the case in 1982 when seven people died after taking Extra-Strength Tylenol that had been laced with cyanide and again in 1990 when Perrier had to recall its flagship soft drink globally when traces of the carcinogen benzene entered the water production process. In many cases, like their spontaneous counterparts, intentional rumors often tend to die quickly when the stressful circumstances surrounding the crisis are mitigated.

Another category of rumor that bears a close resemblance to both the intentional rumor and the homestretcher is the self-fulfilling rumor (Rowan, 1979), which involves an unconfirmed story that predicts a future event. This type of rumor serves to alter perceptions and behaviors in such a way that it increases the probability that the rumored event will indeed come to pass. Stories about the imminent insolvency of a financial institution could result in a run on the bank once anxious depositors begin to question the integrity of its economic structure. In such a way, the rumored event could come to pass as a function of the bank's questionable financial foothold, which the rumor itself helped to create (Esposito & Rosnow, 1983). In a somewhat less serious example of the self-fulfilling rumor, the day after a popular American nighttime television personality mentioned a rumored toilet paper shortage, a national stampede at the supermarket ensued, thereby creating an actual shortage (Rowan, 1979).

Conspiracy and Contamination Rumors

If one considers the examples of commercial rumors already discussed in this book it should be evident that the content of rumors that affect companies, products, or brands typically involves either the theme of conspiracy or contamination. *Conspiracy rumors* tell of policies or practices by a commercial enterprise that are deemed threatening or ideologically undesirable to consumers. The rumors alleging P&G's ownership by the Moonies and that the owner of the company had struck a secret deal with Satan represent examples of this type. Other companies that have been the focus of conspiracy rumors are those alleged to have contributed money to or to have otherwise supported unacceptable causes or positions at odds with the company's (or its customers') philosophy and values. This was the situation with regard to the Snapple Beverage Company, a popular maker of sodas and teas, which in late 1992 was reputed to be actively supporting the Ku Klux Klan and Operation Rescue, an anti-abortion group that attempted to shut down abortion clinics (Noble, 1993).

In another conspiracy hoax, Gerber Foods was rumored to have lost a lawsuit pertaining to false advertising claims that their baby foods were all natural, when in fact preservatives were used. This bogus allegation, which originally emerged in 1997 only to reappear 3 years later, unfolded in the form of messages sent to parents across the United States, informing them that the court settlement of the class-action suit required Gerber to give every child born between 1985 and 1997 a free savings bond. The message recipients were instructed to mail copies of their child's birth certificate and social security card to a post office box in Minneapolis if they had bought baby food from the company during the previous 17 years, arousing suspicions that some elaborate scam was afoot. This rumor was repeated in various forms across fax machines, fliers, and the Internet, with the values of the savings bonds ranging from $500 to $1,400 cash. Apparently, the Gerber hoax sprang from a misunderstanding relative to an actual lawsuit involving the pricing of infant formula by three other manufacturers, who agreed to pay up to $1,400 per claimant as part of a court settlement (Schmeltzer, 1997). As is common in the rumor transmission process, the story mutated into one associated with the better known and more recognizable company, in this case, Gerber.

Another class of rumors in the consumer marketplace is the contamination rumor, which was hinted at by the Gerber hoax. The *contamination rumor*, which is quite common in the food and beverage industry (Brodin & Roux, 1995), claims that a certain feature of a commercial product is potentially harmful or undesirable to consumers (see Box 2.3). In the Gerber case, one aspect of the hoax was the assertion that, contrary to advertising claims, the company's baby foods contained artificial preservatives. The McDonald's wormburger rumor, described in Chapter 1, is an even better example of this form. This rumor beleaguered the famous hamburger restaurant chain off and on between 1978 and 1982. As previously mentioned, the charge that McDonald's was mixing earthworms in its hamburger meat was initially directed at Wendy's, another American fast-food hamburger chain. The Wendy's rumor apparently originated in the state of Tennessee during the summer of 1978 and, as is often the case with such rumors, its retelling was usually accompanied by references to national television broadcasts on which the story allegedly was discussed. Although the target of the rumor during the early stages of its life cycle changed from time to time—for example, McDonald's, Burger King, and Burger Chef were sometimes named—it was Wendy's that received the brunt of consumer attention. This situation changed immediately following a televised news conference featuring company representatives who issued strong denials. From that point on, it was McDonald's that became the primary target for the worm rumor.

Koenig (1985) suggested that the Wendy's worm rumor may have originated as a result of the following flawed syllogism: "A. Raw hamburger looks like red worms. B. Red worms are big and juicy. C. Wendy's burgers are advertised as 'hot and juicy'" (p. 92). With such logic, it was only a small step for the average consumer to conclude that the burgers contained worms. In a more general sense, the persistence of contamination rumors about well-known food products can be partly explained in line with Dery's (1999) arguments concerning the uncertainties and fears linked to our increasingly anonymous

---

Box 2.3. The Pop Rocks Contamination Rumor

In 1974, General Foods began marketing an interesting new candy confection that had been invented nearly two decades earlier by one of their research scientists. Introduced on the market as Pop Rocks, the carbonated candy crystals that crackled (or made "popping sounds") as they dissolved in the mouth became an instant success with children. More than 500 million packages were sold within the first 5 years in selected areas of the United States. By 1979, however, a now-classic rumor spread across the country that eating the candy while drinking a carbonated beverage would cause one's stomach to explode. According to the most common version of the story, this had happened to a young child who had eaten one or more packages and then drank a carbonated soda. The story continued to spread, especially among children, even after General Foods's costly efforts to stifle it, which included taking out full-page advertisements in 45 major newspapers, mailing more than 50,000 letters to school principals, and sending the candy's inventor to explain directly to the public why the product was safe and could not possibly have the effects that the rumor claimed (Brunvand, 1984; Unger, 1979).

Like most stories of its kind, certain details of the Pop Rocks rumor were varied as it circulated; for example, the product contained an illegal drug or spider eggs, that it would cause the stomach to explode if the user swallowed an Alka-Seltzer tablet, that it was declared illegal by the government, and so on (Brunvand, 1984). In the best known variation, the child who supposedly experienced the unfortunate effects of a Pop Rocks–soda combination was identified as the child actor who played the character Mikey in several Life cereal television commercials.

Despite General Foods's efforts, the rumor continued to spread and has never completely gone away—it is periodically retold even today despite the fact that the brand is no longer manufactured. Pop Rocks was taken off the market around 1983, although the rights to the product were purchased by Kraft in 1985 and reintroduced as "Action Candy" through a company identified as Carbonated Candy ("Death of," 2001). Like many such contamination rumors, the wild stories about Pop Rocks no doubt appeal to young children who have a special craving for the mischievous and outlandish. At least in part, the children who spread such rumors and boast that they have themselves consumed such a dangerous product can achieve a kind of hero status among their friends and hone their image as risk takers (Rosnow & Kimmel, 1979).

---

and mass-produced consumer culture (see chap. 3 for a more complete discussion of this point).

Some of the differences between conspiracy and contamination rumors are summarized in Table 2.1.

TABLE 2.1

Conspiracy Rumors Versus Contamination Rumors: Basic Differences

Rumor Characteristics	Conspiracy Rumor	Contamination Rumor
Message focus	An accusation	A target
Circulation	Group under threat	Broad consumer public
Credibility	High credibility; reinforcement of previously held belief	Credibility not necessary; repulsion effect may suffice
Target	Interchangeable; large corporation; often the best known or perceived as the best	Large depersonalizing corporation (service sector, franchises, food outlets, mass distribution)
Effects on sales	Often limited, but bothersome (e.g., consumer boycotts)	Often considerable

Note.   Adapted from Brodin and Roux (1995); Koenig (1985).

Urban Legends

Continuing with our typology, urban legends represent a special form of rumor that is often discussed as a separate category of hearsay altogether. *Urban legends* (also referred to as contemporary legends) are well-developed, untrue stories that typically have an ironic twist or surprise ending that reflects collective fears. Because of their unverified nature, urban legends belong in the general family of rumors, albeit with a special narrative structure (Kapferer, 1990). A number of social scientists view this kind of rumor as a contemporary form of folklore in the sense that the legends represent or reflect an integral part of the traditional beliefs, myths, and tales of a culture that are transmitted orally, often across generations (Victor, 1993).

In distinguishing urban legends from the more typical kinds of rumors previously described, folklorist Jan Harold Brunvand (1981, 1984, 1986), who amassed a vast collection of contemporary legends in their many different versions, argued that a rumor must have certain essential characteristics for it to be regarded as an urban legend and passed on over time. Foremost among these are that an apocryphal story (a) must have a strong narrative appeal; (b) it seems to have a believable, realistic foundation; and (c) it contains a meaningful message or teaches a moral lesson (Brunvand, 1981). Perhaps more so than any other type of hearsay, urban legends tend to be widely told in many different variations over a considerable time period (Brunvand, 1990). According to Wallace and Wallace (1989), urban legends represent an effective means by which people in modern societies "symbolically communicate to each other their anxieties about social issues" (p. 70).

Some rumors in the form of urban legends seem to have become part of the public consciousness and have gained widespread awareness around the world. Such is the case with the contemporary legend commonly known as the microwaved pet. Dating back to 1976, the basic storyline recounts how someone kills a pet out of stupidity, thinking he or she can use the microwave oven as a hair dryer. The most common version of this story tells of an elderly woman who is in a hurry and, thinking she can dry the dog (or cat) she has just bathed, puts the dog in the microwave oven, causing the dog to explode. One variation of this story claims that the pet is "nuked" out of intentional cruelty. Yet another variation has to do with owners putting their pets in the washing machine to clean them (see also Box 2.4). Notice the elaborate plotting details in one retelling of this legend that appeared on an Internet chat site (Healey & Glanvill, 1996):

> I once heard of an elderly lady who used to breed pedigree cats and exhibit them at shows. She specialized in Persian cats and their long hair always made it a difficult task to clean and groom them for showing. In order to cut down the effort involved the old lady had evolved the practice of first washing the cat, toweling it dry and then, finally, giving it a very brief warming in her electric oven. One Christmas her cooker developed a fault and so her son, by way of a Christmas present, brought her a brand new microwave oven. On the day of the next cat show, not understanding the basic difference in the technology between an ordinary cooker and a microwave oven, the old lady industriously washed her prize-winning Persian cat and popped it into the oven for a few seconds. There really was no miaow, nor any noise at all from the cat, for the poor creature exploded the instant the oven was switched on.

Two different interpretations of this legend have been suggested. The first is that it reflects a basic fear of new technology theme, in which the little old lady of lore becomes a symbol of technological incompetence (i.e., the story conforms with the stereotypical image of women and older consumers who have little competence or interest in modern devices and who are at high risk of dangerously misusing new product innovations). The terrible fate of her beloved pet serves as a warning that perhaps it is wise not to let go of traditional ways of doing things too quickly. Thus, the moral: The old ways are safer—convenience be damned (www.snopes.com). Another interpretation of this legend, focusing on an old woman who accidentally eliminates her only companion, reflects fears of growing old alone.

As is commonly the case with more traditional forms of rumor, the source of a contemporary legend tends to be anonymous, with its recounting typically presented as a "true" story that supposedly happened to someone else, such as a friend, a relative, or a neighbor. The incident described in the story so often is linked to at least one person removed from the alleged source that the term *foaftale* has emerged in the contemporary legend jargon (for "friend of a friend"). For example, in the retelling of the Pop Rocks story, children were apt

---

Box 2.4. The "Hippie Babysitter" Contemporary Legend

Marketing professionals are well aware that new product innovations are likely to succeed to the extent that they are seen as having a clear relative advantage over products they promise to supercede. Conversely, if innovations are perceived by consumers as bearing certain risks (e.g., financial, physical, psychological), corresponding fears among potential buyers may serve as barriers that ultimately spell doom for the product. The microwave oven is an example of a product that appeared in the marketplace with great promise (its creators hoped the new cooking device would revolutionize the way meals were prepared in the kitchen), but because most consumers had little understanding about how the product functioned, they also had great concerns about its safety.

One example of a contemporary legend that corresponds to fears about the microwave oven and, more generally, our rapidly changing technological age, is described in the text ("the exploding pet" urban legend). Another rumor linked to the microwave oven, but probably corresponding to other inner fears, is known as the "hippie babysitter" legend. This legend supposedly dates back to 1971, although microwave ovens did not become a widespread consumer commodity until the early 1980s. According to the basic story, a couple hires the hippie friend of their regular babysitter to watch their baby while they go out to eat at a restaurant. They tell her there is part of a turkey in the refrigerator to heat up, but when they come home, the girl is sitting on the floor, tripping on LSD, with the turkey sitting in the baby's swing and the microwave oven beeping. A variation of this story alleges that the parents call the babysitter from the restaurant; when told by her that she had just preheated the oven and was ready to start baking the turkey, the couple realized they had no turkey. By the time they got home, the babysitter was crazed on drugs, had just finished basting the infant with gravy and was about to put her in the microwave oven (www.urbanlegends.com).

Although in part reflecting fears of the explicit dangers of new products that consumers do not fully understand, the hippie babysitter stories also can be traced to some of the inherent anxieties associated with being a parent, including fears about a child's security or feelings of guilt from leaving a child at home alone (or with a stranger). In another sense, the stories also confirm certain highly charged emotions linked to the spread of illicit drugs in society and the unconventional and often threatening lifestyles of cultural outsiders (e.g., hippies).

---

to describe the victim as a friend of another child in the next neighborhood. Further, some more traditional rumors circulate so widely and in so many different variations that they ultimately evolve into a form that can legitimately be labeled as a contemporary legend. Fine (1980) suggested that this was the case with a frequently repeated contamination rumor known as "the Kentucky fried rat." In its different variations, this legend claimed that while eating a piece of chicken purchased from a well-known fast-food fried chicken chain, a person became violently ill. Only later was it discovered that the customer had eaten a piece of a poisoned rat that had been fried and battered along with the chicken. According to Fine, over the years more than 115 versions of this story have emerged and he estimated that approximately half the undergraduates at American universities had heard at least one version. In its retelling, the story gradually evolved from ordinary rumor to urban legend status as it lengthened, took on more details, and touched collective, deeply held fears of dangers beyond one's personal control.

Internal and External Rumors

In characterizing the scuttlebutt that travels through the consumer marketplace and the company grapevine, a relevant distinction differentiates between rumors with content that is of primary interest either to persons within an organization (internal rumors) or external to its operations (external rumors; DiFonzo & Bordia, 1998). Internal rumors, for example, are those that primarily interest people who are involved in the production, distribution, or sale of a company's products and services. By contrast, external rumors primarily interest the persons who purchase or use a company's products, services, and stocks, including consumers, stockholders, and the media.

In an unpublished survey of 74 public relations professionals, DiFonzo and Bordia (1998) noted that their respondents were more apt to report having heard internal rumors (51%) than external rumors (38%), with the remaining 11% either unclassified or having characteristics of both internal and external forms. The most common internal rumors pertained to personnel changes within the organization, job satisfaction (including hearsay about job benefits, transfer of duties, and employee relations), and job security. External rumors tended to focus on product and service quality, the organization's reputation, and the stock market. I obtained similar results in a recent study of French brand managers (Kimmel & Audrain, 2002).

Kapferer's Typology

In distinguishing rumors on the basis of their etiology (i.e., causes or origins), marketing professor Jean-Noël Kapferer (1990) suggested that rumors can vary according to whether they emanate from (a) an event, (b) a detail, or (c) fantasy. The first sort of rumor was the primary focus of Shibutani (1966), who characterized rumors as essentially emerging when formal news channels break down and fail to provide the public with the information or explanations needed to fully understand ongoing events, as during natural disasters or catastrophes. The unexpected sudden rise or fall of a company's stock might constitute an event in the financial marketplace that could be expected to generate rumors about a potential takeover bid or the like.

The second form of rumor develops as a function of a detail or sign that had previously received little attention or gone unnoticed. In an example provided by Kapferer (1990), the birth of a deformed animal near a nuclear power plant could prompt rumors about a radiation leak. Similarly, when the attention of consumers is aroused by unfounded innuendo, the rumor process could be further stimulated when consumers selectively begin to notice details that had long gone unnoticed, such as the P&G man in the moon logo. In the Snapple case, the letter "K" on the company's soft drink labels, which was used to identify the product as conforming to Jewish kosher standards, eventually was interpreted as standing for the Ku Klux Klan once conspiracy rumors began to take shape about the company.

The third type of rumor identified by Kapferer (1990) involves unconfirmed stories that do not stem from any precipitating event or detail, but rather are exclusively a function of fantasy or imagination, despite the fact that in their retelling people often show little inclination to distinguish between fantasy and reality. Urban legends represent examples that can be placed in this category; convincingly told, they may take on a life of their own.

Table 2.2 summarizes the various types of rumors already described, along with corresponding examples of each. It must be emphasized that these rumor classifications should not be taken as mutually exclusive. For example, a rumor that originates due to a particular event could be seen as arising spontaneously as the event unfolds and people crave additional information about what is going on. Instead, the event-based rumor could be perceived as deliberately provoked (or premeditated) in the event's aftermath as a deliberate effort after meaning.

UNDERSTANDING HOW RUMORS START AND WHY THEY SPREAD

Given the many forms that rumors may take, it should be readily apparent to the reader that there is no simple explanation for why rumors emerge, why they tend to be believed, why they are transmitted from person to person in spite of sometimes outrageous or illogical content, and why they represent a significant element of social interaction. The various examples that we have considered to this point suggest the involvement of collective and group needs, personal motives, and situational or contextual forces in the generation and spread of rumors in commercial settings, organizations, and everyday life. It is these forces that have served as the focus of systematic attempts over the years to explain the dynamics of rumor. Foremost among the perspectives that have proven most relevant to our interest in commercial and organizational rumors are the functional approach, the psychoanalytic approach, and the marketing approach.

The Functional Approach

Contemporary researchers tend to regard rumor as a collective (i.e., social) phenomenon with dynamics that can best be explained as involving a combination of psychological and situational variables. This perspective, which emanates

TABLE 2.2

Types of Rumors: Summary

Rumor Type	Example
Pipe Dream	A company's stock is about to rise and now is the time to exercise one's stock options.
Bogie	Because of declining profits a massive layoff is on the way.
Wedge driver	The company's CEO is rumored to be recommending that union members be reprimanded.
Homestretcher	Bill Gates is rumored to be ready to hold a press conference to respond to calls for the breakup of Microsoft.
Spontaneous	During a fuel crisis, it is rumored that alternative reserves soon will be available to consumers.
Premeditated	A new restaurant owner spreads a rumor that a famous rock star will dine at his establishment next weekend.
Self-fulfilling	Rumors of a plant closing so demoralize the workforce that the plant must close due to poor subsequent performance.
Conspiracy	A bank is rumored to be secretly controlled by organized crime.
Contamination	Bubble Yum bubble gum is made from spider eggs.
Urban legends	Elaborate stories allege that alligators are lurking in the New York City sewer system.
Internal	The company's director is about to be replaced by a vice president.
External	A particular brand of breakfast cereal is about to be discontinued in the local market.

from the fields of sociology and social psychology, is classified as functional in nature because it attempts to shed light on the processes of rumor transmission, the factors that lead to individual differences in receptivity, and the role that rumors play in satisfying human needs (Brodin & Roux, 1990). The functional approach was given impetus in the social and behavioral sciences as a result of the ground-breaking work of Allport and Postman, whose seminal book *The Psychology of Rumor* (1947) stood for many years as a definitive treatise on the psychological sources of rumor and the processes of rumor diffusion. Published 2 years after World War II, Allport and Postman's text summarizes the fruits of their investigative labor during the war, when they set out to understand the nature and effects of rumormongering in wartime settings. They viewed such an endeavor as critical in terms of its implications for information management during times of crisis and conflict, and also saw it as a means of identifying how potentially morale-sapping rumors could be controlled. After all, during the war American forces not only had to fight a deadly enemy on the battlefield, but also an unseen enemy in the form of false rumors—rumors that were spreading alarm and threatening national security, on the one hand, and raising false and exaggerated hopes on the other. Rumors also were active among the civilian population during the war. For example, one rumor maintained that whole sides of beef were being thrown away at U.S. Army camps. This was a troubling rumor stateside, where meat shortages were being experienced and people had little awareness of what was transpiring in the Army camps.

Having chosen to investigate a topic that previously had received scant scientific analysis, Allport and Postman (1947) relied on a diverse mixture of potentially fruitful methods, including anecdotal observations, communication studies, and ideas taken from the fields of psychoanalysis, sociology, and psychology. The results of their extensive analysis led them to conclude that the transmission of a rumor is akin to a process of collective problem solving. In their view, rumors are set in motion and spread when there is ambiguity regarding the true facts surrounding a situation and when the theme of the story has some importance to both speaker and listener—their so-called basic law of rumor (see Box 2.5). In other words, situations that are marked by ambiguity or a state of doubt are psychologically aversive, and rumors can be seen as a group's effort to discern the true facts to obtain cognitive clarity and closure—in short, rumors are like hypotheses or tentative explanations after the facts. This effort after clarity could involve the attribution of causes to events, motives to characters, the prediction of future events, and the like. However, Allport and Postman framed their rumor equation as a multiplicative relationship, suggesting that it is not enough for the situation to be characterized by ambiguity—it also must be important enough to prompt people to engage in rumor-generating behavior. This point was clarified in the following example:

> An American citizen is not likely to spread rumors concerning the market price of camels in Afghanistan because the subject has no importance for him, ambiguous though it certainly is. He is not disposed to spread gossip concerning the doings of the people in Swaziland, because he doesn't care about them. (Allport & Postman, 1947, p. 34)

The basic law of rumor was not the result of idle speculation; in fact, its intellectual roots have been traced back to research conducted in the 1930s by McGregor (1938), who cited the variables of ambiguity and importance as integral to the degree to which subjective factors influence people's predictions of future events (cf. Rosnow, 1991). Further, the nature of wartime, which greatly influenced Allport and Postman's (1947) theorizing, is marked by a maximum degree of uncertainty; information about military operations is deliberately withheld and the outbreak of hostilities generally is marked by rampant confusion (Belgion, 1939). In this light, it is not surprising that Allport and Postman would conclude that rumors emerge in ambiguous situations.

Although the basic law of rumor remained the authoritative psychological explanation of rumor for many years, the lesser known work of Indian psy-

---

Box 2.5. Allport and Postman's Basic Law of Rumor

The first general principle of rumor, which appeared in Allport and Postman's (1947) classic book *The Psychology of Rumor*, is conceptualized in a simple two-variable formula that had long been acknowledged by early investigators of hearsay (e.g., Knapp, 1944; Prasad, 1935)—that rumors develop when people have a need for information in ambiguous or uncertain situations. The formula, $R \sim I \times A$, is read as follows:

"The amount of rumor in circulation will vary with the importance of the subject to the individuals concerned times the ambiguity of the evidence pertaining to the topic at issue." (Allport & Postman, 1947, pp. 33–34)

In other words, Allport and Postman (1947) proposed that there are two essential prerequisites to rumor: "first, the theme of the story must have some *importance* to speaker and listener; second, the true facts must be shrouded in some kind of *ambiguity*" (p. 33). According to their further explication of the factors involved, importance was defined in terms of the degree to which people care or feel personally involved by the situation or subject at hand. The variable of ambiguity can be seen as synonymous with general or free-floating uncertainty evoked by a situation in which there is a need for information or cognitive clarity (Rosnow, 1991). The notion that a widespread sense of doubt creates a kind of susceptibility to generate and spread unconfirmed propositions has long been accepted as a critical point to understanding the psychology of rumor.

With Allport and Postman's general principle in mind, it is easier to understand why the majority of rumors emerge in situations characterized by four Cs: crisis, conflict, catastrophe, and commerce (Koenig, 1985). Whether we are considering a wartime context, the aftermath of a devastating earthquake, a feared explosion at a nuclear power plant, or a contamination scare involving a popular soft drink, in each situation there is likely to be an unsatisfied need for information and a strong desire to achieve a clearer sense of what is going on. This is particularly true for people who are significantly involved in the situation (e.g., earthquake survivors, residents in the communities surrounding the power plant, and loyal buyers of the soft drink). Despite the fact that the validity of their basic law was never empirically demonstrated, Allport and Postman deserve a great deal of credit for shining light on two critical variables involved in the rumor transmission process.

---

chologist Prasad (1935) may have been equally enlightening (cf. Rosnow & Kimmel, 2000). On the basis of an analysis of rumors that appeared following the devastating earthquake of 1934 in Bihar, India, Prasad concluded that in addition to ambiguous, unfamiliar, and unverifiable elements, rumors are generated and transmitted when conditions are emotionally disturbing or fear-arousing for group members. Presumably, the anxiety induced by emotionally unstable situations provides a motivating force for rumormongering.

Thus, Prasad was influential in adding a third factor—anxiety—to Allport and Postman's ambiguity × importance formula. In light of the fact that there never was any direct evidence that rumors relieve the tension of uncertainty, the recognition that an emotional factor is integral to the rumor dynamic was a critical step in understanding.

Several aspects of these early views have been empirically examined in recent years, leading to some important modifications. In his reconceptualization of the basic law of rumor, social psychologist Ralph Rosnow (1991, 2001) gave greater emphasis to the role of anxiety in the rumor generation process, and his arguments coincide well with the notions presented earlier in this chapter that suggest that fear is a natural outcome of a rapidly changing world that is progressively more difficult to fully understand. In Rosnow's (2001) view, rumors represent a logical outgrowth of a world in flux:

> because people's assumptions about how the world works are often confronted by unexpected events or challenged by unforeseen favorable or unfavorable consequences of anticipated events. The more perplexing these events, the more that people need to invent stories to put their anxiety to rest (even if the attempt proves unsuccessful, or the positive effect is only temporary) and to furnish cues to guide their future behavior. (pp. 212–213)

In this way, rumors function as a means of establishing control over situations when the status quo or established order is put at risk by some external threat:

> the flux of social change can give rise to emotional crises whenever some novel event cannot be understood in terms of established assumptions. Once people's expectations are violated, new sensitivities and new ideas emerge along with other ongoing changes in society. For people to act in concert, they must alter their orientations together, which they do by consulting with each other via rumors and then comparing one another's impressions of their experiences and conjectures. (Rosnow, 2001, p. 213)

If rumors indeed serve as a communication mechanism that assists people in reducing their shared fears, it is also recognized that in some circumstances, rumors also can give rise to anxieties (e.g., Naughton, 1996; Turner, 1992). This is the case when reports begin to circulate about allegedly contaminated consumer food products. Clearly, such rumors would not be expected to reduce fears. Further, unlike the implication derived from the basic law of rumor that the underlying factors in rumor generation operate independently, it now is understood that they are more likely to be intimately linked (Rosnow, 2001). For example, as the uncertainty surrounding a situation increases, we might also anticipate a heightening of anxieties; similarly, uncertainty becomes more difficult for people to tolerate under highly stressful circumstances.

What keeps rumors going once they begin to circulate? Although this is a complex question that requires an in-depth consideration of the nature of information diffusion during interpersonal communication, Rosnow and his colleagues argued that belief in the rumor (i.e., credulity) serves as a critical triggering mechanism for transmission. That is, unless rumors are believable or at least somewhat plausible to their recipients, they are unlikely to be passed along to others. However, in situations of extreme anxiety, the rumormonger's critical judgment may be blunted so that belief plays a less active role. The role of belief in the rumor transmission process is discussed in greater detail in Chapter 4.

Since the early 1970s, a body of scientific evidence has emerged that largely supports these suppositions (e.g., Anthony, 1973; Esposito, 1987; Jaeger, Anthony, & Rosnow, 1980; Kimmel & Keefer, 1991; Rosnow, Esposito, & Gibney, 1988; Rosnow, Yost, & Esposito, 1986; Walker & Beckerle, 1987). For example, in an early study conducted by Anthony (1973), Philadelphia high school students were given a standard test to identify who among them were either highly anxious or relatively calm by nature. Shortly thereafter, during a meeting with the school's guidance counselor, they heard a rumor that budgetary limitations might force the curtailment of activities in the student clubs to which they belonged. Later, when the students were asked whether or not they had discussed the rumor, Anthony found that the highly anxious students spread the rumor more frequently than the calm ones did. In subsequent studies, including one carried out by Rosnow et al. (1988) following the murder of a university student and a survey conducted by myself and Robert Keefer (Kimmel & Keefer, 1991) to determine the factors that are associated with rumors about AIDS, it was revealed that the more frightening and personally relevant the situation was for the individuals questioned, the more likely they were to spread rumors. Further, in our AIDS study, when we asked our respondents why they chose not to pass on a rumor they had heard, their most frequent response was that they simply did not believe the rumor to be true.

In sum, the current understanding from a functional perspective suggests that rumors are generated under conditions marked by an optimal combination of anxiety (an affective state characterized by apprehension about ongoing or forthcoming events), uncertainty (free-floating doubt or ambiguity pertaining to unstable situations), and involvement (i.e., importance or relevance of the situation). Thus, an atmosphere conducive to the spread of rumors requires that (a) individuals are experiencing a state of doubt due to unexplained events or ambiguity concerning other aspects of a situation—that is, they are filled with questions about what is happening and what will happen next; (b) they are worried, upset, or nervous about the situation; and (c) the situation is personally involving for them. In this view, rumors arise out of logical reasoning or popular imagination to restore a sense of stability when events turn unpredictable and are psychologically threatening. If the rumor adequately explains unanswered questions or sufficiently fills in gaps in people's understanding about what is going on, this may serve to reduce their anxieties and eliminate their fears. However, if the rumor itself arouses anxiety—that is, it is of the bogie or wedge

driving variety—it can escalate fears. As a result, rumors often are self-perpetu-
ating in the sense that they can create anxiety in the recipient. This explanation is
important in understanding why it often is so difficult to control or eliminate rumors. Finally, rumors are likely to endure—provided that the communications
are credible and not easily verifiable—until contrary facts emerge that prove the
rumor is false or underlying anxieties are alleviated.

The Psychoanalytic Approach

The psychoanalytic approach to studying and understanding rumor goes beyond a consideration of the social-psychological variables previously described by focusing on unconscious psychic forces as underlying the onset of
rumors (e.g., Gayda, 1992). In this view rumors are seen as psychological defense mechanisms or fantasies produced by the unconscious mind that assist
in integrating the individual within the group, at the same time allowing one
to maintain a unique personality (Ambrosini, 1983). Fantasies enable individuals to satisfy their desires in an unconscious, personal way.

Although the best known proponent of the psychoanalytic approach,
Sigmund Freud, never directly addressed the phenomenon of rumor in his writ-
ings, his analyses of the unconscious, fantasy, and hysteria certainly bear an indirect relevance to the subject. Nonetheless, it was Freud's contemporary, Carl
Jung, who explicitly cast rumors within the palette of activities related to fantasy
and as an outlet for the expression of dreams (Brodin & Roux, 1990). In an early
paper on the psychology of rumor, Jung (1917) classed rumors into two categories: (a) ordinary rumors that are temporary and reflective of strictly individual
needs, and (b) visionary rumors that are recurrent and reflective of collective
needs. According to this distinction, legends (including contemporary legends)
and wild stories about mythical creatures, monsters, or extraterrestrial visitors
that people have shared for centuries would be considered as falling within the
second category—visionary rumors or living myths that traverse both time and
generations. Whereas ordinary rumors, in Jung's view, depend on the presence
of individual desires, curiosity, and sensation seeking, visionary rumors require
deeply felt emotion shared by many people.

Jung's notions about rumor stem from his theory of analytical psychology.
Like Freud, Jung (1936/1969) emphasized the unconscious mind and its influence on dream processes in his theory; however, his most unique contribution
was to suggest that the unconscious mind is comprised of two forms, the personal unconscious and the collective unconscious. Whereas the personal unconscious is created from a person's experiences and thus is idiosyncratic to
the individual, the collective unconscious represents the inherited portion of
the unconscious mind that is identical in all humans. According to Jung, the
collective unconscious consists of primitive images and patterns of thoughts,
feelings, and behavior, which together serve as a kind of ancestral memory of
the human race.

In partial support of these notions, Jung pointed to similarities in religion, art, symbolism, and dream imagery across cultures and historical periods as representing aspects of our inherited unconscious. He referred to the basic symbols contained in the collective unconscious as *archetypes*, or mythological motifs that reflect basic human needs and are apparent in dreams, fantasies, and cultural practices. The images of the mother or wise elder represent two examples of archetypes consistent with Jung's theory. In this context, the content of visionary rumors provides further examples of primitive archetypes that, for example, might signify collective fears and anxieties in facing a complex world or an expression of the universal desire for redemption and survival.

In his paper "A Visionary Rumor," Jung (1959) applied his analytical psychology notions to an interpretation of rumors about flying saucers. He saw tales of UFOs as visionary rumors founded on an emotional tension stemming from a collective distress over the world situation. Further, the stories signify an unconscious wish for a redeeming savior or supernatural force that could allay our fears. Sightings of flying saucers have been reported since the 16th century, but have really only become a staple of worldwide fascination and curiosity since the mid-1900s. In recent decades, stories of UFOs and alien visitors to our planet have provided grist for the rumor mill as churned out by American tabloid newspapers and have emerged as a mainstay of science fiction literature and cinema. Consistent with Jung's explanation, these contemporary versions of UFO tales either tell of benevolent, superior beings from another planet who have come to save humanity, or of menacing creatures who threaten the planet and thereby serve to unify people of diverse ideologies against a common foe.

Other cases of long-standing rumors can also be interpreted as reflections of archetypal images or projected fantasies. For example, the death of innocents emerges from time to time as an underlying theme in a variety of rumors and urban legends that are culturally transmitted from one generation to another. In one contemporary version of this theme, a rumor spread across American university campuses in late 1969 that Paul McCartney of the Beatles had been tragically killed in an automobile crash and replaced in the rock group by a double (Reeve, 1994). This story has been compared to the legend of the Greek god Dionysus, who was said to have suffered a violent death and then to have been later resurrected (Rosnow & Fine, 1976). A somewhat similar theme that can be interpreted as another example of a projection of our collective unconscious pertains to child kidnapping rumors. One common version describes the strange disappearance of a young girl whose mother has taken her shopping at a K-Mart store located in a suburban shopping center. Following a search, the little girl is found in a restroom with a woman who had cut off the child's hair and dressed her as a boy in a bizarre kidnapping attempt.

A variation of the child abduction rumor with racial overtones recounts the story of a young boy who, while shopping with his mother at an inner-city department store, is attacked and castrated in the store's lavatory. This so-called castration myth has reappeared in various forms throughout history, although in its modern-day versions the victim and perpetrator are described as being of different races, with the victim's race always matching that of the person who tells the story (Rosnow & Fine, 1976). In France, similar stories of child abduction have been framed within the context of fears concerning the White slave trade. For example, in his book *La Rumeur d'Orléans*, French sociologist Edgar Morin (1971) recounted the rumors that spread throughout the city of Orléans and surrounding towns in the center of France beginning around the late 1960s. In these stories, young women were alleged to have been drugged while shopping in fashionable clothing stores and then taken to foreign cities and sold into a life of prostitution. According to certain variations of this rumor, it was suggested that this activity was organized by Jewish boutique proprietors who paid off local authorities and police to maintain their silence about the scheme. Each outbreak of the rumor appears to have been sparked by a different incident: in Laval, it corresponded to the arrival in town of an anti-White slave trading activist who warned members of the community about the danger, whereas in Orléans, it seems to have originated after a fictitious kidnapping plot was graphically presented as a real event in a popular French tabloid newspaper. The rumor emerged once again in 1985, with a popular clothing store in the town of La Roche-sur-Yon serving as the site where the druggings allegedly took place. In his analysis, Morin explained that such rumors likely were the result of a simple projection of a feared scenario devised by active imaginations. He traced the incubation of the rumor to all-girls religious high schools where, as Kapferer (1990) observed, the isolated setting served as a fertile environment for the rapid spread of the sexually charged story:

> This adolescent population, isolated from social reality and closed off from the rest of the world, is fertile ground for the production of sexual fantasies—imaginary scenarios embodying repressed desires—that one girl tells her friends as if they had really happened to her, and that the friends in turn envy and make into their own experiences. (p. 28)

Consistent with the sorts of stories that served as the focus of his analyses, Morin (1971) confined his definition of rumors to stories lacking a factual basis, associating rumor with mental disease or, in his words, a "psychological cancer." Without any basis in reality, rumors are like hallucinations that emerge in the minds of mentally disturbed individuals; however, once they enter the social environment and begin to circulate, they are accepted as truthful information because of the trust placed in the teller. Although this view is not a widely accepted one today, it may be particularly useful in helping us understand why many urban legends and, to a lesser extent, ordinary rumors appear to emerge spontaneously, without any apparent relation to precipitating events or ambiguous and anxiety-provoking situations in real life (Kapferer, 1990).

The Marketing Approach

Marketing is a field of inquiry that covers a wide range of phenomena related to the identification and satisfaction of consumer needs. In a recent process-oriented definition, Kotler et al. (1999) described marketing as "a social and managerial process by which individuals and groups obtain what they need and want through creating and exchanging products and value with others" (p. 10). This definition reflects a dramatic evolution since the time when marketing was narrowly understood as pertaining solely to selling and advertising. In addition to promotion, other marketing activities involve the identification of consumer needs, the development and introduction of new products and services, strategic planning, building customer relations, pricing considerations, and the management of distribution channels.

Whether one considers marketing as a managerial process or as a formalized field of inquiry, it is clear that it is interdisciplinary in nature, with strong links to a variety of disciplines, including sociology, psychology, communications, and consumer behavior. Not surprisingly, this interdisciplinary nature is reflected in what has been dubbed the "marketing approach" to rumor (Brodin & Roux, 1990). Rather than being singular in nature, the marketing approach draws from several perspectives, including the functional approach (described earlier) and notions derived from sociology, social psychology, and communication studies. The objective of this approach is to integrate the concepts and empirical data derived from multiple sources to shed light on rumors that pertain to consumer products. This pluralistic perspective is essentially the approach we have adopted in this book, although our focus on marketplace and organizational rumors is broader in scope.

Given its multidimensional nature, the marketing approach is difficult to pin down exactly because it actually involves a combination of different theoretical views; however, the integration of these views is for the most part oriented toward the identification and application of strategies for controlling rumors. Among the theoretical perspectives that have proved particularly applicable to marketers in terms of suggesting strategies for rumor control are attribution theory, information processing theory, and theories of information diffusion and word-of-mouth communication.

Attribution theory has been utilized by marketers to better understand some of the circumstances under which people tend to believe others who tell or deny rumors. Specifically, this approach has shed some light on the variables that contribute to rumor credibility and helps explain why rumor denials are often ineffective (Brodin & Roux, 1990). Attribution theorists (e.g., Ajzen, 1977; Kelley, 1973) have argued that people have a tendency to utilize available information likely to prove useful in making a judgment about the cause of a behavior or an event and to ignore information that does not appear useful in ascertaining causality. In one view, according to social psychologist Harold Kelley (1973), information about consistency, distinctiveness, and consensus tends to influence whether we attribute someone's behavior to internal (i.e., something about the person) or external (i.e., something about the situation) causes. For example, if we want to explain why a friend is having trouble with her new computer, we might ask whether our friend usually has trouble with this computer (consistency), whether she has trouble with other computers or only this one (distinctiveness), and whether other people have similar problems with the same model of computer that she is using (consensus; Myers, 1996). If we learn that our friend alone usually has trouble with a wide range of computers and not just her new computer, we are likely to conclude that she is to blame for the difficulties and not defects in the computer.

Applied to the rumor transmission process, let us assume that it is not the case that our friend is having difficulties with her new computer, but rather that she has just informed us that she heard that a new line of computers has been manufactured with a dangerous computer "worm" that will destroy all files stored on the computer's hard drive within 1 year of use. In deciding whether or not to believe this story, we might consider whether our friend usually conveys unconfirmed stories that turn out to be true (or false; distinctiveness), whether she has repeated this story on other occasions (consistency), and whether we have heard the same story from other sources (consensus). We are likely to accept the rumor as credible if we recognize that our friend has never spread false rumors in the past and others have told us the same story.

Of course, judgments about products are dependent on a wide range of other considerations likely to have some impact on whether we accept product-related rumors. For example, negative evaluations of product attributes often have a stronger influence on consumers' judgments than positive evaluations of the same attributes (e.g., Folkes, 1988; Mizerski, 1982; Weinberger, Allen, & Dillon, 1981). That is, we generally expect companies to convey only positive information about the goods and services they are offering, so it is not surprising when we are constantly bombarded by promotional messages telling us about the high quality of those goods. After a while, however, we may stop listening, because the information is no longer seen as informative (so-called advertising burnout has occurred). Conversely, when we hear a negative rumor about the product—even given its unconfirmed nature—that message is likely to capture our attention and have a significant influence on our perception of the product involved. This is one reason rumor denials often are ineffective in the marketplace: We expect companies to issue them when the reputation of the company or its goods and services are being threatened by malicious talk. On the other hand, it is often hard to imagine how someone not affiliated with the company could benefit from making false assertions about the company's products, especially if that person happens to be someone close to us whom we tend to trust. As discussed in later chapters, attribution to a credible source is an essential quality underlying both a rumor's evolution and the efficacy of rumor denials.

In addition to the relevance of attribution principles, the marketing approach also draws on information processing theory for insights into how rumors might be effectively combatted. Not entirely dissimilar in nature, both attribution and information processing focus on rational thinking processes and the ways in which people cognitively utilize the information they receive from the situation and previous experience. Consumer researchers and advertising professionals have long used cognitive decision-making theories in their attempts to accurately predict consumer brand selection and reactions to promotional messages (cf. Solomon, Bamossy, & Askegaard, 1999). For example, according to compensatory decision-making rules, consumers take note of the attributes that come to mind when thinking about a particular product category; they evaluate each brand in their consideration set in terms of how well the brands rate on each attribute; and they select the brand that does best overall on the ratings, after weighting each attribute according to importance. Thus, if I believe that Porsche performs better than BMW on the attributes of automobiles that are most important to me (e.g., prestige, value, and durability), I will be more likely to select a Porsche the next time I purchase a car (assuming my budget allows it!), even though I may have assigned BMW higher ratings on some of the other attributes. This sort of rational approach to decision making would suggest that in their attempts to dispel an outrageous rumor (e.g., that a hamburger chain adds worms to its meat), a company should develop a credible and persuasive communication clearly describing reasons why the rumor is untrue. Given the rather incredible nature of the rumor, we might expect message recipients to rationally conclude that the rumor is false (Tybout, Calder, & Sternthal, 1981). Why then does this approach often fail?

In their analysis of the McDonald's wormburger rumor, Tybout et al. (1981) suggested that information processing theory can provide insight into how consumers react to rumor-relevant information. In this view, it is assumed that when we receive a new piece of information, it is represented without alteration in active memory (i.e., the store of readily retrievable information), where it may activate previously stored thoughts about the same object. Because of the limited capacity of active memory, both incoming information and previously processed information about an object can be moved to long-term storage. This occurs as a result of the repeated active association of attributes to the object (so-called rehearsal). As Tybout and her colleagues posited, recipients of the McDonald's rumor were likely to have associated the alleged product attribute (worms) with the object (McDonald's) in their minds repeatedly (depending on how many times they heard or thought about the rumor), and this association was then stored in their memory. Next, whenever they subsequently thought about the object (e.g., "Shall we lunch at McDonald's today?"), object-relevant thoughts about the object were retrieved from memory ("When I think about McDonald's, I remember the worms."). Had the rumor not been heard, the corresponding thoughts retrieved from memory surely may have been more positive in nature ("McDonald's burgers are tasty and juicy" as opposed to "McDonald's burgers have juicy red worms") and the evaluation of the object (McDonald's) would have been more favorable.

According to Tybout et al. (1981), "Consumers are affected because they process the rumor, not because they necessarily believe it" (p. 74). In their view, this is why even the most implausible rumors can have an impact on consumers' behavior and why logical denials may actually have a countereffect to what was intended—that is, the refutation increases rehearsal of the rumor and the likelihood that rumored attributes will be linked to the object in the recipient's memory. As Koenig (1985) suggested, even if we reject the McDonald's rumor as incredulous, when it comes time to choose between lunching at McDonald's or a local pizza parlor, just the thought of worms in hamburgers is enough to steer most people in the direction of the latter. We consider the implications of this explanation further when we focus on specific strategies for combatting rumors in subsequent chapters.

Another useful direction that marketers have taken for understanding rumors and developing strategies for their control focuses on the areas of information diffusion and word-of-mouth communication. Drawing from the literature on diffusion of innovation (i.e., the ways in which acceptance of a new product, service, or idea spreads across a social group or community), a rumor can be viewed as having a distinctive life cycle (see chap. 3). At some point during its spread, a critical mass (or "tipping point") may be reached, when the rumor begins to take off and spread rapidly in an uncontrolled fashion, not unlike a contagious disease. During its spread, the rumor is likely to undergo certain modifications, which ultimately may add to its plausibility. Given the fact that much product-related information, including unconfirmed information in the form of rumors, is conveyed through word-of-mouth, this process of interpersonal communication is also viewed as crucial for understanding how rumors spread and how they might be controlled. Because of the informal nature of these processes, companies often find it an uphill battle to try to influence their course. What marketers have learned about these concerns represents the focus of Chapter 4.

CONCLUSION

Given the range of possible forms that rumors may take and the various explanations that have been proposed to unveil their dynamics, it is easy to understand why rumors are considered to be such elusive and slippery subjects. We can also appreciate the difficulties that companies face in controlling their spread and limiting their potentially negative consequences. In our view, as there are multiple perspectives for understanding different aspects of the rumor dynamic, there are also multiple ways to approach rumors in attempts to control them and limit their adverse effects. In the next chapter, we take a closer look at the nature of rumors that spread through the marketplace and in organizational settings, in light of the notions presented here.

CHAPTER THREE

Commercial Rumors
and Organizational Grapevines

McDonald's just announced that 30 cents out of every dollar of purchases
in its 60 branches in Saudi Arabia will be donated as of today to the Palestin-
ian intifada against the Israelis. Please BOYCOTT their stores (it tastes like
s - - t anyway). Please send this message to all your e-mail pals.
—Internet posting (January, 2001)

As you no doubt recognize, this McDonald's message, which circulated on the
Internet as tensions were rising once again in the Middle East, is fictitious. Regardless, it is exactly the kind of false rumor that rattles company officials because in the minds of most people it *could* be true and, as such, it could serve to
undermine the McDonald's image and influence consumer behavior. No matter how much money the restaurant chain spends on advertising and promotions, there is no guarantee that such falsehoods can be prevented in the future.

Now that we have placed the concept of rumor under the microscope to
better understand its characteristics and dynamics, in this chapter we apply
some of these notions to examine the nature of marketplace and organizational rumors in greater depth. This requires that we reconsider the role of
some of the psychological and situational forces (e.g., anxiety, uncertainty,
need for information, unconscious needs, projective fantasies) that we identified in Chapter 2 in our overview of the basic approaches to understanding the
rumor process. More specifically, this chapter focuses on several compelling
questions that should help us better appreciate the kinds of rumors that represent the focus of this book and put us in a better position to be able to recommend strategies for controlling them:

- Why are rumors so prevalent in business-related settings?
- Do rumors that circulate in the consumer marketplace operate the same
  way as rumors that flow through organizational grapevines?

- What functions and human needs do business-oriented rumors satisfy?
- Why do people spread rumors that they know are likely to prove to be false?
- Why is belief in rumor content more often the norm rather than the exception?
- Why do some marketplace rumors reappear over time, whereas others do not?

Prior to addressing these questions, it is important to bear in mind the fluid and malleable nature of rumors: Not only is the content of a rumor likely to be altered in the retelling, but so too are rumor targets, which at times are interchangeable, jumping from one company to another. These organic qualities add to the difficulties many companies encounter in attempts to control rumors before they can inflict serious damage. Nonetheless, depending on the circumstances, rumors in marketplace and organizational contexts can have positive as well as damaging effects for companies, customers, and employees.

EXPLAINING COMMERCIAL RUMORS
IN THE CONSUMER MARKETPLACE

Although several forces are probably at work in the spread of commercial rumors, in the majority of cases we can assume that such rumors are to some extent the offspring of uncertainties, anxieties, and a natural desire for inside information—three psychological ingredients that researchers have found to be at the root of rumormongering (see chap. 2). These factors are likely to influence the development and course of both contamination and conspiracy rumors. For example, rumors like the ones involving Tropical Fantasy soft drinks, Jockey shorts, and AIDS-tainted Domino's pizza that focus on Black Americans and gays correspond to racial tensions, an uneasiness regarding gay rights, and threats to the status quo arising out of gains made by disenfranchised groups. People with AIDS represent a more recent group to fear, which may explain why AIDS-related rumors have become more prevalent since the 1980s (e.g., Fine, 1987; Kimmel & Keefer, 1991).

Contamination Rumors

The persistence of contamination rumors about well-known food products, such as the "wormburger," exploding candy, and fried rat rumors, in large part may be explained by the widespread uncertainty and anxiety in contemporary society about additives, cholesterol, and other health risks contained in food. As I previously suggested, these rising fears are linked to modern-day developments in the ways food and beverage products are produced and distributed. Such tensions are communicated from parent to child, thus implicating people of all ages in the rumor-spreading process.

In the past, prior to industry developments that have led to the emergence of enormous corporations and the internationalization of markets, the consumption of food was a much more personal and intimate activity. In the morning, a household member would purchase beef or poultry for that evening's family dinner from the local butcher, who was a familiar neighbor and perhaps even a friend. They could have confidence that the butcher would provide fresh and risk-free meat because his livelihood depended on their continued patronage and because over the years they had learned to trust him.

Now, the neighborhood butcher may have long been squeezed out of business due to the influx of large, anonymous supermarkets and fast-food restaurant chains. The meat you purchase for dinner is apt to be mass produced and packaged, originating from points unknown, and having a quality that is difficult to assess (cf. Schlosser, 2001). The Big Mac or Whopper that you order in one of the many fast-food restaurants in town is prepared, served, and eaten in an impersonal setting among strangers. At the same time, we are overwhelmed by reports of the latest evidence from medical studies demonstrating the potentially cancer-producing (and other) risks from everyday products and scientific advances. Many of these studies at times contradict the findings of previous research that recommended as healthy the foods and beverages we now are told to avoid (cf. Evenson, 2001). The fears and uncertainties engendered by these developments often are exacerbated by sporadic crises that occur unpredictably, such as the recent outbreaks in Europe of the Creutzfeldt–Jakob (mad-cow) and hoof-and-mouth diseases. In this context, it is not surprising that contamination rumors are common in the contemporary marketplace. However, although the blame—if that is the correct word—for such rumors should be laid on socioeconomic changes and in some cases simply bad luck, in actuality they represent an attack on the manufacturer, given that the focus of the rumors tends to be placed on the target (i.e., the product or brand; Brodin & Roux, 1995).

The rumor that fast-food hamburger chains add worms to their hamburgers to increase protein levels probably did not emerge out of thin air. One possibility is that this false rumor began circulating after someone found something that looked like a worm in his or her hamburger (e.g., a tubular-shaped piece of blood vessel). To add credibility to this conjecture the consumer may have surmised that the worm was added as a protein supplement. This "discovery" would be difficult to keep to oneself; discussing it with friends would be one way to have the explanation either confirmed or disconfirmed. This could be enough to add fuel to a rumor about wormburgers. In this scenario, what promulgated the story was a need to know—that is, a desire for information to placate one's fears and reduce the uncertainty surrounding an uncommon situation. Of course, there is probably nothing harmful about eating worms (even uncooked juicy ones) along with one's hamburger. Nonetheless, the idea is unpleasant enough to most people that even those who initially rejected the story as ludicrous may have had second thoughts about its veracity.

Keeping in mind the rather innocuous way this story may have emerged (e.g., a teenager telling his friends, "I found something peculiar in my burger today"), it is often awe inspiring to recognize how quickly a rumor can expand and take off, sometimes even sweeping the nation. Shortly after the onset of the McDonald's story, a questionnaire pertaining to the rumor was distributed among university students in the state of Georgia, a particular hotbed of activity for the rumor (Goggins, 1978). All but 4 of 247 students reported having heard the wormburger rumor, with 63% claiming to have heard it from a friend and the remainder through the media. More than half (57%) admitted that they had passed on the rumor after hearing it, although it is not known how many of these individuals disbelieved the story. From the company's perspective, one other finding no doubt raised the greatest concern: Slightly more than 7% of the respondents claimed that the story had influenced their decision not to eat at the restaurant, an important finding that is probably greatly understated (Koenig, 1985). In fact, one owner of four McDonald's franchises in Atlanta saw his sales plummet by 30% in 1978 when the rumor was at its peak in that area, forcing him to lay off about one third of his employees (Mikkelson, 2001).

McDonald's has been hit particularly hard by contamination rumors over the years and several other related rumors subsequently involved the company in addition to the story about worms (see Box 3.1). Of course, the fast-food hamburger chain is not alone in being targeted by contamination rumors, but it is one of many companies that have suffered similarly at the hands of false rumor campaigns. I have previously discussed the Pop Rocks contamination rumor in some detail and numerous other examples could be cited. Some of the widespread stories making the rounds during the summer of 2001 included unfounded reports of flesh-eating bacteria on banana peels; soda cans contaminated by poisonous rat urine; a toxic sponge infected with the so-called Klingerman virus and mailed to people at random; crayons containing asbestos; and claims that infected syringes were found pasted to gas-pump handles, pay phones, or vending machines. Each of these stories have appeared in the form of inquiries forwarded to medically oriented Internet sites, such as the Web site for the American Cancer Society, suggesting that such rumors reflect suspicions and lack of sophistication concerning rapid developments in fields of medicine.

Contamination rumors perhaps can best be explained in terms of a general distrust of major corporations or the government. Market leaders represent bigger symbolic targets, and the "antibigness" rumors often merge with rumors that can be traced to other anxieties (see Box 3.2). A large corporation represents a depersonalized presence in many communities—an intruder that threatens traditional values and ways of operating. When successful fast-food

---

Box 3.1. McDonald's Deserves a Break Today?

Although we have already considered some of the rumors that have targeted McDonald's in the past, the rumor mill has not stopped churning out new stories about the company. Here are some of the stories that have appeared since the mid-1990s:

1. McDonald's milkshakes are not made out of dairy products, which is why the menus refer to them as "shakes" rather than as "milkshakes."
2. McFlurries, McDonald's blend of whipped vanilla ice cream and branded candies, have a feathery appearance because they contain bird feathers.
3. McDonald's uses the fluid of cow eyeballs as a milkshake thickener.
4. McDonald's apple turnovers do not contain any apple, but instead are made out of potatoes or pears plus flavoring.
5. McDonald's milkshakes contain seaweed.

The snopes.com Web site has refuted each of these outrageous stories: The milkshakes do indeed contain milk, but are referred to as "shakes" so as not to confuse consumers who might otherwise expect a beverage made with ice cream. The only story that bears some degree of truth pertains to seaweed in the milkshakes. In actuality, the milkshakes contain a substance that is derived from carrageen, a type of seaweed that is commonly used as an agent in foods, beverages, and frozen goods.

To counter allegations that unmentioned ingredients are included in their product offerings and at the same time to allay the fears of customers allergic to them, each McDonald's restaurant will provide on demand a complete ingredient list for every item on their menu. The company also has established a toll-free telephone hotline and Web site specifically for responding to consumer concerns.

Box 3.2. The Bigger the Company, the More Likely the Rumor

A few years ago, a truly bizarre story circulated on the Internet. It took the form of a message that was made to look like a wire service release and it bore the following title: "Microsoft Bids to Acquire Catholic Church." The story told of Microsoft's attempt to buy the Roman Catholic Church in exchange for an unspecified number of shares of the company's common stock. Pope Paul II was to become a senior vice president of the combined company's new Religious Software Division and, in turn, Microsoft's senior vice presidents were to be invested in the College of Cardinals. Although no doubt intended as a joke, before long the story was repeated countless times throughout print and broadcast media and people who had obviously fallen for the prank began to contact Microsoft's offices for confirmation.

(continued)

As it turns out, companies as large and profitable as Microsoft probably cannot hope to elude the web of rumor networks. Because rumors often reflect a distrust of large corporations, the larger the company, the more likely it is that rumors will circulate about it. This tendency also has been noted in the urban legend literature where, according to Fine (1980), "the frequency of attachment of an urban legend to the largest company or corporation is so common as to be considered a law of urban folklore" (p. 228).

McDonald's and Coca-Cola have for many years appeared at or near the top of listings of the world's most powerful global brands, with Microsoft not far behind in the top 10 (Kotler et al., 1999), and it is no surprise that they consistently have served as easy targets for rumormongers. In the case of Coca-Cola, there have been so many stories circulating about its leading soft drinks that the company's public relations department simply expects rumors as the norm and has developed a form letter to respond to consumer queries (Fine, 1979). The following stories have circulated at one time or another about Coke:

1. The New Coke fiasco was actually a clever marketing ploy.
2. Coca-Cola became carbonated by accident.
3. Coca-Cola was once considered anti-Semitic for refusing to do business in Israel.
4. The modern image of Santa Claus was created by Coca-Cola.
5. Coca-Cola used to contain cocaine.
6. Coca-Cola is an effective spermicide.
7. A tooth left in a glass of Coca-Cola will dissolve overnight.
8. The shape of the Coca-Cola bottle was mistakenly based on the cacao tree seed pod.
9. Coca-Cola's name was translated into Chinese as "bite the wax tadpole."
10. Combining Coca-Cola and aspirin will get you high.
11. Only two people in the company know Coca-Cola's formula, and each of them only knows half of it.
12. Coca-Cola was originally green.
13. The Mormons own the Coca-Cola Co.
14. The cursive script of the Coca-Cola label includes an image of a person snorting cocaine.

According to the snopes.com Internet site (www.snopes.com/cokelore), an investigation into the veracity of these claims revealed all to be false with the exception of Items 3 and 5; insufficient evidence was available to determine the accuracy of Items 6, 8, and 9.

franchises like McDonald's and Wendy's become targets, the rumors suggest anxieties about the trustworthiness of large business enterprises. In their attempts to cut costs, such companies may choose to use cheaper ingredients, even if some of the substitute substances are noxious, unpleasant, and potentially unhealthy (Schlosser, 2001). Mikkelson (2001) summarized these points very clearly in her interpretation of recent McDonald's rumors:

> All large corporations are by their very nature suspect simply due to their size, and this holds even more true in the fast food industry. The public harbors a deep mistrust of Big Business, seeing it as impersonal and profit-driven to the point of irresponsibility. Couple this with lurking fears about what might be hidden in food not personally prepared by the ingestee, and rumors about large corporations dumping anything they can get away with into their fast food offerings will surely result. And just as surely, because it is the largest of the large, McDonald's will star in most of them.

Conspiracy Rumors

Underlying fears and uncertainties also lie at the heart of conspiracy rumors like those that have plagued P&G and other major corporations, as well as governments (see Box 3.3). The P&G Satanic rumors were most active among religious groups in the United States when their members were finding their positions on abortion, prayer, and other issues threatened and under increasing attack. The rumors may have served as a dramatic vehicle for rallying Christians against the devil, justifying their fears and explaining their anxieties. Similarly, the rumors that targeted Snapple are easier to understand when placed in the social context of the 1990s, a time when racial tensions, gay rights, abortion, and other emotionally charged issues received prominent attention in the American media. From a psychoanalytic perspective, creating a common enemy could serve as a defense mechanism for group members who fear that their group's values, philosophy, or agenda are at risk. The "enemy"—whether it is Satan, homosexuals, or the media—could unconsciously serve as a justification for any difficulties or frustrations the group may have been experiencing.

I briefly mentioned Snapple's difficulties with rumors in Chapter 2. Although several different rumors swirled around the alternative soda and natural iced tea producer during a relatively brief period in 1992 (including the claim that Snapple was brewing some of its teas in South Africa), the most vexing were the ones asserting that the company was contributing to prolife causes and the KKK. The whispering campaign was fueled by the appearance of anti-Snapple fliers near local universities, where students were likely to be highly politicized and concerned about such issues as abortion and minority rights. Snapple's drinks were very popular and considered to be rather trendy among young people at that time; thus, it must have been particularly traumatic for the students to hear stories suggesting that they were financially supporting a company with al-

---

Box 3.3. Big Government and Rumors

Like large corporations, in the minds of many people government has simply gotten too big for comfort in recent years, and the complex and apparently overwhelming bureaucracy arouses anxious feelings and uncertainties about the government's motives, trustworthiness, and efficiency. As we have found with firms, the fears and uncertainties about government also serve to spark the emergence of rumors.

One example of a government-related rumor that has emerged periodically since the 1940s is the "great cabbage hoax," which originally appeared in Washington, DC as a reaction to price controls during World War II (Hall, 1965). The essence of the story was the claim that the Office of Price Administration had issued a memo to announce the regulation of the price of cabbages—a very long memo of 26,911 words! Although this false story was largely restricted to government circles at the time and quickly faded, it received much greater circulation when variations reappeared during subsequent decades; in each case, the story was widely reported by dozens of national media outlets. The basic version of the great cabbage hoax typically stated that the Gettysburg Address contained 266 words, the Ten Commandments, 297 words, the Declaration of Independence, 1,348 words, and the government's cabbage memo, 26,911 words. One twist that sometimes occurred was the suggestion that the memo concerned the regulation of the price of foghorns.

The cyclic pattern of the cabbage rumor reflects the ebb and flow of societal uncertainties and anxieties about big government. When people become skeptical about the intentions and capability of their government, as happened in the United States in the post-Watergate era, this rumor is likely to reappear in one form or another. The cabbage story reinforces old feelings about the inefficiencies of government and the often frustrating, bureaucratic tendency of government agencies to issue verbose and incomprehensible regulations (Rosnow & Kimmel, 1979).

---

leged ultraconservative or racist positions. One of Snapple's distributors posited that the rumors probably were passed on by "people who believe in good things but don't know the truth" (Noble, 1993, p. D7).

It may not be surprising, due to the fact that rumors tend to be context specific and that the brands are lesser known outside their domestic markets, that the P&G and Snapple rumors never really circulated outside American borders. Apparently, a 1987 translation of one of the P&G rumor leaflets briefly appeared among religious groups in France, but that is the only instance that I am aware of. According to Jerome Francois, a P&G brand manager in Paris, the devil rumors never represented a problem in Europe (personal communication, September 12, 2000). This is not to say that Europeans do not share some of the same underlying fears and uncertainties as Americans, but that their concerns are made salient at different times and by different personally threatening situations and events. As an example, a steady outbreak of rumors transpired on the heels of developments in Europe leading up to the introduction of a single currency (the euro) in January 2002 and the growing realization that the European Union (EU) was more than a set of abstract treaties but a reality that soon would directly affect the lives of all Europeans ("European Topics," 1994; "With Euro on the Way," 2001). These unfounded stories—dubbed "Eurorumors" by sociologists—have become more and more prevalent since the early 1990s and have included the following:

- Brussels was going to require European growers to give up the curved cucumber in favor of a rectangular version that would be easier to stack and ship.
- Camembert cheese was going to be outlawed.
- The Bank of France was deliberately causing a shortage of franc coins to facilitate the approaching changeover to the euro.
- EU bureaucrats planned to ban noisy toilets.
- Cigarette sizes would be regulated.
- Firefighters would be required to wear navy blue trousers.

Together, these sorts of rumors reflect concerns about an uncertain future. For many Europeans, the rumors represent a natural response to the profound feelings associated with a feared loss of national identity engendered by the loosening of border restrictions, the elimination of national trade barriers, a common currency, and other related EU developments. These events also are beginning to raise fears that are likely to give rise to contamination rumors, particularly in light of concerns in continental Europe about genetically modified food imports and the recent outbreak of mad-cow disease (see Box 3.4).

As we found with contamination rumors, a number of recurrent conspiracy rumors also seem to reflect a distrust of powerful corporations; in fact, for either form of commercial rumor it usually is the case that allegations originally involving smaller companies or lesser known products shift, over time, to larger and better known targets (see the section "Convergent and Divergent Rumor Processes"). We saw that this was the case with regard to the worm-burgers rumor, which first was linked to Wendy's and only later became associated with McDonald's. Conspiracy rumors also tend to increase as uncertainty over the economy and related fears about layoffs and plant closings grow. Not surprisingly, the P&G rumors were particularly prevalent in regions marked by high unemployment and economic depression.

Another motive underlying the spread of conspiracy rumors, which also applies to the contamination variety, is that rumors can enable frustrated or hostile consumers to vent their anger or obtain the satisfaction of getting even with a company for real or imagined grievances (see the section "Motives for Spreading

Box 3.4. Contamination Rumors and the French

In recent years, Europe has begun to see an influx of contamination rumors not unlike those that have beset some of the best known American firms—the targets may be different, but the themes generally are the same. In his book *Rumor in the Marketplace*, Koenig (1985) accurately predicted that although contamination rumors had not yet emerged as a problem in Europe at the time of his writing, they were on the way. He attributed this to the fact that the depersonalizing presence of corporations, in the form of fast-food franchises and discount chains, was only just beginning to have an impact in terms of setting the stage for the onset of rumors. American-style food retailers now are common throughout the EU, as are many of the rumors associated with them.

The loosening of EU trade barriers, which has led to the arrival of genetically modified foods from the United States and contaminated meat from the United Kingdom, has been a significant development, creating an atmosphere of fear, uncertainty, and a distrust of government. French citizens, for example, are more fearful than they have been in the past about the quality of their food products. Recent surveys have revealed that 63% of French consumers check the ingredients of the food they buy, 73% admit being worried about the presence of genetically modified organic matter (referred to as OGM in France) in their food supply, and 58% claim that they do not trust their government in handling the OGM issue.

Adding to these contemporary anxieties, the French still may be suffering some lingering effects from a major contamination rumor that dates back to the mid-1970s. In 1976, a one-page flier falsely attributed to a hospital in the town of Villejuif, near Paris, listed a number of innocuous food additives as carcinogenic, leading to suspicions about the healthfulness of a number of popular products, including La Vache-qui-Rit (Laughing Cow) cheese and Amora brand mustard. By the mid-1980s the "Villejuif flier" was still circulating in France and had begun to appear in other regions of Europe. No one ever found out where the flier originated from, but it is estimated that more than 7 million people had seen it and been "poisoned" by the false rumor and that one out of every three French households had been affected (Kapferer, 1989).

The longevity of the Villejuif rumor has been attributed to various factors, including the apparent credibility of the flier, which made explicit reference to having been authorized by the esteemed Gustave-Roussy Institute in Villejuif. However, a careful examination of the flier, along with a minimal amount of knowledge about food additives, would have readily revealed the suspect nature of the rumor. Many of the food additives prohibited in France were listed in the "safe" category on the flier, whereas harmless substances such as E330, a natural citric acid found in oranges and lemons, were listed as carcinogenic. The rumor received additional impetus as a result of newspaper reports that reprinted the flier in its entirety, and by the inclusion of the list of supposedly carcinogenic products in a 1984 popular book on cancer written by a French doctor who had failed to investigate the actual harmfulness of the substances.

Untrustworthy Rumors"). This sort of motive has been suggested as a possible reason that the food seasoning monosodium glutamate (MSG), which is extremely popular among Chinese people, has such a negative image in the United States. For most Americans, the very mention of MSG conjures up the notion of "Chinese restaurant syndrome," a malady of headaches, flushing, and dizziness that has long been attributed to MSG added to a meal. By contrast, for the average Chinese person, who eats an estimated 1.3 pounds (½ kilo) of it a year, MSG is considered a flavor enhancer with positive health effects (Rosenthal, 2000). Although there have been some concerns raised even in China about possible side effects, there are some Chinese officials who suspect that a long-standing conspiracy is at the root of MSG's bad reputation in the West. In this view, which is unsubstantiated, rumors about problems associated with MSG use were started by some restaurant owners who were jealous of the successful business of Chinese restaurants in their locale. (The intentional spreading of negative messages, including the possibility that some commercial rumors may be started by competitors, is discussed further in the following section.)

Convergent and Divergent Rumor Processes

The many marketplace examples we have considered to this point reveal that commercial rumors differ from other types of rumors in terms of the tenuous nature of the links between the rumor target and the allegations associated with the target. This important distinction is clarified by the so-called convergent and divergent rumor processes (Koenig, 1985). The *convergent rumor process* refers to the possibility that a single company may be targeted by more than one different rumor, although not necessarily at the same time. For example, shortly after the rumor began circulating that P&G was secretly owned by the Moonies, a second and more troublesome rumor alleging the company's link with the devil began to take precedence as the Moonie rumor died out. Similarly, we saw that at least three different rumors circulated about Snapple roughly around the same time (see Fig. 3.1). Additionally, more than one target company may be victimized by the same rumor (although, again, not necessarily at the same time) in what is referred to as the *divergent rumor process*. For example, both McDonald's and P&G were targeted by the same devil rumors; later, McDonald's became the focus of the wormburgers rumor, which had earlier been associated with Wendy's. Of course, it may happen that a company initially implicated by a rumor campaign as a function of the divergent rumor process may later find that it has become ensnared by a convergence of rumors. This is because once people believe one rumor about a company it becomes that much easier for them to believe another, especially if the rumors are logically related. Thus, it must have seemed readily plausible to people who had heard and believed that Snapple was contributing to anti-abortion groups that the company also was supporting the KKK.

A. <u>Convergent Rumor Process</u> = the same company is targeted by more than

one rumor:

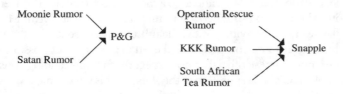

B. <u>Divergent Rumor Process</u> = different companies are targeted by the same rumor:

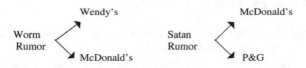

FIG. 3.1. The convergent and divergent rumor processes.

The fact that rumor allegations and company targets tend to be somewhat interchangeable for marketplace rumors highlights the dangers inherent in a company's attempts to start rumors about its competitors. There is little hard evidence suggesting that companies actually do initiate negative rumor campaigns against rival firms, although this no doubt does occur from time to time, at least indirectly. For example, although the source of the Tropical Fantasy rumors (see Box 2.1) has never been identified, the producers of the soft drink line, the Brooklyn Bottling Company, have maintained that they acquired evidence pointing to vindictive former employees or unscrupulous competitors as the culprits who either started or actively perpetrated the rumors. We also have seen that there were scattered cases in which independent Amway distributors engaged in rumormongering against P&G, although these incidents were not part of a concerted effort by Amway. In short, the evidence seems to indicate that although company representatives for the most part probably do not start rumors about their competitors, they probably do very little to assist their rivals in fighting the rumors and in some cases actually may give the stories a little push.

The problem with engaging in the process of spreading false stories about competitors, in addition to obvious ethical concerns and practical difficulties in starting a rumor in the first place, has to do with the distinct possibility that ultimately the rumor could come back to haunt the company that launched the rumor campaign. This has much to do with the fallibilities of human memory. When we repeat an unconfirmed story we have heard or read about to someone else, we may do a pretty good job of remembering the story, but have difficulty recalling which firm was involved. In that case, we are likely to simply fill in the blank for the forgotten company by replacing it with the name of another company that happens to be more salient in our minds. This is another reason why larger and better known firms so frequently serve as rumor targets, and why rumors tend to shift from smaller to larger companies—the names of market leaders are more likely to be retrievable when a rumor is transmitted. A similar process occurs when we watch a provocative or funny television commercial. How many times did you remember the commercial, but either not notice or immediately forget the name of the company that was advertised? In short, the tendency for people either to forget or unintentionally switch the names of products and corporations represents a difficult challenge for companies attempting to plant favorable stories about their own product offerings or unfavorable stories about those of their competitors. Koenig (1985) adroitly described the dangers of starting rumors about one's rivals by suggesting that "the risk is much like that in using poison gas in warfare: The wind may change and blow all the gas back onto the initiating forces" (p. 101).

The suggestion here is that when we are discussing commercial rumors with others, our focus often is placed firmly on the message content, and only minimal attention is given to the name of the company (or other target). However, it is important to point out that this tendency is less likely to occur in the case of contamination rumors, where attention tends to be directed to the target rather than the allegation (e.g., "I heard that McDonald's puts weird things in their burgers."). Conversely, for conspiracy rumors, what captures our attention is the alleged conspiracy and how threatening and far reaching it may be (Koenig, 1985). The extent of the conspiracy is what is of particular concern, and the company that is named is of interest only in the sense that it illustrates the point (e.g., "Do you know that Satan has now even gotten P&G to join his conspiracy of evil?").

Rumor Credibility

We have seen that credibility or belief is an important variable leading to the transmission of a rumor from person to person (see Box 3.5). That is, the more the rumor appears to be trustworthy to an individual, the greater the likelihood that person would be prone to pass the rumor to someone else. An exception to this basic principle is found in situations that arouse very high levels

Box 3.5. Rumors and Credibility

When a rumor is received we might imagine that one of the first steps the recipient takes before deciding whether to pass the message on to others is to evaluate its credibility or trustworthiness. If the rumor has been received from a trusted source, the recipient will probably be less skeptical about the story's veracity than if the contrary is true, and more willing to accept any evidence, no matter how weak, to establish a level of belief.

Rumor recipients may seek evidence to support the trustworthiness of a rumor from any number of sources. Repetition tends to foster belief, so the more times we hear a rumor, the more likely we are to assume it is credible. Internet chat groups and bulletin boards also represent a fruitful source of information for evaluating a rumor, although because the messages are anonymous, there is a question of credibility in the content of the discussions. Consumers are also prone to seek physical cues that appear to support the rumor's message content, such as through a careful examination of brand names, logotypes, product labels, and packaging. This occurred in the context of the P&G devil rumors, in that the company's logo was seen as bearing certain Satanic cues. In the case of the Snapple rumors, in addition to consumers interpreting the letter K (the kosher mark) on the label as evidence of the company's support for the KKK, a drawing of a ship on one of the brand's teas was said to represent a slave ship. (In fact, the ship was intended to represent the Boston tea party.) Similarly, a rumor that circulated a few years ago that Reebok, the athletic shoe company, was involved with South Africa during apartheid was given impetus by the British flag on the logo and the firm's name, which sounds African. In the case of the P&G Satan allegations, one way that the company slowed down the spread of the falsehoods was by undermining their credibility. This was done by presenting evidence that the alleged television appearance of the company owner during which he supposedly admitted his partnership with the devil never actually took place.

One of the first lessons that companies hit by rumor crises tend to learn is that even the most outrageous stories often are believed by consumers. For example, in the case of the Kentucky fried rat legend, Fine (1980) observed that "some might see the possibility of a major restaurant chain serving a rat to a customer as ludicrous and beyond credibility" (p. 235). Yet Fine's research revealed that the legend was widely accepted. In his examination of 115 accounts of the rumor, he found that 76% of the 51 informants who indicated their belief in the story claimed that they believed that the event definitely or probably happened. In fact, some took their belief so seriously that they admitted to actually changing their eating habits.

Of course, it is difficult to anticipate how some apparently innocuous marketing materials could ultimately give rise to rumors or be used to justify the trustworthiness of stories that already are in circulation. Prior to adopting a brand name, logo, label, or package design, firms routinely con-

> duct consumer research to assess how these things influence brand image. Given that consumers' tastes and perceptions may change over time, it would probably be in the best interest of a company to conduct additional studies periodically over time to identify rumors in the making.

of anxiety, because in such cases people are apt to give less critical attention to the message content (Rosnow, 1991). Nonetheless, most people are reluctant to spread information to others if there is a good chance the message is not truthful, for fear of either raising people's false hopes (in the case of wish rumors) or scaring them for no good reason (in the case of dread rumors).

To illustrate, Rosnow (1991) pointed to the scenario that is likely to transpire in the case of rumors that invoke hoped-for consequences, such as those involving quick killings in the stock market or speculations about the size of a year-end bonus in the workplace. Individuals may be tempted to pass such rumors along to validate their own fantasies or wishful thinking or to show off that they are in possession of privileged inside information. According to Rosnow:

> In either case, if the involving outcome failed to materialize as predicted ... the frustration or annoyance that resulted could lead recipients to harbor resentment, even anger, toward the teller. Hence, there should be a vested interest in not passing a positively involving rumor unless the teller felt it contained a kernel of truth. (p. 488)

Rosnow explained that a similar process likely would occur for dread rumors, only in this case the rumors invoke feared or disappointing consequences; when the predicted events do not come to pass, recipients might respond by doubting the teller's reliability or stability, or even by reacting more aggressively toward that individual.

The problem with this logic, however sound it may be, is that it does not explain why so many widely circulated commercial rumors tend to prove false. In fact, Rosnow (1991) suggested an answer when he concluded that people will not ordinarily transmit an untrustworthy rumor "unless perhaps motivated by some ulterior or devious personal objective" (p. 488). When it comes to commercial rumors (or, as discussed later, the organizational grapevine) rumormongers do indeed often have ulterior motives for actively participating in unfounded rumor campaigns.

Motives for Spreading Untrustworthy Rumors

There are probably several reasons people would be interested in spreading untrustworthy or false information about a company to others. One compelling motive is that this behavior provides an outlet for venting any frustrations or anger one may experience in a consumer-related situation. In fact, consumers are well aware of their potential influence in the marketplace when it comes to the power of word-of-mouth communication. The informal discussions we have about products often can have a greater influence on product evaluation than information obtained from a company's marketing communications or from more objective sources, such as *Consumer Reports* (Herr, Kardes, & Kim, 1991). One reason that this is the case is that, unlike advertising or formal sales pitches, word-of-mouth communications often include negative evaluations of a company or its offerings, which enable consumers to express their dissatisfaction following an unpleasant experience (Richins, 1983; Rosen, 2000; Swan & Oliver, 1989). In this way, negative word-of-mouth provides a means for the consumer to exact a measure of revenge, especially when the grievance is not dealt with seriously by company representatives. Because the teller is likely to be perceived as having nothing to gain by talking poorly about a company, negative word-of-mouth can serve to reduce the credibility of a firm's advertising and have an influence on consumer attitudes and purchase intentions (Bone, 1995; Smith & Vogt, 1995).

Several research studies have demonstrated the power and prevalence of negative word-of-mouth following unpleasant experiences in the consumer marketplace. One study revealed that up to 90% of disgruntled customers chose not to do business again with the offending company, and on average, each discussed their negative experience with at least 9 other people. Further, 13% of the unhappy customers told more than 30 people (Walker, 1995). In another study, conducted during the late 1970s, the market research firm TARP (now e-Satisfy) surveyed 1,700 Coca-Cola customers who had complained or made an inquiry to the soft drink company for any reason. Customers who were satisfied with the way the company handled their complaint told an average of 5 other persons about their positive experiences. However, those who complained to Coca-Cola and were dissatisfied with the response told on average 9 to 10 people about their negative experiences, and in 12% of the cases, they told more than 20 other people. Further, 30% of the dissatisfied consumers said they stopped buying Coca-Cola products and another 45% said they would buy less in the future (TARP, Inc., 1981).

Other research seems to confirm the general finding that consumers tend to convey negative information to more people than positive information. At one time it was believed that the ratio of those who receive negative messages to positive ones was two to one. However, it now appears that the ratio varies widely depending on the industry. The automobile industry, for example, tends to conform to the two to one ratio, whereas for other consumer categories, for every one person who hears about a positive experience, up to six hear about a negative one. Dissatisfied customers for electronic products were found to be nearly four times more likely than satisfied customers to share their story with online chat groups (cf. Rosen, 2000). As Rosen and others have pointed out, the Internet provides unhappy consumers with the ability to convey negative word-of-mouth almost immediately to an incredibly vast audience.

Given these points, it goes without saying that many firms are particularly concerned about the flow of negative word-of-mouth, particularly when the message conveys unfounded or false information in the form of rumors. What makes matters even more troublesome for businesses is that it is exceedingly difficult to exercise any influence or control over word-of-mouth because of its informal nature. Nevertheless, there is some good news in all this for companies. In a series of studies examining the interpersonal consequences of transmitting negative and positive rumors, Kamins et al. (1997) found that consumer-oriented messages identified as rumors were evaluated less favorably than other word-of-mouth communications. Further, when the information was labeled as a rumor, both its credibility and likelihood of being passed on to others decreased. When the rumors were positive in nature, the teller tended to be more favorably evaluated than when negative rumors were transmitted.

Kamins et al. (1997) also reported an interaction between the valence of a rumor and the personal relevance of the rumor to the teller, such that there was a greater propensity to spread positive rumors that reflected well on oneself, as opposed to passing on negative rumors that reflected poorly. Consistent with previous findings, however, respondents reported that they were exposed on average to more negative rumors than positive rumors, and more likely to spread the negative ones. The researchers concluded that their findings provide some insight into effective marketing strategies for combatting rumors, including labeling the unfounded message as a rumor to use the generally negative image of rumors in the consumer marketplace to one's advantage. We return to these ideas again in later chapters on managing commercial rumors.

If we next consider the motives underlying participation in the word-of-mouth process, it is possible to identify some of the potentially beneficial effects of spreading commercial rumors, at least from the rumor teller's perspective. There are certain underlying needs that motivate a person to talk about a product or service. This is particularly clear in the case of *opinion leaders* (i.e., consumers who are knowledgeable about one or more product categories and who offer advice and have influence over others in a social system), who may be motivated by one or more of the following (Schiffman & Kanuk, 1994):

- Self-enhancement (i.e., to achieve status by appearing to be "in the know" and demonstrating one's expertise).
- To gain attention and show off.
- Product involvement (i.e., when one has a very good experience with a product or service, there often is a strong desire to share this with others).
- Altruism (i.e., to assist a friend, relative, coworker, etc., by providing advice).

We might imagine that any of these motives also would be applicable to the decision to transmit a commercial rumor, assuming that the rumor has an adequate level of credibility. In this sense, although the rumor may not be advantageous for the targeted company (especially when the message is unfounded), it nevertheless may have beneficial outcomes for the teller.

In some cases, consumers who have recently made an important purchase are compelled to convey positive messages about the product and the company to others. This tendency is linked to the fact that a common side effect of the purchase, especially if it is an expensive one, is the psychological discomfort or tension that stems from having second thoughts about whether one has made a correct decision. One way that consumers can overcome this phenomenon, known as cognitive dissonance or buyer's remorse, is to talk to others about the product's advantages. In this way, consumers can reduce the postdecisional dissonance they are experiencing and convince themselves that they made the right choice.

There is one other positive aspect to transmitting rumors that I have yet to address. It should be noted that there is some degree of entertainment value that comes from participating in the rumor transmission process, especially for rumors that are not particularly believable or personally relevant. For many people, the wormburgers or Pop Rocks rumors, and others of their ilk, lack any degree of credibility; even so, they may be viewed as amusing topics to talk about. In fact, in some cases we might imagine that what makes a rumor so useful as a diversion is the recognition that the story *is* in fact a rumor. In other words, the topic of discussion may focus more on the fact that people are spreading a ridiculous rumor than on the content of the rumor itself. Discussions about rumors per se also could provide the participants with a means of establishing their superiority, by putting down the people who believe such nonsense while boosting their own self-images as intelligent people who cannot be taken in by falsehoods.

Brand Equity and False Rumors

In Chapter 1 I briefly described some of the potentially damaging consequences unfounded rumors can have for a company. Aside from purposeful actions taken by consumer groups to intentionally undermine a firm's profit margin through organized boycotts and related activities, perhaps the most serious consequence of a negative rumor can be seen in the way it can influence how consumers think and feel about a company's brands. This influence is best understood through a consideration of the marketing concept known as *brand equity*, a term used to refer to the value added to a brand by its name and symbol. More specifically, David Aaker (1991), who has studied the concept extensively, defined brand equity as "a set of brand assets and liabilities linked to a brand by its name and symbol, that add to or subtract from the value provided by a product or service to a firm and / or to that firm's customers" (p. 15). In Aaker's view, the assets underlying brand equity consist of brand loyalty, name awareness, perceived quality, brand associations, and other proprietary brand assets (e.g., patents and trademarks). Brand equity can provide value both to the firm (e.g., by enhancing competitive advantage, prices and margins, and trade leverage) and to the firm's customers (e.g., by enhancing confidence in the purchase decision, use satisfaction, and the process of brand decision making).

The world's top brands, such as Coca-Cola, McDonald's, Sony, Kodak, and Mercedes-Benz, are characterized by high levels of brand equity because they successfully provide the assets that Aaker (1991) identified. In contrast to many of their competitors, these brands are well known and readily identified by consumers (i.e., brand awareness), they are characterized by high levels of customer loyalty (i.e., they are purchased repeatedly by consumers who feel a strong sense of commitment to the brand), they are perceived as having a high level of overall quality, and so on. Each of these brand names also conveys a ready set of associations in the consumer's mind. For example, the Mercedes name is linked to a variety of positive associations in memory for many consumers, such as well engineered, durable, safe, and high in prestige level. The same can be said about the McDonald's name, which may conjure up in one's mind images of Ronald McDonald, the golden arches, cleanliness, speedy and efficient service, and the like. Regardless of whether a person views these associations as positive or negative, the point is that they add depth to the brand represented by the company name.

With these points about brand equity in mind, we can better understand how rumors can cause serious harm to a brand as well as to a company's overall image in the marketplace. Negative rumors about the company and its products and services, when believed, can clearly undermine consumer loyalties. The trust that is inherent in loyalty to a firm can be shattered when rumors appear because the rumors would suggest to consumers that the company has something to hide. As in human relationships, this sort of basis for mistrust could undermine a loyal consumer's relationship with a favored brand (Fournier, 1998). This outcome would prevail whether the rumor claims that the company is involved in an alleged conspiracy (because conspiracies are by nature based on secrecy) or that its product offerings are contaminated in some way (e.g., by using cheaper and unhealthy substitute ingredients without the consumer's knowledge to cut costs). Perhaps even more damaging is that negative rumors can influence brand associations by serving to replace positive associations in the consumer's mind (developed through direct experience with the brand, positive word-of-mouth, or the company's marketing campaigns) with negative ones (suggested by the rumor content). This possibility is consistent with the notions about how rumors work from an information processing perspective (see chap. 2). Thus, whereas an association for McDonald's in a consumer's memory prior to having heard the wormburgers rumor might have been "big juicy burgers," after hearing the rumor the association would be more along the lines of "juicy red worms" (see Table 3.1).

The brand equity perspective also helps us recognize that strong brand awareness can actually represent a liability for a company when it comes to rumors because, as we have seen, rumors tend to attach themselves to better known and more successful firms. The implications for fighting rumors that can be derived from brand equity notions highlight the necessity to initiate public relations campaigns that reinforce the original brand image and corresponding associations (i.e., prior to the onset of the rumors), without strengthening the new associations attributed to the rumors. This is exactly what McDonald's accomplished when they launched an antirumor campaign emphasizing that their burgers contained "100% pure beef," without ever mentioning the word *worms*.

FINANCIAL RUMORS

There is perhaps no other milieu as persistently fraught with the preconditions that predict the emergence and spread of rumors than that of finance. Although financial markets, at least theoretically, are supposed to operate according to models of rationality and informed decision making, in reality rumors and speculation are the order of the day. Financial rumors are fueled by the inevitable anxieties and uncertainties that surround big capital when economic livelihoods are at stake. Although fear, uncertainty, and importance are the same key underlying variables that I have identified at the root of rumors that circulate in the consumer marketplace, financial rumors are more likely than the former to be localized and fleeting—they vanish almost as quickly as they arise, though their effects can be dramatic.

TABLE 3.1

Suggested McDonald's Associations Before and After the Wormburger Rumor

Before	After
Pure 100% beef	Juicy red earthworms
Big Mac	Big worms
Reliable and friendly service	Unreliable and secretive
Clean and efficient	Unclean, dirty
Nice place to take your kids for a meal	Place to avoid

Note. A brand association is considered to be anything in the consumer's mind linked to a particular brand (Aaker, 1991). These associations can be positive (e.g., based on an advertising campaign or a satisfying purchase) or negative (e.g., based on an unfounded, negative rumor).

The fact that rumors exist at all in the financial marketplace suggests that traders and investors are not operating on a level playing field. Receiving some inside information via informal communication channels can put one at an advantage that can quickly be converted into profits. By implication, this means that rumors, once received, will have their impact on behavior and decision making almost immediately. Thus, the relatively truncated life span of a financial rumor has a lot to do with the fact that the rumor content is likely to be acted on or not by recipients, with the rumor then becoming rapidly irrelevant. This is largely a function of the way the stock exchange functions, whereby events themselves quickly confirm or refute the veracity of a rumor (Kapferer, 1990). This is exactly what happened in the Emulex case: The rumors emerged, had their impact on trading, and then disappeared (after being refuted), all within a 24-hour period (see Fig. 1.4). As Kapferer (1990) pointed out, the situation is quite different for commercial rumors. Rumors such as the ones that have plagued P&G and other companies, such as the Satanic conspiracy theories, may extend over many years or cyclically reappear as the social or psychological climate provides the appropriate context for their reemergence. Such rumors may be linked to significant fears and uncertainties, but they rarely have as immediate or direct an impact on the consuming public as do financial rumors. Additionally, people tend to put forth relatively little effort, at least in the short term, to actively attempt to uncover the truth about a consumer-oriented conspiracy. In fact, we might expect that by their very nature conspiracy rumors are such that it would be virtually impossible to provide evidence that would adequately convince some recipients that the stories are false—if people are motivated enough to believe such rumors, they may not be very open to any contrary information that would deny them. Such conditions tend not to characterize the preponderance of financial rumors. Within just a few hours, it was possible to satisfy investors that the rumored events concerning Emulex (that it was under federal investigation; its CEO had resigned; etc.) clearly were false.

During any particular day, financial rumors are likely to emerge concerning corporate acquisitions and takeovers, mergers, stock movements, and the like. Rumors are such a persistent phenomenon in the world of finance that numerous mass media outlets have been created specifically to report them, including the Wall Street Journal's "Heard on the Street" and "Abreast of the Market" columns, Business Week's "Inside Wall Street" column, SmartMoney's Web site, and Dan Dorfman's Jagnotes.com Web site, to name a few. In most cases, the speculation generated by these unfounded stories never pans out, which does not mean that they do not cause a market reaction (see Table 3.2). According to Jon Najarian, founder of the investing site 1010 WallStreet.com, it is less of a gamble for investors simply to follow trading patterns for a takeover target, for example, than to rely on takeover rumors. This is because savvy traders who believe that a rumor might have some merit are more likely to buy call options relative to the

TABLE 3.2
Rumored Takeovers That Never Happened

Rumor Date	Buyer	Target	% Price Gain of Target on Day of Rumor	Closing Price on Day of Rumor	Price as of 7/22/99
6/11/99	Staples	CompUSA	8.9	$8.44	$6.69
6/18/99	Safeway	K-Mart	11.9	17.00	15.56
6/18/99	Wells Fargo	Associated Banc Corp	11.7	41.19	40.16
6/25/99	America Online	Juno Online	17.7	26.13	21.81
7/2/99	Amazon.com	Onsale	35.6	25.25	17.50
7/9/99	Fleet Financial	Advest	14.8	23.75	21.38
7/16/99	Wal-Mart	Rite Aid	6.9	23.38	22.50

Note. From La Monica (1999b). Reprinted with permission of SmartMoney, 1999.

targeted company. These options to buy in at a fixed price tend to have a higher return than the actual stock (La Monica, 1999b).

Based on their content, it is possible to distinguish three main types of financial rumors, depending on whether the rumor concerns companies, people, or the economic and political environments. Company-based financial rumors directly concern the financial behavior of certain firms, as when Company X is rumored to be readying a takeover bid for Company Y. In mid-July 1999 just such a story emerged when the beleaguered drug store chain Rite Aid was rumored to be on the verge of selling out to Wal-Mart. Almost immediately, Rite Aid's stock gained nearly 7% on a slow trading day, despite the fact that if people had taken the time to assess the rumor's veracity they would have recognized that its claim did not really make much sense. After all, Wal-Mart already had pharmacies in its discount stores and thus had little need for a drug store chain; the discounter's acquisition strategy was focused on international markets; and the company had only 1 month earlier acquired the British supermarket chain Asda Group for $10.8 billion and probably was not ready to pay out another $6 billion so soon to acquire Rite Aid (La Monica, 1999b). Another example of a company-based financial rumor appeared in October 2000, when Deutsche Bank AG shares fell 7% on the heels of a rumor that it had lost $1 billion on a junk-bond deal that had soured ("Junk-Bond Rumors," 2000).

The second category of financial rumors are those that are people-oriented, focusing on personalities in the business world whose activities could have implications for the economic stability of their firms or financial markets in general. These rumors might describe a director's decision to step down from his or her post, internal dissension among the rank and file, conflicts between the main shareholder and CEO, and the like. A recent example concerns rumors that circulated during November 2000 that the database software giant Oracle's chief financial officer was unhappy with the firm and was about to leave. Such speculation was determined to have caused a drop in Oracle shares of as much as 15% on the Nasdaq, which responded by voiding some "erroneous" trades that occurred amidst confusion surrounding the rumors ("Oracle Hit," 2000). Apparently, shareholders were particularly nervous about the company in light of recent events, including a dispute at the management level leading to the resignation of Oracle's longtime president and CEO and recent industry scuttlebutt about the release date for Oracle's next major product.

The third type of financial rumors are those that are dependent on events occurring in the economic and political environments. Any number of events in these arenas can pose a threat of instability capable of influencing trading activity on stock exchanges, including speculation about the health of world leaders, elections, coffee production in Brazil, and so on (see Table 3.3). For example, during the mid-1970s, rumors proliferated that Soviet leader Leonid Brezhnev, who had not been seen in public for several weeks, was suffering from more than 20 different maladies, ranging from a toothache to leukemia (Rosnow & Fine, 1976). Each rumor was met by another response in trading on Wall Street. In another case, the rumored return to professional basketball by Michael Jordan, after his initial retirement from the game, resulted in investor actions that significantly increased the stock market value of firms whose products were endorsed by Jordan (Mathur, Mathur, & Rangan, 1997; see Box 3.6).

TABLE 3.3
French Elections and the Paris Bourse

Date	Election Winner	Paris Bourse (same day)
12/22/58	De Gaulle	+1%
6/16/69	Pompidou	−1.8%
5/20/74	d'Estaing	−1.3%
3/13/78	General election (first-ballot right-wing victory)	+9%
5/11/81	Mitterand	Unquotable; downward trend
5/9/88	Mitterand	11:15 a.m.: +2.35% Closing: +1.31%

Note. Elections are the sorts of political events that are rife with rumors. Note how the Paris stock exchange ("Bourse") evolved on the heels of important French national elections (data from Frémy & Frémy, 2002).

Box 3.6. The Michael Jordan Phenomenon

In 1993, Michael Jordan, one of the most talented and successful professional athletes of his era, announced his retirement from the Chicago Bulls basketball team to pursue a career as a professional baseball player (Hammonds, 1995). At the time, Jordan was actively involved as a product endorser with no less than 14 different companies, earning him in excess of $32 million per year, in addition to his other business ventures (Mathur et al., 1997). By early March 1995, following his mediocre performance as a baseball player, rumors began to circulate on Wall Street that Jordan was contemplating a return to basketball. The rumors were confirmed shortly thereafter, and on March 20 Jordan began playing once again for the Bulls.

Marketing researcher Lynette Mathur and her colleagues examined the impact of rumors of Jordan's impending return to basketball on the profitability of five of the top firms with products endorsed by the athlete: General Mills (Wheaties), McDonald's (Quarter Pounders, Value Meals), Nike (Air Jordan), Quaker Oats (Gatorade), and Sara Lee (Hanes Underwear). Assuming that these firms were in mature markets with limited growth potential, the investigators assumed that the positive outcomes of the rumors for these client firms would perhaps best be revealed through a consideration of the market shares of competing companies with non-Jordan-endorsed products (e.g., Kellogg's, Wendy's, Coca-Cola, Reebok). To test this, the authors utilized an approach known as event study methodology, which identifies the valuation effects of marketing decisions. With this method, it is presumed that investors evaluate and use all relevant new information that comes to them prior to making an investment decision. Although most of this information will not be considered significant enough to influence investment strategies or stock prices, occasionally some new information will be received that seems important enough to influence the assessment of investment strategies and subsequent actions. Information that is viewed positively tends to lead to investor buying that serves to increase the price of the stock, whereas negatively evaluated information puts downward pressure on stock prices. Based on this approach, Mathur et al. (1997) were able to examine the "Jordan phenomenon"—investors' evaluations of the potential impact of Jordan's return to basketball on the share prices of Jordan's endorsement firms. In short, their findings were consistent with expectations: Investors of Jordan's firms reacted very favorably to rumors of his anticipated return to the NBA and, coupled with his increased visibility in the media, this resulted in an average increase in the market-adjusted values of his client firms of more than $1 billion (2%) in stock market value. A corresponding negative reaction to the rumors was noted for the stock prices of non-Jordan firms. Given the very special stature accorded to Michael Jordan, this case may be an exception when it comes to rumors of this kind; nonetheless, this example highlights the impact that rumors pertaining to events of national interest can have on the financial markets.

Whatever their specific nature, financial rumors serve an important function for traders in a context in which new information is highly valued. It is presumed that any change in price or volume of sales for stocks, bonds, or commodities should only come in response to new and relevant facts about such things as changes in competitors' pricing structure, fluctuations in interest rates, labor difficulties, takeover activity, announcements of layoffs, new products, and related factors. For traders to profit from new information they have to respond before the rest of the market receives the news. Thus, in the financial marketplace, the pressure to respond quickly and its attendant anxieties lead to a ready body of consumers for indications of future events. Such a situation is particularly conducive to the reception of rumors, which frequently bear messages of managerial decisions and market activity that have not yet been publicly announced (Kimmel et al., 1992).

In today's global marketplace, traders have grown increasingly desirous of information pertaining to potential takeover targets. In recent years, researchers have begun to examine the influence of takeover rumors on trading activity (e.g., Pound & Zeckhauser, 1990; Zivney, Bertin, & Torabzadeh, 1996). For example, Pound and Zeckhauser (1990) assessed the impact of 42 takeover rumors appearing in the *Wall Street Journal* column "Heard on the Street" from 1983 to 1985. Their analysis of investment opportunities, based on an examination of a 1-year buy-and-hold trading strategy following the rumor publication date, revealed insignificant risk-adjusted excess returns. This finding led the researchers to conclude that the market reacts efficiently to rumors. In a replication and extension of that study, Zivney et al. (1996) examined nearly 900 takeover rumors for the period 1985 to 1988 by additionally considering those appearing in the *Wall Street Journal* column "Abreast of the Market." Their results similarly revealed that the market reacts efficiently to initial rumors, showing negligible excess returns in the postrumor period. Interestingly, however, the investigators found different market reactions depending on the newspaper column in which the rumors appeared. Short-term overreactions in the market were associated with the "Abreast" column as opposed to rapid price stabilization following rumor publication in the "Heard" column. Based on their analyses, the authors concluded that shrewd investors would stand to benefit not by buying on the rumor date and holding for some period of time, but by short-selling on rumors appearing in the "Abreast" column for a postrumor period of about 100 days. On this basis, traders could expect a 20% annual excess return with about 70% of the trades being profitable.

In addition to their information function, the content of rumors can have an impact on financial markets by influencing sentiments of optimism or pessimism. Consumer researchers have long recognized the influence of consumers' optimism or pessimism about the future on their willingness to make purchases (e.g., Katona, 1975). Further, as illustrated by the Michael Jordan phenomenon, it also is clear that the stock market reacts to headlines of positive or negative events, even when the events are not directly linked to financial affairs. It seems reasonable to expect rumors, which typically bear content reflecting hoped-for or feared future events, to influence consumer and trader sentiments accordingly.

EXPLAINING ORGANIZATIONAL GRAPEVINE RUMORS

We next turn our attention to an examination of organizational rumors. As previously described, such rumors tend to circulate through the company grapevine, the informal and unofficial network of communication that exists in virtually all organizations. The functions of grapevine rumors and the motives for spreading them have much in common with commercial rumor transmission, but as I explain, there also are some apparent differences.

The term *grapevine* dates back to the American Civil War, when soldiers would string vinelike telephone lines from tree to tree across battlefields for use by Army intelligence (Kreitner, 1983). Apparently, this rudimentary communication system proved quite inadequate and the messages that were transferred were so often garbled or inaccurate that eventually any rumor was said to have come from the grapevine (Mishra, 1990). In contemporary parlance, the grapevine describes an interpersonal network of communication that in many ways resembles word-of-mouth communication, the difference being in the content of the exchange and the nature of the participants. Word-of-mouth involves the informal communication between consumers about products, brands, stores, promotions, and other commercial matters. Rumors about any of these elements of the consumer marketplace, such as messages involving contamination or conspiracy allegations, constitute one form of word-of-mouth content. By contrast, grapevine participants are members of the same organization and the information they share is pertinent in one way or another to the company or to other members of the workforce. This might include conjectures about forthcoming changes in management or work conditions, rumors pertaining to certain details about an anticipated merger, the sharing of unconfirmed stories about an office romance, and so on.

Like the antiquated telegraph system from which it got its name, the organizational grapevine can often seem similarly haphazard and disrupted—information can flow in any direction across different hierarchical boundaries and, because the informal information tends to be communicated orally, it is subject to increasing inaccuracies as it passes from person to person. Nonetheless, messages pass more quickly through the informal network and often have a greater impact than those transmitted through formal channels.

Like commercial rumors, organizational rumors can satisfy multiple needs and functions, including these:

- To know.

- To convince.
- To boast.
- To get even.
- To feel relief.
- To entertain.
- To receive job performance feedback.
- To learn about employment opportunities.

Despite the collective nature of the rumor process, these motives are capable of satisfying individual or group needs. For example, a single employee can set off a trial balloon to test reactions to the rumor that he or she is the top candidate for an important, recently vacated position in the company. Similarly, an entire department can launch the unconfirmed message that their group has been selected to win an esteemed award at the end-of-the-year corporate dinner. Other functions of the grapevine primarily are group-oriented; for example, an active informal network of exchange can serve to make work groups more cohesive, it provides opportunities for human contact that help make the workplace a more stimulating environment, and it can help to create corporate identity (Davis, 1969; Greenberg & Baron, 1997).

The role of the organizational rumor network in bringing a group together and contributing to its performance, motivation, and satisfaction is, of course, more relevant in organizations than in the commercial marketplace, where rumors occasionally are shared among complete strangers (e.g., anonymous people who participate in Internet chat groups). However, this was not always the case. As Kapferer (1990) observed, in the past the marketplace was a basic setting where friends and neighbors would gather to exchange information about themselves and other matters of interest to the community. This still is the case in tightly knit professional communities, such as the medical profession and academia, which are rumor-rich fields where information travels exceedingly fast. In certain areas of Europe, such as France, the grapevine concept is referred to by the expressions "the Arab telephone" and "the bamboo telephone," terms that acknowledge the fact that in some Mediterranean or Asian communities, the oral tradition of information exchange and rumor transmission represent efficient means of communication. Thus, the outdoor marketplace, community festivals, clothes-washing areas, and other communal settings served not only as settings to shop, to celebrate, or to clean one's clothes, but also as situations in which one could obtain valued information. Especially in the Western world, these locales no longer function as primary areas for information exchange—the local outdoor market has since given way to the sterile and anonymous shopping mall; people avoid contact in impersonal laundromats, and neighborhoods are less tightly knit communities than clusterings of familiar strangers. In business settings, however, the grapevine is alive and well.

Beyond these social considerations, we find that organizational rumors function similar to commercial ones in a psychological sense. The important personal motive listed as "to know" represents one of the most basic forces that gives rise to the emergence of rumors in any context. The grapevine is useful in the business setting because of its capacity for organizational sense-making, particularly in ambiguous and anxiety-provoking situations. Conjectures in the form of unfounded rumors can be passed to others in the organization who may be in a better position to shed light on the story's accuracy. These rumors also can provide a sense of closure when official communications transmitted through a company's formal networks are filled with gaps or inconsistencies. In these ways, rumors can provide a sense of cognitive consistency and clarity about the work environment and can relieve the tension caused by uncertainty. Stories about people in the firm and what happens to them when they behave in certain ways also can clarify which actions are considered acceptable or unacceptable according to the organizational culture (Kelly, 1985). Not surprisingly, the grapevine tends to be most active during anxiety-provoking periods of change, as well as when economic and labor conditions are in flux or characterized by a slowdown. Grapevine activity and organizational rumors can be expected to increase to the extent that information important to the workforce is either not forthcoming from formal communication channels or when trust in management is lacking and information releases from official channels lack credibility (Simmons, 1985).

Despite its potential benefits, in poorly managed companies the grapevine can fuel anxieties and misunderstandings among a workforce, breed hostilities among employees, and contribute to poor morale. In such situations, rumors can become part of a potentially disruptive cycle, whereby anxiety over ongoing events leads to rumors and the rumors then lead to demoralization and greater anxieties, which in turn create more rumors. While this is going on, members of the workforce may spend so much time tuning into the grapevine that their productivity is negatively affected. Clearly, in such a scenario, the rumors are harmful in the sense that they serve as self-fulfilling prophesies for feared future events, such as layoffs or a plant closing. It is for these and other reasons that some managers believe the grapevine is too dangerous to the company to allow it to operate freely and without some sort of controls—it can sap morale and conflict with the need for secrecy in the development of new products and policies (Rowan, 1979). However, corporate attempts to rein in the grapevine by reducing opportunities for workers to engage in informal discussions (e.g., by discouraging extended lunches or breaks) can seriously impair their ability to gather essential information. As Rowan (1979) related, one advertising professional's amusing reaction to the trend to substitute the traditional three martinis with a glass of white wine at lunch was to complain that "the grape is shrinking the grapevine" (p. 134). I have more to say about how the grapevine can be managed effectively to avoid the destructive effects of organizational rumors in Chapter 7.

CONCLUSION

In this chapter we have seen that much of what has been learned about commercial, financial, and organizational rumors conforms well to rumor theory and our understanding about how business works. As suspected, the emergence and spread of such rumors typically can be traced to a compelling need to obtain information in situations characterized by uncertainty and fear. To the extent that rumors appear to be trustworthy, they no doubt will be passed on through relevant rumor networks, at least until the underlying psychological and emotional needs that gave rise to them in the first place have dissipated. Further, depending on the circumstances, rumors in marketplace and organizational contexts can have positive as well as damaging effects, particularly in terms of their potential for satisfying needs and their influence on the way consumers perceive companies, products, and services.

How Information Spreads: Word-of-Mouth, Opinion Leadership, and the Media

As a rumor travels, it tends to grow shorter, more concise, more easily grasped and told. In successive versions fewer words are used and fewer details are mentioned.

—Allport & Postman (1947, p. 75)

Fama crescit eundo. [The rumor grows as it goes.]

—Virgil, *Aenis*

Implicit in these quotations are two logical but conflicting descriptions of what happens to rumors as they are passed along a rumor network. On the one hand, Allport and Postman's (1947) observations, based on some simple demonstrations they carried out during the early days of rumor research, suggest that rumors become more simplified as they spread. Given the inherent limits of human memory and the desire most of us have for simplicity, coherence, and closure in our thinking, Allport and Postman's assertions seem well taken. Yet the opposing view, as expressed in the often cited Latin maxim, *fama crescit eundo*, also seems quite plausible—that rumors expand as they circulate. In other words, as a rumor is passed along, more details and evidence are added and the rumor mutates into something more substantial than its original formulation. Which of these perspectives on rumor transmission is more accurate? Are these views mutually exclusive, or is there some degree of truth in both?

In this chapter we examine these and other questions related to the transmission and circulation of rumors, such as whether rumors have a typical life cycle, whether it is possible to trace the origins or original source of a rumor, whether certain people are more apt to spread rumors than others, and the role of the media in the rumor transmission process. In addressing these issues, it is helpful to return again to the subject of word-of-mouth communication for gaining insight into how information spreads through consumer groups and rumor networks. A good place to begin this discussion is to reconsider the early investigations into rumor transmission conducted by Allport and Postman (1947) shortly after World War II. Once again we can appreciate that although these two rumor pioneers made some important early contributions to our understanding about how rumors circulate, they apparently only had part of the story right.

HOW RUMORS SPREAD

In addition to their ground-breaking basic law of rumor (see chap. 2), Allport and Postman (1947) are perhaps best known for their descriptions of what happens to a message as it is passed from person to person. Their ideas about how information changes as it is conveyed across a set of people were derived from the results of some basic rumor simulation studies modeled after an established psychological approach for studying memory.

Rumor Distortions: Leveling, Sharpening, and Assimilation

Early psychologists (e.g., Bartlett, 1932; Kirkpatrick, 1932) recognized that human memory is not as reliable as we might hope; it does not provide a fixed image like a snapshot taken from a camera, but instead is porous and changes from the moment we process something we encounter in our environment. In the modern era, the most vivid evidence for this can be found in the extensive laboratory research on the accuracy of eyewitness testimony to crime (cf. Wells & Loftus, 1984). Across hundreds of studies conducted by psychologists in recent decades, results consistently have revealed that eyewitnesses are imperfect in their memories and that a long list of identifiable factors can systematically influence their recall.

The original experiments for studying memory involved having research participants read an innocuous story or look briefly at a picture; several months later, they were asked to return to the laboratory and reproduce to the best of their ability what they had originally processed. Without fail, certain predictable distortions and eliminations emerged in the participants' memory for the story or picture. Allport and Postman (1947) reasoned that a modified version of this methodology could be exploited for studying rumor transmission. Essentially, the method they developed involved having a small group of volunteers (usually six or seven male university students) participate in an experiment reminiscent of a children's diversion known as "the telephone game." While the rest of the participants in the demonstration waited outside the room, a member of the audience (e.g., from a classroom of students) was asked to look at a slide projected onto a screen and, at the same time, to describe it to the first participant, making sure to include about 20 different details in the description. During this "eyewitness" account, the participant was placed in a position where he could not see the picture being described, although it remained plainly evident to the audience. Next, a second participant was brought into the room and also placed in a position of not being able to see the screen. The first participant then repeated as fully and accurately as possible the description he had just heard from the audience member. This second participant then gave his account of the picture to a third participant, and so on down the chain until the last participant's report. The experiment ended with a comparison of the final version of the description with the original picture on the screen. Each time the simulation was conducted the results revealed, not surprisingly, that the final version differed significantly from the original image. For example, the number of details presented in the first account was reduced to only a handful by the end of the transmission chain.

In one variation of this line of research, Allport and Postman (1947) utilized a slide depicting a scene on a subway car. The image showed a handful of people of different nationalities seated along the side of the car (see Fig. 4.1). Standing in the forefront were two men—a White man and a Black man—who were apparently confronting one another. In one noteworthy detail, the White man brandished a razor blade in his hand. By the time the sixth person in the chain received a description of the image, the razor blade usually had shifted from the White man's hand to the Black man's hand, indicative of how cultural expectations, beliefs, and past experiences affect the way people per-

FIG. 4.1.   Rumors and perceptual expectations. This example of a slide used in the early Allport and Postman (1947) rumor simulation experiments revealed how message distortions are a function of characteristics of the perceiver. From Buckhout (1974). From THE PSYCHOLOGY OF RUMOR 1st edition by ALLPORT, G. © 1947. Reprinted with permission of Wadsworth, a division of Thomson Learning: www. thomsonrights.com. Fax 800 730-2215.

ceive and remember a situation and how they ultimately report it to others. Allport and Postman (1947) summarized their findings from these rumor simulations in the following way:

> There was a marked tendency for any picture or story to gravitate in memory toward what was familiar to the subject in his own life, consonant with his own culture, and above all, to what had some special emotional significance for him. In their effort after meaning, the subjects would condense or fill in so as to achieve a better "Gestalt," a better closure—a simpler, more significant configuration. (p. 150)

In short, it was this patterning in the way serially reproduced messages were transformed that led Allport and Postman (1947) to the conclusion that appears at the outset of this chapter—that is, rumors become more simplified as they circulate. More specifically, the researchers identified three processes by which this occurs: leveling, sharpening, and assimilation (see Box 4.1). *Leveling* involves the tendency to eliminate or leave out certain details, even those that could be essential to understanding the true meaning of the message. As a result of this process, rumors become easier to pass on to others. By contrast,

---

Box 4.1. How Rumors Change: Leveling, Sharpening, and Assimilation

In their book, *The Psychology of Rumor*, Allport and Postman (1947) described the typical changes that rumors undergo as they are passed by recounting a story that spread shortly before Japan's surrender to the Allies at the end of World War II. The rumor involved a Chinese teacher who was vacationing in Maine during the summer of 1945. Following a recommendation in his travel guidebook, the traveler requested directions from some local townspeople for a hilltop from which a marvelous view of the countryside could be had. This simple request immediately led to the generation and spread of a rumor that a Japanese spy was in the area to photograph it. In this case, the distortions in the story began immediately. First, the narrative was leveled as a result of a number of essential details having been left out: the timid nature of the visitor when asking for directions, the fact that his nationality was unknown, and his willingness to be identified by the townspeople. Certain details then were pointed up through the process of sharpening: The man's camera was emphasized, the fact that he was an Asian led to the conclusion that he was Japanese, and his sightseeing suggested that he was engaged in espionage activity. Assimilation occurred when the story was interpreted in a way that was more believable to the rumor spreaders, in terms of their current frame of reference. Given the wartime Zeitgeist, it was easier for the townspeople to believe that a Japanese spy was engaged in espionage activity in the area rather than to grasp the reality that an Asian scholar, employed by an American university, was vacationing in their town.

sharpening means that those details that remain are accentuated or made more specific. By underlining or emphasizing a small set of details, rumors maintain their "hook"—that is, the element that makes them capable of capturing the interest of others and adding to their apparent reliability. The third process, *assimilation*, involves incorporating certain changes into the message so that it makes more sense to those spreading the rumor. The structure of the story is altered so that it becomes more coherent and more consistent with the expectations and beliefs of the participants involved in its transmission. With these processes in mind, we might expect that the more complex a message is, the more transformations it will undergo.

As an example, consider that the following incident occurred during a management-only meeting at a major corporation: During the meeting, the male CEO made some derogatory comments about the job performance of female employees at the firm, and some of these comments could have been interpreted as sexist in nature. Further, assume that one of the male senior managers protested and a somewhat heated exchange followed, some of which could be overheard in the offices outside the meeting room. Following the exchange, the CEO acknowledged that his comments were inappropriate and apologized for making them.

Once word about this incident gets around, we might expect it to undergo certain predictable distortions. As the story becomes a rumor, some details would become more vivid and sharper, perhaps for the purpose of adding drama. Thus, we might find that the story becomes one about a fistfight that broke out between the CEO and the manager over a sexist joke told by the CEO. With each retelling, both the joke and the fight are emphasized and exaggerated. As the story spreads, it becomes shorter and more concise, as certain details are leveled in the retelling, such as the point about the CEO apologizing for his remarks. Finally, the details are reinterpreted so that they conform more closely to the worldview or stereotypes of the teller. Through assimilation, the story might be transformed into one about a female manager who, having slapped the CEO after a sexist remark he made during the meeting, broke down and began to cry.

It is likely that the overall process of rumor distortion described by Allport and Postman (1947) is quite common in the spread of many rumors. Not only is it consistent with the way memory tends to operate, but it also reflects the fact that during the transmission process, rumor spreaders must be able to strike a reasonable balance between the volume of details that must be conveyed and the message content's informational and emotional potential for the recipients. According to Gladwell (2000), similar processes in message transmission underlie why certain individuals (who he described as "connectors," "mavens," and "salesmen") seem to have such a significant impact on whether a new product or idea catches fire in the consumer marketplace. In his view, such persons can make an idea contagious by dropping certain nonessential points (i.e., leveling) and exaggerating others (i.e., sharpening) so that the message acquires a much deeper meaning:

> If anyone wants to start an epidemic, then—whether it is of shoes or behavior or a piece of software—he or she has to … find some person or some means to translate the message of the Innovators into something the rest of us can understand. (p. 203)

In this light, the role of these processes in the spread of marketplace rumors takes on added significance. In fact, a number of analogies can be drawn with regard to the contagion effects or social epidemics that characterize cases of both successful new product diffusion and marketplace rumors.

Simplified Linear Rumor Models: Some Limitations

Over the years, a number of critics have pointed out some important limitations in Allport and Postman's (1947) explanation of how rumors spread (e.g., Koenig, 1985; Rosnow, 1991). The main thrust of the arguments is that the demonstration method they used, which was dependent on a chain sequence of rumor transmission involving a small number of people, did not adequately simulate how rumors actually are communicated outside of controlled situations. To be fair, Allport and Postman (1947) recognized the constraints imposed by their experiments: "Laboratory control can be achieved, we admit, only at the expense of oversimplification. By forcing serial reproduction into an artificial setting we sacrifice the spontaneity and naturalness of the rumor situation" (p. 64).

Nonetheless, these limitations are significant in terms of what we now know about rumors and why they spread in the first place. The early simulations involved "rumors" that had little if any particular interest for the participants, who themselves lacked compelling incentives for either passing the story accurately to others or listening attentively as it was told (e.g., to obtain information about what was happening in the situation, to reduce anxieties, etc.). Further, the processes of distortion identified by Allport and Postman (1947) do not necessarily imply that rumors become briefer as they are passed. Although it is likely that when we repeat a story to another person we are apt to leave out certain details that do not seem to add to or fit the general thrust of the account, there also is a natural tendency to embellish the story by adding our own personal stamp, including points that keep it interesting, fresh, and more credible. This is just what one finds in the retelling of many contemporary marketplace rumors and in the passing of messages through the organizational grapevine. Instead of shrinking in details, rumors like those pertaining to P&G, Snapple, Tropical Fantasy, and the like took on improvised details as they circulated. For example, idle speculation about a conspiracy between P&G and Satan eventually snowballed as invented facts about national television appearances by the company's owner and allegedly hidden messages in the product logotype were added to the basic story. In other cases, rumors expand as a function of the convergent rumor process. Thus, after a while, rumors claimed that Snapple was not only contributing to anti-abortion causes, but to the KKK as well.

As suggested, the most serious problems with Allport and Postman's (1947) simulations is that they relied on a serial chain of transmission—a model that rarely applies to the way rumors are passed in natural settings. That is, when we receive an unconfirmed story from some source and are motivated to pass it along, it is rare that we tell one other person and leave it at that. Moreover, communication typically involves a two-way interaction. We rarely choose other persons at random to pass the rumor to, but instead select recipients with whom we would be comfortable enough to engage in a discussion about the rumor, whether these individuals are intimates (e.g., relatives or friends), acquaintances, or anonymous members of an Internet chat site who share a mutual interest relevant to the rumor content. One reason people decide to retell a rumor in the first place is to receive feedback about it, perhaps from someone who has additional evidence or expertise to either confirm or refute the story. This feedback component is lacking in rumor simulations that involve the passage of a message across a chain of individuals, from Person A to B, B to C, C to D, and so on, without any possibility of elaboration, adaptation, or refutation of the message in a two-way exchange (see Fig. 4.2). As Koenig (1985) noted, the survival capacity of most rumors would be very limited if they spread in a one-way direction to one person at a time, because if any one person in the chain was not interested or did not believe in a rumor, the transmission would reach a dead end and be stopped.

Given these points, it makes sense for us to consider some alternative models that more adequately describe the spread of rumors. One possibility is that rumors spread rapidly because they are diffused in a branching pattern, which suggests that a rumor will be passed on to two or more people who, in turn, tell it to two or more people, and so on, as might characterize social contagion during a crisis. Consistent with this pattern, rumor transmitters are selective in terms of who they choose to pass the rumor to, and some recipients could serve as dead ends by choosing not to retell the rumor to others (Degh & Vazsonyi, 1975). In other words, unlike the simple linear model that holds that Person A tells the rumor to Person B, B to C, and so on, according to the branching model, A might communicate the rumor to D and E, but not to B and C. Person D might choose to tell the rumor to F and H, whereas E might decide not to pass it on at all. Although this so-called rumor conduit pattern involves more people and thereby speeds up the rumor diffusion process, it also implies a unidirectional and noninteractional circulation. It is likely, given what we currently know about the communication process, that the unidirectional models are overly simplistic and that rumors are more likely to circulate

FIG. 4.2. The serial transmission chain. This famous Norman Rockwell painting, "The Gossip," which appeared on the cover of a 1948 edition of the *Saturday Evening Post*, perfectly illustrates the unidirectional pattern of transmission, as suggested by early rumor simulation studies. From The Curtis Publishing Co. (1948). Printed by permission of the Norman Rockwell Family Agency. Copyright © 1948 the Norman Rockwell Family Entities.

through complex networks characterized by multiple interpersonal links and a two-way interactive transmission of information.

Word-of-Mouth Communication and Rumor Networks

To better understand how rumors spread in the consumer marketplace, it is particularly instructive to review how marketing communication experts conceive the flow of word-of-mouth through the opinion leadership process. In the preceding chapter, we introduced the concepts of word-of-mouth communication and opinion leadership, two processes that underlie how personal influence takes place in consumer-related situations. *Personal influence* means that consumers have the capacity to affect each other's attitudes and behaviors relative to something in the marketplace (e.g., a brand, a store sale, an advertisement) through their informal word-of-mouth exchanges.

The term *word-of-mouth* was originally coined by William H. Whyte, Jr. in a *Fortune* magazine article entitled "The Web of Word-of-Mouth." In his article, Whyte (1954) reported an interesting phenomenon regarding room air condi-

tioners, which at that time had just been introduced into the American consumer market. He observed that if one passed through urban neighborhoods
(where the air conditioners typically were mounted in a front window), the
appliance appeared to be distributed in clusters of homes rather than in a random fashion. That is, six houses in a row might have an air conditioner,
whereas three on either side would not. A similar patterning was apparent
with the distribution of televisions, as indicated by antennas on rooftops
around the same time. Whyte concluded that the ownership of such consumer goods reflected patterns of social communication within the neighborhoods. The people who talked together about products and services showed
similar purchase and usage behaviors.

Whyte's observations seem to conform very well to the linear model of rumor transmission described earlier. We might imagine one innovative family
daring enough to take a chance with an expensive new product, and thus becoming the first in the neighborhood to purchase an air conditioner. The family members then talk about their recent purchase to their next-door
neighbors, who then tell their next-door neighbor, and so on, down the block,
until a family is reached that decides not to make a similar purchase. Of
course, communication tools were much more limited than they are today, so
it is understandable that this pattern of communication prevailed in analyses
of interpersonal exchange during the early 1950s.

The traditional linear model of communication originally placed the mass
media in a predominant role in the way information was thought to disseminate to an aggregate of consumers (see Fig. 4.3). This view, the so-called
one-step flow of communication model, posited that information is directed
from a source (e.g., a broadcaster or journalist) to prospective audiences, like
bullets propelled from a gun. The decision of each member of the audience
about whether or not to act on the message was viewed as the result of a passive role in the process—if they got in the way of the "bullet," they would be
hit. Accordingly, companies were thought to be able to communicate efficiently with different target audiences simply by varying the message and the
type and frequency of channels used for conveying the message. This model
was soon recognized as an oversimplification of the communication process
for two basic reasons: (a) it ignores the possibility that through personal influence consumers can have an impact on each other, and (b) it does not take into
account the fact that some consumers, for a variety of reasons, may not receive the intended message.

The one-step flow model was eventually supplanted by another view that
was widely held until somewhat recently. The two-step flow of communication model can be traced back to a famous study of voting behavior conducted
by Lazarsfeld and his survey research team during the 1940 U.S. presidential
campaign (Lazarsfeld, Berelson, & Gaudet, 1944). Initially carried out as a test
of the one-step flow of influence from the media, Lazarsfeld's study found

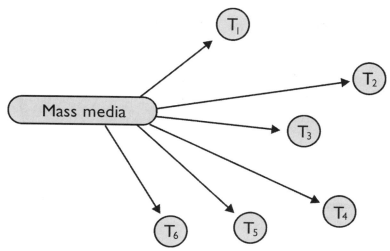

FIG. 4.3. The one-step flow of communication model. T_n is a member of the target audience. From Fill (1995). Reprinted with permission of Pearson Education Limited.

that campaign advertisements transmitted through radio and print channels had negligible effects on actual voting behavior and only minor effects on changes in candidate preference. Apparently, people were very selective in terms of attending only to aspects of the messages that conformed to their preexisting opinions. Importantly, the study revealed that the main factor in determining voting decisions was the informal social group to which an individual belonged and, more specifically, the influence of someone in the group who was more tuned in to the media than the others. This so-called opinion leader (or "influential") was better informed than other members of the group and more likely to pass on information (either solicited or unsolicited) to the others.

Returning to our consideration of the two-step flow model of communication, we see that opinion leaders are recognized as playing a critical role in the flow of information from mass media sources to other consumer targets (see Fig. 4.4). The original version of this model posited that information flows in two steps to a mass audience: In the first step, the message passes from the media source to the opinion leader, and in the second step, from the opinion leader to the rest of the group. According to later versions of this model, information originating from the mass media not only reaches opinion leaders, but others as well, who may not be influenced until they check with their group's opinion leaders. Thus, in Fig. 4.4 we see that Consumer T4, who represents an opinion leader for a consumer group, serves as the original source of information for Persons T5 and T6, who were not reached by the original transmission of the message, and as a message reinforcer for Targets 1, 2, and 3. In short, the

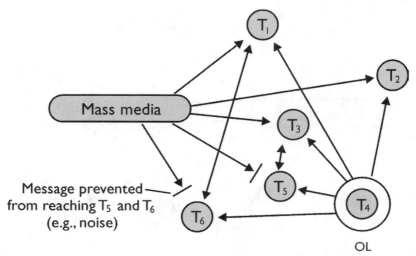

FIG. 4.4. The two-step flow of communication model. From Fill (1995). Reprinted with permission of Pearson Education Limited.

two-step flow model rejected the notion that the mass media alone influence product purchase, brand selection, and the transmission of ideas and other information to a mass audience. Rather, the personal influence attributed to influential members of the group also plays an important mediating role in the communication process.

The currently accepted multistep flow of communication model goes beyond the two-step model by proposing multiple, often complex patterns of influence within the group (see Fig. 4.5). It is understood that the mass media is more efficient than ever in successfully reaching most people directly, including opinion leaders and information receivers. However, the significant role of interpersonal relations in the flow of mass communication has undermined the image of a passive audience at the mercy of omnipotent media (Weimann, 1982). Although the opinion leader is given an important role in this model, opinion leaders and members of the target audience all influence each other through a complex pattern of two-way communication. The bidirectional nature of the interpersonal interactions is suggested in the figure by double-headed arrows, thereby adding the feedback notion that was missing in the earlier communication models and in Allport and Postman's (1947) rumor simulations. Another interesting aspect implied by this model is that an individual consumer may receive the same information from more than one source. For example, in the figure we see that Person T3 could have received the original message directly from the media (e.g., a television program), the group's opinion leader T4, and another group member T2, and then could have discussed the story with Targets 1 and 5. This multiple source element

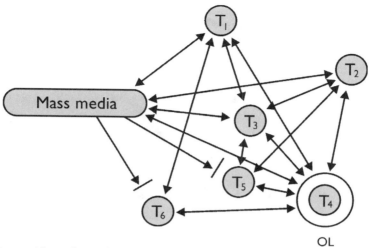

FIG. 4.5.   The multistep flow of communications model. From Fill (1995). Reprinted
with permission of Pearson Education Limited.

has important implications for rumor transmission because it implies that a
person may receive the same rumor from more than one source. This is significant because it is likely that the more times a person hears a rumor, the more
apt he or she is to believe it (Allport & Lepkin, 1945; Kimmel & Keefer, 1991).

This more complex multistep model of communication, when applied to
word-of-mouth networks, is useful for identifying the nature of referral relations (i.e., word-of-mouth connections depicting "who told what to whom"
pathways) among consumer audiences, whether the message that is passed
from person to person is a product or service recommendation, a description of
a new product, a suggestion about product usage, or a commercial or organizational rumor. An example of a word-of-mouth network appears in Fig. 4.6, depicting referral connections along which information about a new service
might be spread (Mowen, 1995). In such networks, it is important to understand
that a social tie between two individuals may be strong (e.g., two close friends
who get together on a regular basis) or weak (e.g., neighbors who infrequently
meet in passing, but who one day happen to have a brief discussion about the
new service). In Fig. 4.6, we see that an individual may pass a message on to persons with whom one has strong ties or weak ties, and the fact that one has strong
ties with someone does not necessarily mean the message will be shared with
that person. Additionally, within the word-of-mouth network, smaller
clusterings of interconnected consumers who share strong ties with one another may exist (e.g., in Fig. 4.6 Persons B, C, and D form one such group,
whereas F, G, and H form another). The more tightly knit such groups are, the
more likely it is that a message will spread rapidly among group members.

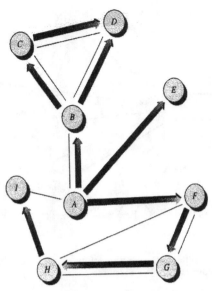

FIG. 4.6.   A word-of-mouth network. Lines with arrows represent referrals. Lines without arrows represent strong ties. From Mowen (1995). Mowen, John C., CONSUMER BEHAVIOR, 4/E, © 1995, p. 622. Reprinted by permission of Pearson Education, Inc., Upper Saddle River, New Jersey.

In typical word-of-mouth discussions, the opinion leader plays a significant role in informally offering advice or guidance to other consumers by providing information about a specific product or product category, product acquisition and usage, brand attributes, and a wide range of other consumption-related topics. Marketers have learned quite a bit about opinion leaders and the opinion leadership process since the early work of Whyte and Lazarsfeld (cf. Rogers & Shoemaker, 1971; Venkatraman, 1989; see Box 4.2). For example, opinion leaders should not be thought of as absolute leaders who tell everyone else what to think and who others blindly follow; rather, they are persons from whom others informally receive information or advice about products and services. Opinion leaders are typically considered highly credible sources of consumer-related information, because they are perceived as neutral and objective (unlike, for example, company representatives or advertisers) and equally apt to convey unfavorable information about a product or brand as favorable. In this light, because credibility often is doubtful, an opinion leader is likely to be chosen as an initial contact for verification or feedback about a rumor.

Although it has proven somewhat difficult to draw a profile of characteristics of the typical opinion leader—in large part because opinion leadership tends to be product-category specific—there is evidence that such individuals are likely to be high in innovativeness (i.e., they are more likely than others to try new

---

Box 4.2. Network Hubs

Given their central role in communicating with large numbers of other consumers about products, services, and companies, it is not surprising that opinion leaders have also been referred to by consumer industry insiders as influencers, power users, lead users, and influentials. In his informative book on the creation of word-of-mouth marketing, Rosen (2000) preferred to use the term *network hubs* when speaking about connected individuals who are in a central position to further the buzz about a product, change a message, or perhaps block a message from spreading. In Rosen's view, four types of network hubs can be distinguished:

1. *Regular hubs.* These are average people who represent sources of information for only a few other consumers or a few dozen, but who nevertheless can serve to influence a product category.
2. *Megahubs.* These are professional opinion leaders such as journalists, celebrities, analysts, and politicians, who, like regular hubs, have many two-way links to others, but also have thousands of one-way links with people who receive their messages through the mass media. The American television personality Oprah Winfrey is considered to be such a hub because of her ability to reach and influence millions of people.
3. *Expert hubs.* These are specialized opinion leaders who have demonstrated significant knowledge of a certain area and thus represent authorities on the subject for other consumers. A friend who you go to for advice and information about cars because you know that person will be extremely knowledgeable about the product category represents this kind of hub. In short, expert hubs are identified on the basis of what they know.
4. *Social hubs.* These are members of groups who are particularly central within their group because of their charisma, trustworthiness, and high level of social activity. It is usually possible to identify at least one person like this in a wide range of social groupings, including one's neighborhood, company, town, and so on.

What these different varieties of network hubs have in common is that they communicate more information about particular product categories, with greater frequency, than do other people. In fact, as Rosen (2000) pointed out, it is probably appropriate to speak about an individual's degree of opinion leadership: "If an average Palm user tells twenty other people a year about the device, and another user tells eighty people about it, that second person is clearly a hub" (p. 46).

Just how influential is the network hub in the consumer marketplace? Rosen (2000) offered some statistics:

(continued)

- 58% of young people rely to some extent on others when selecting a car.
- 53% of moviegoers follow the recommendations of friends.
- 65% of the people who bought a Palm organizer did so on the basis of recommendations from others.
- 43% of travelers cited friends and family as basic sources of information in deciding places to visit and which airlines, hotels, and rental cars to use.
- 70% of Americans rely on the advice of others in selecting a new doctor.

products and services), self-confidence, and gregariousness, and are also heavy users of special-interest media (Schiffman & Kanuk, 1994; Summers, 1970). For example, financial opinion leaders are more likely to be regular readers of such publications as *Money, Barron's,* or *The Wall Street Journal* and frequent viewers of television programs like *Wall Street Week* (Stern & Gould, 1988). It also appears that opinion leaders tend to influence others who are very much like themselves in terms of age, socioeconomic status, and educational background. Moreover, certain predictable conditions in the social context are expected to give rise to the opinion leadership process (see Box 4.3).

This brief overview of word-of-mouth networks and opinion leadership is informative in helping us understand how rumors spread throughout a social community. The multistep flow model suggests that rumor networks are likely to be much more complex than early rumor researchers may have imagined. A rumor is not simply a message that is received and then automatically passed on to one other person; rather, rumors are shared and evaluated as part of a two-way interaction between the transmitter and the recipient. Rumor recipients may receive an unconfirmed message from more than one source and the message may or may not be passed on to both strong and weak ties, depending on the trustworthiness of the rumor content, the nature of one's social relationships, and one's attentiveness to the content of mass media. Certain persons—whether we choose to call them opinion leaders, influentials, or network hubs—are likely to play a more central role in the rumor's evaluation and diffusion, but these persons are themselves potentially influenced by less centrally located individuals (or marginals) in the social network. Complicating the process even further is the recognition that many people belong to more than one social network, thus accounting for the tendency for message diffusion to branch out not merely by diffusing within groups, but between them as well.

THE LIFE CYCLE OF RUMORS

Traditionally, the typical rumor tends to have a clearly identifiable life history. Although this may be less true today, due largely to new technological tools

---

Box 4.3. Conditions That Give Rise to the Opinion Leadership Process

According to Engel, Blackwell, and Miniard (1990), who extensively studied opinion leadership, one or more of the following conditions must be present if opinion leadership is likely to occur:

1. The consumer lacks sufficient information to make an adequately informed choice.
2. The product is complex and difficult to evaluate using objective criteria.
3. A consumer lacks the ability to evaluate the product or service, regardless of how the information is disseminated and presented.
4. Other sources of product- or service-related information (e.g., salespeople or advertisers) are perceived as having low credibility.
5. An opinion leader is more accessible than other sources and thus can be more easily consulted.
6. Strong social ties exist between the consumer and the opinion leader (e.g., the opinion leader is liked and respected).
7. The consumer has a high need for social approval (i.e., cares about what others think).

Although Engel and his colleagues specified these conditions as pertaining to opinion leadership, it is interesting to consider how they might similarly operate as determinants of whether a person chooses to pass on a rumor to a personal relation.

---

that have served to speed up their evolution and devolution dramatically, for most rumors it is possible to identify specific life stages. However, because of the amorphous nature of rumors, the demarcation between the different stages of the life cycle often is blurred.

French sociologist Edgar Morin may have been the first to suggest that rumors follow a predictable life course. As mentioned in Chapter 2, based on his analysis of the rumor of Orléans, Morin (1971) likened rumors to diseases which pass through such stages as incubation, propagation, metastasis, opposition, resorption, and residua. (Along these lines, the reader might recall the quotation at the beginning of chap. 1 in which La Monica noted how *rumor* rhymes with *tumor*.) Simplifying this disease analogy, Rosnow and his colleagues (Rosnow & Fine, 1976; DiFonzo et al., 1994) distinguished among three general rumor stages: birth, adventures (i.e., evaluation and dissemination), and death. In the *birth stage*, conditions are such that they are likely to give rise to the emergence of rumors; that is, various aspects of the social and psychological contexts provide a fertile breeding ground conducive to rumor generation. This is likely to be true of situations marked by a high degree of collective excitement and a corresponding strong demand for information, as occurs during information blackouts, unexplained or partially explained events, unpredictable occurrences, and the like. As we discussed in Chapter 2, rumors are especially likely to emerge when these occurrences are associated with high levels of fear or anxiety. In business contexts, rumors also can emerge as a result of intentional actions on the part of individuals motivated by specific grievances or competitive interests.

One of the most basic and frequently asked questions that inevitably is voiced when a rumor begins to circulate is "Where did that story come from?" This typically is an exceptionally difficult question to answer, given that the specific origins of a rumor are in many cases impossible to pinpoint. As some authors have suggested, tracing the origins of a rumor is a lot like trying to determine where a joke came from. In many cases, an attribution to a specific source is indeterminable, as suggested by a lead-in remark along the lines of "I heard that …", or left ambiguous (e.g., "A friend of a friend said that …"). To add legitimacy to the story a reference may be made to "having heard on good authority," a person in a high position in the social network, or the media.

From the standpoint of those who are charged with dealing with the rumor from a managerial or public relations perspective, the specific origins are far less important than determining where specific hotbeds of rumor activity are located. By the time the rumor becomes recognized as a problem by the organization, the story usually will have evolved to a point far beyond its original version. As Fearn-Banks (1996) pointed out, because each person who passes on a rumor may alter it to some degree, they in essence can be implicated as contributing at least in part to its source. Typically, a commercial rumor problem will be perceived once the company begins to receive letters or phone calls from concerned customers who are seeking verification of whether something they heard is true. This is something that predictably tends to occur rather early in the rumor life cycle. In the case of organizational rumors, a situation meriting some action usually becomes apparent when a senior manager hears about a story that is circulating through the company grapevine.

During the *adventures stage* of the rumor life cycle the credibility of the story is evaluated and, if it appears trustworthy enough, rapid and widespread dissemination usually follows (see Box 4.4). During the evaluation, there is a tendency for people to compare the rumor content with readily accessible cognitions (the latter of which may be stimulated by the rumor itself). In this way, we might expect the rumor to be interpreted—and perhaps even modified—in a way that is more consistent with one's beliefs or needs. Consistent with this process, rumors need not be considered completely believable prior to an individual's decision about whether or not to share it with others. In fact, it is more appropriate to think of rumors not as either true or false, but as falling somewhere along a continuum ranging from very likely to very unlikely to be true. In short, because of the difficulty in determining with certainty the truthfulness of a statement, most people are willing to suspend judgment when they evaluate a rumor. As long as there is confidence that the rumor contains some kernel of truth, and thus *could* eventually be confirmed, the de-

Box 4.4. **Six Degrees of Separation**

The flow of information through interpersonal communication networks can be incredibly swift. Within less than 1 hour of the first announcement that John F. Kennedy had been shot, more than 90% of the American
public was aware of the event and approximately 40% claimed to have heard
about it from another person and not via the mass media (Greenberg, 1964).
Immediately after receiving news of the assassination, 54% of the population expressed a desire to talk about it (Sheatsley & Feldman, 1964).

The extent of connectedness among human beings in contemporary society is effectively illustrated by the concept of six degrees of separation.
This well-known notion can be traced back to an experiment conducted in
the late 1960s by social psychologist Stanley Milgram (1967) on the
small-world problem. Milgram was interested in determining how an idea
or piece of news travels through a population to shed light on the nature of
the interpersonal links between people. Milgram hypothesized that the two
most plausible possibilities are that we are either connected by autonomous
links with a limited number of other people or we are joined by a vast and
complex interlocking web.

Using the idea of a chain letter, Milgram mailed a small packet to 160
people in Omaha, Nebraska, along with the name and address of a stockbroker who lived and worked in separate cities in Massachusetts. He asked
each person to put their name on the packet and then to mail it to someone
they knew who would get it closer to the stockbroker, who would then try
to do the same. The idea was to get the mailing to its final destination in the
fewest number of steps possible. If, for example, you lived in Omaha and
had an ex-college roommate living in nearby Lincoln, Nebraska, who had
family in Boston, you might choose to mail the packet to that person. Even
though Lincoln is somewhat further from Massachusetts than Omaha, your
ex-roommate would probably stand a better chance of getting the packet to
the stockbroker than you would. Once the stockbroker received the mailing, Milgram checked to see how many persons were listed on the packet to
ascertain how closely connected two strangers on different sides of the
country were to each other. What he learned was that only five or six steps
were required for most of the mailings to reach their destination—the
so-called six degrees of separation. In short, Milgram's study revealed that
the world in which we live indeed is a small one, particularly in terms of the
interpersonal communication of information.

cision may be made to transmit it. The P&G devil rumors circulated widely
among conservative religious groups no doubt because the stories confirmed
fears among these groups and thus were likely to be believed. The decision to
transmit the rumors to warn others about the growing Satanic conspiracy
then became a foregone conclusion.

As discussed earlier, as a rumor is disseminated it tends to undergo modifi-
cation to conform more closely to current beliefs, expectations, and previous
experiences of the persons involved in its spread. We might expect that as the
rumor becomes more and more refined as a result of this process it gradually
mutates into a form that is easier to believe. Further, the longer the rumor is
active and the more people become involved in its circulation, the likelihood
of hearing it from more than one source can be expected to increase as well,
thus lending further credibility to its content. There is some evidence that people have a tendency to wait until they have heard a rumor a second or third
time before they decide to communicate it to others (Weinberg et al., 1980).

During the *death stage* of the life cycle, a variety of circumstances can lead to
a rumor's demise. According to Rosnow and Fine (1976), these boil down to
three basic forms: irrelevance, dissipation, or disproof. A rumor can die a natural death if circumstances change and the rumor becomes irrelevant. Such
cases typically are limited to those messages that are predictive in nature. For
example, rumors of an imminent closing of a plant or a manager's firing at the
end of the next business cycle are likely to cease once the deadline passes and
no change has been made. At that point, the rumor may simply be modified,
along with a new deadline and suspected reason for the delay, but eventually
participants in the rumor network either will recognize that the story is unreli-
able or they will grow weary of it. Of course, if the rumored event does come
to pass, the story will have been confirmed and the content of the communication will no longer be recognized as rumor, but as news.

Rumors that have been in circulation for some time are likely to dissipate
when they grow tiresome for the public, unless new details are forthcoming or
different audiences become susceptible to their spread. Here we find another
reason why many unconfirmed reports do not become more concise as they are
transmitted—people often lose interest rather quickly in an unchanging story,
especially if underlying tensions that fueled the rumor in the first place begin to
dissipate or if attention is diverted elsewhere, such as to another rumor. The addition of new details or clues can serve to keep the rumor interesting.

In addition to irrelevance and dissipation, rumors may disappear when
they are forcefully and effectively denied by a credible source. One reason that
the anti-abortion rumors targeting the Snapple Beverage Corporation were
extinguished so quickly is that the company moved immediately to initiate a
counterrumor campaign as soon as the seriousness of the situation became
apparent to management (Noble, 1993). Every letter received from concerned
customers, even those praising the company's rumored stance, was personally answered with a statement about the company's neutral position on abortion. Additionally, Snapple representatives contacted prochoice organizations
to underline the fact that there was no truth to the rumors and affidavits were
forwarded to distributors, retailers, and relevant established political groups
to that effect. As soon as anti-Snapple fliers began to appear, the company re-

sponded with their own counterfliers. The combination of these activities effectively stifled the rumors within less than 5 months of their initial appearance and before consumer boycotts were organized.

Because people expect targeted companies to deny rumors, the tactic must be implemented quickly and efficiently (see chap. 6 for specific guidelines). The speediness of a response is especially critical: If it is too late in coming, people will have time to conclude that the company has something to hide and also will be more apt to receive the rumor from multiple sources. In such cases it will be that much more difficult to convince them that it is the rumor—and not the denial—that is false, and the denial will merely serve to worsen an already bad situation. Finally, whichever scenario leads to the demise of a rumor, it is important to keep in mind that the battle may only have been temporarily won. As we have seen with the P&G rumors and the great cabbage hoax, once certain rumors enter the public psyche they may simply become dormant when conditions of uncertainty and anxiety pass, only to be revitalized at a later time when similar circumstances emerge again.

The Nervous Impulse Analogy

To better illustrate the nature of rumor dissemination during the life cycle just described, Rosnow and Fine (1976) likened the process to the way neural messages are transmitted through the human nervous system. Nerve cells, or neurons, transmit information in the form of electrical impulses that travel from one neuron to another through a complex system of interconnections. When a nerve cell is sufficiently stimulated and a threshold for conductivity is reached, an electrical impulse moves rapidly down the length of the cell to minute cell endings. The message then carries over to the next cell in the form of a chemical interaction. However, before a chemical can effectively stimulate the next neuron in the chain, it must travel across the synapse, a tiny gap separating the two neurons. The more stimulating chemicals that pass to the receiving end of another neuron, the more likely that cell's threshold will be surpassed and the message will be communicated to another cell. According to Rosnow and Fine (1976), this process is not unlike that which occurs when a rumor is transmitted:

> In a similar way, social and psychological "excitations" stimulate the formation of rumors which leap from person to person at a speed that is dependent on the social chemistry. The greater the news value of an event, the more rapid is the process of diffusion. (p. 32)

The sorts of "excitations" that Rosnow and Fine had in mind include a variety of possible factors that may serve to stimulate a transmitter to pass on the rumor to others, such as anxiety and ambiguity, variables that subsequent research has clearly implicated in the rumor generation process.

The neuron metaphor is somewhat limited given that rumors do not travel nearly as fast as the electrochemical events that occur in the nervous system, even in light of the way the Internet has served to speed up the rumor transmission process. Also, communication in the nervous system involves one-way transmission; as we have seen, rumor transmission is more likely to involve a two-way exchange. Nonetheless, like the nervous impulse, which travels at full speed whatever the nature of the external event that provoked it, rumors can be seen as "igniting" a contagion effect once the excitation that preceded it is sufficiently strong (Rosnow & Fine, 1976).

The Diffusion of Innovations Analogy

In addition to the neuron analogy, the rumor life cycle can be further appreciated through a comparison with the process by which new products are adopted and diffused through consumer networks. *Diffusion of innovation*, as elaborated in the marketing literature by Everett Rogers (1962), refers to the process by which something that is perceived as new, such as a product, service, or idea, is communicated through the consumer population. Diffusion is a group process that can be thought of as unfolding like a social contagion that spreads through a delimited social system, in the same way that a contagious disease may diffuse through a population. Successful products, for example, are first known, acquired, and used by only a small number of people, referred to as innovators. Approximately only 2.5% of the consumer population is comprised of innovators, who tend to be risk takers or adventuresome individuals who are on the cutting edge of developments within one or more product categories. For example, in a famous early diffusion study following the introduction of hybrid seed corn in Greene County, Iowa, during 1928, only a handful of 259 farmers had started using the new seed by 1932 (Ryan & Gross, 1943). By 1941, all but two of the farmers studied were planting the new seed. The new seed probably never would have eventually caught on the way it did had it not been for the small group of adventurous farmers—the hybrid seed innovators—who were open to trying something new.

Within a particular social system, people do not adopt something new—if they adopt it at all—at the same rate. Innovators are followed by a larger group of consumers who are rather quick to take up new ideas or products that they have seen accepted by the innovative consumers. This group, the early adopters, typically represents around 13.5% of the consumer market and includes a large proportion of respected opinion leaders who play a critical role in speeding up the diffusion process. This group consists of individuals who are very tuned in to marketplace developments, given their heavy use of mass media and frequent consultations with salespeople. The next group of adopters is the early majority, approximately 34% of the population, who can be considered "average" or "typical" consumers. This group consists of persons who rely heavily on informal sources of information and who are relatively careful in their purchasing behavior. Although consumers in this group tend to follow the lead of early adopters, they are not blind followers, but must be independently convinced of the quality of a new product, service, or idea. The late majority (approximately 34% of the population) consists of skeptical and cautious consumers who generally adopt out of economic necessity or reaction to peer pressure. These are persons who adopt only those items in the consumer marketplace that they perceive to be already acceptable to others. The final group of adopters, comprising the remaining 16% of the population, ir represented by the laggards, who are very traditional and set in their ways. These persons tend to be suspicious of new ideas and may wait so long to adopt an innovation that the innovation itself may already have begun to be phased out, only to be replaced by another innovation. For example, as many consumers had begun to replace their VCRs with DVD players, some laggards may have just gotten around to purchasing their first VCR.

Given these five groups of adopters, the diffusion process tends to take the shape of a normal distribution when depicted graphically (see Fig. 4.7). As shown in Fig. 4.7, the diffusion process may be fast (e.g., the rapid diffusion of portable phones and DVD players) or slow (e.g., the use of the Internet in some European countries, such as France and Spain). As it turns out, the same behavior that causes the adoption and diffusion of new products is, to a great extent, responsible for the new product's life cycle. That is, for a majority of consumer products, most sales are made once the product already has been around for a while, and only after it is purchased by more venturesome consumers who, if satisfied, can be expected to spread the word about the product's value. For this reason, it is of great interest to marketers to be able to identify the innovators for their product category. Eventually, once the product has matured and most consumers who will ever buy it are already doing so, the possibility of further purchases comes either by convincing current customers to buy more or by modifying the product to appeal to current nonbuyers. In other words, for the life cycle of most products the time will come when there is a point of diminishing returns in terms of profits and new sales.

The diffusion process mirrors rather well the way that many rumors spread across a consumer population. At the outset, rumors tend to be localized among a rather small group of individuals, whom we can dub the rumor innovators. It is these persons who tend to be the first to get the inside scoop on a story or who perhaps are themselves responsible for issuing conjectures about a product or firm. Assuming the rumor is neither confirmed nor disconfirmed at this stage, we can expect it to disperse across the wider population in the manner depicted in Fig. 4.7. By the time the rumor reaches the rumor laggards, interest in the story may already have begun to fade or else been disconfirmed. In some cases, such as for conspiracy rumors about consumer-oriented companies (e.g., the P&G Satanic rumors), we might expect

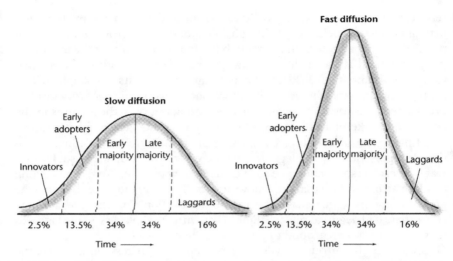

FIG. 4.7.   The diffusion of innovation process and adopter categories. From Fill (1995). Reprinted with permission of Pearson Education Limited.

the diffusion process to be rather slow, with the story gradually spreading across the country or across different consumer communities or types. In the financial marketplace, where events unfold at such a rapid pace, rumors are apt to flame and then burn out in an extremely quick fashion, as we saw occur in the Emulex case. Just as some products become hits again with consumers long after their initial demise (e.g., children's scooters, Hush Puppies), some rumors reappear in a cyclical fashion as the underlying needs and emotions that originally gave rise to the rumors reappear.

Unlike the diffusion of innovation process, whereby the objective of marketers is to speed up the adoption of something new across a population, the opposite goal prevails in the case of commercial rumors, where the interest is in bringing the diffusion process to a halt before the rumor spirals out of control. Similarly, marketers have a strong interest in identifying persons who may serve as rumor innovators or opinion leaders to curtail the influence of these individuals in getting the unfounded message out to a much larger number of consumers. Marketing communications typically are differentially adapted and targeted to appeal to various consumer groups at different phases of a product's life cycle. This is an important point to keep in mind for companies attempting to develop effective antirumor communications programs.

PARTICIPANTS IN THE SPREAD OF RUMOR

The diffusion process points out the importance of attempting to distinguish between different kinds of participants in the rumor process. Are certain persons more prone to spread rumors than others or more apt to serve as rumor innovators? Although there has been relatively little attention to this question in the research literature, some authors have offered typologies to character-ize the various players in the rumor transmission process. For example, orga-nizational studies (e.g., Davis, 1969; Sutton & Porter, 1968) have identified three types of individuals relative to rumors: bridgers, baggers, and isolates. *Bridgers*, also referred to as key communicators, are the most active partici-pants in the organizational grapevine and they are largely responsible for the grapevine's success. These persons serve as liaisons or passers-along of ru-mors, making use of their multiple connections in the organizational system. They are key communicators in the sense that they represent the ones who are responsible for initially introducing information into the organization's infor-mal communication networks.

By contrast, *baggers* or "dead-enders" are those individuals who receive ru-mors but do not pass them along to others, or else they communicate them to one or two other dead-enders. Organizational studies have revealed that this sort of person is not uncommon in organizations. In fact, according to some estimates, only about 10% of an organization's workforce tend to be active participants in the grapevine (Mishra, 1990). Most of a company's rank and file employees essentially are unmotivated to pass on the rumors they receive. Many of these individuals do not pass on rumors because they never receive them in the first place. This third category represents the organization's *iso-lates*—persons who are not privy to rumors and thus are incapable of passing them along even if they had the motivation to do so. Isolates remain outside the rumor network because they lack the interpersonal connections within the organization that would allow them to receive information circulating through the grapevine.

Where in this typology a person would be classified appears to be a func-tion of a combination of social factors, personality characteristics, and per-sonal motives. For example, as briefly described in Chapter 2, Anthony (1973) revealed the personality factor of chronic anxiety (i.e., the degree to which a person tends to be nervous and easily upset across a wide range of situations) to be a reliable predictor of whether a person had heard a specific rumor. After having planted a rumor among a sample of high school girls, Anthony re-ported that 93% of the girls previously identified as high in anxiety (as a result of their scores on a psychological test) claimed to have heard it, whereas only 31% of the girls in the low-anxiety group reported hearing it. In another study that attempted to discern the characteristics of rumormongers, it was re-vealed that university students who dated and got together with friends less of-ten than their peers were more likely to spread a rumor, perhaps as an attempt to increase their esteem and thereby widen their circle of interpersonal rela-tionships (Rosnow & Fine, 1974). In this sense, we might imagine that persons within an organization who feel that they lack power or success might be more apt to believe and spread rumors (Fearn-Banks, 1996). However, it also has been observed that people tend to be more active in the grapevine when their close friends and colleagues are actively involved (Mishra, 1990).

In addition to chronic anxiety and self-esteem, there are other personal characteristics that appear to be factors influencing the degree to which a person is motivated to believe and transmit rumors. Earlier, we noted how conspiracy rumors in the commercial marketplace tend to reflect a general mistrust of the government and powerful corporations. Suspicious or skeptical persons thus may be more prone to participate in the spread of such rumors. However, the way in which someone responds to a rumor may depend very much on that person's state prior to rumor reception. Along these lines, Buckner (1965) identified three "sets" or states of readiness a person may have, including a *critical set*, whereby the rumor recipient possesses both the ability and motivation to critically evaluate a rumor's claims prior to deciding whether to repeat it. By contrast, an *uncritical set* describes a person's lack of critical ability to evaluate a rumor that, as a result, may simply be passed on in one form or another. The third condition, a *transmission set*, characterizes rumor recipients who are neutral toward the rumor content and repeat it to conform to the expectations or demands of others. Buckner's notions regarding these prior states were derived from an early paper by Chorus (1953), who introduced the concept of *critical sense* to describe an individual's willingness to accept and spread a rumor. According to Chorus, the higher a person's level of this personal factor, the less likely that person would be to repeat the rumor. As we suggested earlier, for many commercial and organizational rumors, critical sense is likely to be diminished when emotions (e.g., fear and anxiety) run high, thereby increasing the likelihood that the message will be repeated.

Another factor that merits further research scrutiny is self-monitoring—the ability to observe and control one's expressive behavior and presentation in social situations (Snyder, 1974). People who are labeled as high self-monitors are those who tend to be very adept at adapting their behavior to fit the social situation. In a sense, they are like social chameleons who are capable of reading others and then altering their own behavior to make a good impression. The suspected link between this characteristic and rumor comes from research suggesting that high self-monitors have a great interest in social information, apparently because it is useful to them in determining how to behave in particular situations (Fiske & Taylor, 1991). Unlike low self-monitors, who lack either the motivation or ability to fit in, high self-monitors are more likely to seek out and consider information that is relevant to norms for self-presentation in a situation. This, of course, could include rumors, which might be interpreted by high self-monitors as special sources of "inside information" regarding the parameters of a situation and relevant behavioral cues for social conduct.

In another classification of the actors involved in the rumor process, Kapferer (1990) distinguished between various roles that people may play in the instigation or dissemination of rumors. This includes the instigator, who essentially creates a rumor by attempting to explain an ambiguous or otherwise confusing situation or who may be motivated to harm a competitor, and the interpreter, who follows the instigator by shaping the explanation into something more convincing and credible. Because they are respected and listened to by others, opinion leaders then play an important mediating role in determining whether or not the rumor will spread across the social group. Other roles include that of apostles, the devotees of a rumor who become committed to its dissemination; profiteers, who may not believe a rumor but see an advantage to having it circulate; opportunists, who use a rumor to moralize or prove a point; and flirters, who are disinterested in the credibility of a rumor but enjoy talking about it and recognize its entertainment value. Conversely, there are individuals who work against rumor circulation: The passive relays are persons not convinced about a rumor's trustworthiness and remain suspicious about it without taking action, and the resisters actively fight against a rumor because of vested interests or disbelief in its content.

THE INFLUENCE OF THE MASS MEDIA

Although our focus in this chapter until now has been devoted to the role of interpersonal forces in the communication of rumors, the power and influence of the mass media in the rumor process cannot be overlooked. In prior chapters we have discussed how contemporary and emerging communication technologies have sped up the means by which rumors circulate. In the remainder of this chapter, we consider further how mass media may be involved in the emergence and spread of rumors in the marketplace.

That the media play any role at all in the spread of commercial rumors is somewhat contrary to certain assumptions and expectations about the dynamics of rumor transmission. For example, one common assumption is that rumors arise when there is an absence of news transmitted through formalized communication channels. This would be the case in situations in which the news media have literally broken down (as during a natural disaster) or else cannot be trusted (e.g., due to censorship). Not long after the turn of the 20th century, it was believed that the development of mass forms of communication (beginning with the electric telegraph) would essentially put an end to rumors. This view was based on a conception of rumors as a medium of information when there was nothing else. Nonetheless, reports of the demise of rumors proved premature, in large part because they failed to consider the human element in mass communications. The electronic and print media basically exist as channels for the transmission of information; it is up to people to determine and direct the flow of content through these channels.

   In Chapter 1, we described how the line between rumor and news often is difficult to discern. One reason these forms of communication are often confused has to do with the context in which information appears. It is not uncommon to find rumors appearing as front-page "news" in responsible newspapers, with the reported information attributable to vaguely identifiable sources. Evidence for this was obtained in a study by Levin and Arluke (1987), who analyzed the content of the front page of every Sunday edition of *The New York Times* from October 1985 to September 1986 and observed that 70% of the stories during that period contained at least one anonymous source (described as "key officials," "government sources," "witnesses," and "delegates"). Clearly, reporting based on "informed" or "reliable" sources has become a normative practice among journalists in recent years, particularly with the emergence of the Internet, where the flow of news is largely uncontrolled and often lacking in verification. In short, although much reported news is of publicly verifiable facts, it also is the case that much is secondhand information or hearsay.

   Mass-mediated rumors often are not apparent as rumors because they either are perceived as something else (such as news) or given credibility by their juxtaposition alongside verified news. When transmitted through formal media channels, rumors tend to appear believable because the media typically are viewed as more reliable, authoritative, and credible sources than are most persons who convey unsubstantiated information in their everyday conversations. A rumor that is reported through one channel is likely to be picked up and reported through other channels, which is precisely what happened when various wire services picked up and disseminated the Emulex rumors. Repetition of the story is likely to contribute to the rumor's apparent credibility as well.

   Several commercial rumors have been falsely linked to mass media sources as they have been transmitted. Such attributions to the media are typical and often serve to foster belief in and the spread of unfounded stories about a firm and its products. For example, tellers of a rumor that Church's Fried Chicken Corporation was owned by the KKK and that the product was being contaminated so as to cause sterility in Black male consumers typically attempted to authenticate the story by claiming that a friend had seen a television news magazine exposé about the plot (de Vos, 1996). Similarly, as discussed in Chapter 2, the McDonald's and P&G Satan rumors were embellished by allegations that a company official or owner had appeared on a network TV broadcast to admit to his relationship with the devil.

   The electronic and print media not only serve as channels for rumor transmission, but also may play a significant role in initiating and perpetuating rumors. The potential of the mass media as mechanisms for fighting rumors already in circulation (e.g., by exposing them as untrue) also should not be overlooked (see Box 4.5). In this light, it is possible to identify at least three

---

Box 4.5. The Mass Media and Rumors

In an analysis of the popular press, folklorist Paul Smith (1992) identified six basic approaches used by newspapers in their presentations of contemporary legends. It would appear that these approaches can also apply in a more general sense to other types of rumors and other forms of mass media:

1. *Reporting* rumors as "factual" news.
2. *Exposing* rumors as "untrue" stories.
3. *Retracting* rumors previously reported as factual "news."
4. *Educating* the audience via the presentation of rumors.
5. *Entertaining* the audience via the presentation of rumors.
6. *Advertising* commercial products for sale using rumors.

According to Smith, these categories are not mutually exclusive; rather, a single presentation of a rumor can combine one or more of these approaches.

---

mechanisms by which the media play a role in the rumor process: (a) by serving as conduits of verifiable and unverifiable information, (b) by instigating rumor, and (c) by acting as "catalysts" to accelerate the effects of rumors (Kimmel et al., 1992).

The Media as Rumor Conduits

The diffusion of mass-mediated rumors can occur rapidly, reaching and influencing tremendous numbers of people almost instantaneously. Previously, we provided an example of how the mass media can serve as powerful conduits of rumor in our description of the reports that consumers were finding syringes and hypodermic needles in Diet Pepsi cans. Although eventual evidence revealed the tampering claims to be phony, reports of product tampering initially were carried in newspapers and local televised news broadcasts in the cities affected and soon thereafter were reported nationwide. Similarly, in a study of the Villejuif rumor, newspapers and magazines were most likely to be cited as the sources from which people first learned of the rumor, far ahead of leaflets slipped into mailboxes or posted in schools, workplaces, and hospitals (Kapferer, 1989). Some print outlets simply reproduced the Villejuif leaflet word-for-word in alarmist articles.

With the emergence of the Internet as a communication tool, never before have people been linked to such a vast network of information and misinformation (see Box 4.6). As Dery (1999) argued, "the wildfire spread of conspiracy theories ... would be impossible without Information Age innovations such as computer bulletin boards, desktop publishing, and shortwave radio broadcasting" (p. 20). One might predict that the prevalence of commercial

---

Box 4.6. Rumors and the Internet

Throughout this book we have made the point that the emergence of the Internet has begun to change to a great extent the playing field in terms of how rumors operate and have their effects in business-oriented contexts. According to Emanuel Rosen (2000), an expert on how "buzz" develops in the consumer marketplace (see Box 4.2), the Internet has shifted a great degree of power to the consumer in terms of having a positive or negative influence on the purchase behavior of others. Although as recently as 10 years ago customers might have shared their purchase experiences solely with family and friends, the Internet now provides options for venting one's joys or frustrations concerning a company with millions of people. These options also apply to the communication of rumors:

- Customers can e-mail the rumor to all their friends.
- They can participate in chats or newsgroups to discuss the rumor.
- They can annotate the Web site of a firm with their own comments about the rumor they heard about the company and its offerings.
- They can discuss the rumor on a consumer Web site devoted to product ratings, such as Deja.com or Epinions.com.
- They can publish information about the rumor on their own Web sites.
- They can start a Web site dedicated to a company (either as a fan site or a protest site) that highlights the rumors concerning the company.

Referring to the Internet's role in generating word-of-mouth about a car company, Rosen (2000) related the opinions of the president of a PR firm who commented, "If [the car company] had their way ... owners would be forbidden to speak to each other. We know too much" (p. 17). Now, thanks to the Internet, consumers engage in thousands of conversations in public newsgroups and online forums, in addition to their offline word-of-mouth exchanges.

---

rumors will increase in coming years as the technology of rumormongering continues to develop. Such a trend already has been observed in the financial marketplace. In recent years, the frequency of financial rumors reported as fact through various media outlets has shown a steady rise. For example, the periodical *Business Week* carries a column entitled "Inside Wall Street," which frequently reports on financial deals that never come to fruition. Another outlet for unfounded financial stories is the Jagnotes.com Web site. The growth of this stock-tip service essentially mirrors the technological developments that the mass media have undergone in recent decades. Originally formed in 1990, JagNotes began as a telephone service, with employees contacting subscribers with hot financial tips. It then became a fax service, providing its customers with a daily report on marketplace trends, tips, and rumors, prior to evolving into a Web site in early 2000 (Gordon, 1999). In light of such developments, La Monica (1999b) concluded, "I'm not trying to suggest that the press is fabricating rumors. It is our job, after all, to report what people are talking about. But a news account of a rumor is not a buy recommendation for the stock." By late 2000, certain antirumor measures had begun to emerge to counter the proliferation of financial services that regularly report unconfirmed rumors, including Web sites specifically intended to evaluate and report on the trustworthiness of such rumors.

The Media as Rumor Instigators

Some mass-mediated rumors have turned out to be complete fabrications from the outset—false stories that have been intentionally or unintentionally perpetrated by editors, reporters, and the like. One example of the media creating false information from scratch occurred in the wake of the Chernobyl nuclear reactor accident in 1986 (Lecerf & Parker, 1987). A false rumor was instigated by the media alleging that the death toll from the accident had reached more than 2,000 victims. This rumor was reported by the French Press Agency (AFP), and appears to have originated from a dispatch sent by an American press agency from Moscow, citing an unconfirmed report from the area of the accident. In reality, only 31 people had died from the accident by the end of 1986.

Cases such as these, in which "news" stories without a shred of truth appear in various media outlets and are repeated as facts, are sometimes referred to as *factoids*. The great cabbage hoax rumor, described in Chapter 3, represents a classic commercial-related factoid. Such fabricated stories now appear with alarming regularity on the Internet. One recent consumer products example, which apparently first emerged in 1999, involved the potential dangers of the microwave oven. This story, referred to as the exploding water rumor (see Box 4.7), seems to have originated from a widely disseminated e-mail letter from an unknown source. It then served as the focus of much discussion throughout various Internet chat groups. At present, there remains some debate as to whether the events described in the initial e-mail account actually could have occurred (cf. Glazer, 2001).

The Media as Rumor Catalysts

In addition to serving as rumor conduits and instigators, the media ultimately can play a role in affecting attitudes and behaviors toward rumor targets. Similar to the way a catalyst serves to modify and accelerate a chemical reaction, the media can speed up or otherwise influence the public's reaction to a news event. Perhaps the clearest illustration of this catalytic role can be seen in rumors that act as self-fulfilling prophesies (see chap. 2). Once again, the Diet Pepsi scare serves as a relevant example. Less than 2 weeks after the first re-

---

Box 4.7. The Exploding Water Rumor

This rumor, also referred to as the nuked water or microwaved water rumor, was in widespread transmission over the Internet during 1999. Its origins and rapid dissemination were predominantly limited to various Internet discussion forums, including bulletin board postings and chat groups. Its origins have been attributed to a widely distributed e-mail message, which reads as follows:

I feel that the following is information that any one who uses a microwave oven to heat water should be made aware of. About five days ago my 26-year-old son decided to have a cup of instant coffee. He took a cup of water and put it in the microwave to heat it up (something that he had done numerous times before). I am not sure how long he set the timer for but he told me he wanted to bring the water to a boil. When the timer shut the oven off, he removed the cup from the microwave.

As he looked into the cup he noted that the water was not boiling but instantly the water in the cup "blew up" into his face. The cup remained intact until he threw it out of his hand, but all the water had flown out into his face due to the buildup of energy. His whole face is blistered and he has 1st and 2nd degree burns to his face which may leave scarring. He also may have lost partial sight in his left eye.

While at the hospital, the doctor who was tending to him stated that this is a fairly common occurrence and water (alone) should never be heated in a microwave oven. If water is heated in this manner, something should be placed in the cup to diffuse the energy such as a wooden stir stick, tea bag, etc. It is however a much safer choice to boil the water in a tea kettle.

Please pass this information on to friends and family.

According to an authoritative evaluation of this rumor, the AFU & Urban Legends Archive (www.urbanlegends.com) advised that liquids heated in a microwave oven may indeed unexpectedly boil after becoming superheated and then triggered by something added to the glass; however, this phenomenon occurs infrequently. There is not sufficient information in the original e-mail to verify if the injury described actually occurred. Of course, this supposedly firsthand account is much more memorable than the dry safety warning included in the microwave oven's instructions.

---

ports that syringes had been found in Diet Pepsi cans, more than 50 people from 20 American states came forward with similar stories in what turned out to be copycat hoaxes.

Media reports can create a vicious circle or feedback loop, in the sense that the rumor contributes to the situation and the situation then contributes to more rumors. Television may exacerbate the feedback loop more so than any other information medium because one small aspect of an event can be magnified for viewers who are lacking in intellectual antibodies to resist rumors. In fact, a comment along the lines of "I saw it on TV" often can provide the appearance of credibility to even the most outrageous stories. Rumor control programs need to be capable of enlightening the public about the nature of mass-mediated communications to reduce people's susceptibility to be uncritically accepting and to better resist unfounded rumors.

The Media as Rumor Combatters

All the news is not bad regarding the role of the media in the commercial rumor transmission process. Effectively developed and carefully implemented antirumor campaigns have been waged successfully by firms, and many of these campaigns have involved the mass media in one form or another. Although these approaches are detailed in the second half of this book (see Part II, "Combatting Rumors"), we return one more time to the Diet Pepsi tampering hoax.

In the Diet Pepsi case, a crisis team of company executives was assembled as soon as the syringe claims began to receive national media attention. The next day, the company's North America president, Craig Weatherup, appeared on network telecasts with video footage showing how Pepsi-Cola products are canned during the production process. The video clearly demonstrated how the canning process makes it virtually impossible for foreign objects to be inserted. Weatherup followed the video presentation with six personal appearances on morning and evening national news shows, where he earnestly explained how a syringe could not possibly find its way into a can. He next appeared on a late-night TV broadcast along with the commissioner of the U.S. FDA. Both men attempted to calm consumers by describing FDA reports that the needles and syringes reportedly found in Pepsi cans were not contaminated. They advised consumers to pour canned drinks into a glass before drinking them and warned of the maximum penalty for making false complaints (including a 5-year prison term and $250,000 fine). Together, these actions represented a quick, consistent, and highly credible mass-mediated attack that effectively squelched the syringe scare ("Right Moves," 1993).

Other media-related strategies have been successfully utilized by firms to counter rumors, including the circulation of counterfliers, denials in print ads, televised press conferences, and threats of lawsuits. The corresponding risks associated with each of these approaches, including the possibility that there will be a boomerang effect that serves to exacerbate the situation, are detailed in subsequent chapters.

CONCLUSION

The images of neighbors sharing rumors across the picket fence separating their backyards or passing along a story in a serial chain of telephone calls (as depicted in Norman Rockwell's famous painting) no longer suffice to adequately characterize the much more complex ways in which information spreads in contemporary society. Today, a rumor can be disseminated almost instantaneously by a person with minimal computer skills through the click of a mouse and, within a span of several hours, a company could experience disastrous financial consequences as a result. Certain persons are likely to be more prone than others to believe and transmit rumors. Others are centrally connected to extensive interpersonal networks and, as a result, are capable of playing a more significant role in the paths that rumors take and the speed with which they disperse. The mass media can serve a variety of roles in both the rapid spread and possible control of rumors. With this sort of insight into the processes that account for the spread of rumors, it is clear that the task that faces companies that are moved to develop and launch effective rumor control programs indeed is a daunting one.

Part II

Combatting Rumors in the Marketplace and Workplace

Open your ears; for which of you will stop
The vent of hearing when loud Rumour speaks?
—William Shakespeare, *Henry IV*

CHAPTER FIVE

Managing Commercial Rumors: How Can Marketplace Rumors Be Prevented?

The most efficient way to quiet a rumor is a denial by the general manager.
Play with the rumors ... show that one isn't afraid.
Ignore the rumor and let the others talk.

These comments are representative of some of the recommendations I obtained from French product and brand managers in response to a recent survey I conducted dealing with rumors the managers encountered in the conduct of their business and the effectiveness of strategies used to counter them (Kimmel & Audrain, 2002). As reflected in these brief suggestions for handling rumors, there are a variety of methods for rumor control and what works for one manager (or in one business sector) might not necessarily be the most effective strategy for another. This fundamental point is consistent with the discussion pertaining to the nature of rumor in Part I of this volume.

In this and the following chapters, basic measures for the prevention and management of commercial rumors are described and evaluated. Given that rumors are about as much a part of business life as profits and losses, it is virtually inevitable that managers will be required to select from a range of rumor control strategies at one time or another. In fact, the management of rumors should represent a basic component of day-to-day business operations, rather than merely something that is considered in crisis situations, which is currently the modus operandi for most consumer goods companies.

Short of ignoring a rumor and hoping it will disappear on its own, which is a strategy considered in Chapter 6, most successful approaches to dealing with marketplace scuttlebutt require the establishment of an atmosphere of trust and credibility among the firm's various publics. This is easier said than done and, as emphasized here, each approach brings with it certain risks. We begin our discussion of rumor control tactics by focusing in this chapter on procedures oriented to the prevention of rumors, including means for anticipating rumors before they occur and monitoring early effects during their formative stages. We then turn our attention in Chapter 6 to the specific strategies and tactics that can be employed to fight rumors once they have begun to pose serious problems for a firm.

RUMOR PREVENTION: DEALING WITH UNCERTAINTY AND ANXIETY

Business activities that involve approaches to preventing and neutralizing rumors must focus on the reduction of, to the greatest extent possible, the conditions that tend to give rise to rumors and the motives that compel people to communicate unsubstantiated messages. The challenge at the outset, then, is for company personnel to focus their efforts on the situational preconditions that create a fertile atmosphere for rumors to fester and to establish detection mechanisms for identifying emerging rumors during their formative stage.

As we have seen, it is essential to recognize that the psychological, situational, and marketing forces that tend to influence the rumor process are more or less likely to play a role at different stages of the rumor life cycle. Thus, as a framework to guide our discussion of rumor prevention and control, it is useful to consider once again the stages through which a rumor typically passes. A model based on our earlier discussion of the rumor life cycle (see chap. 4) appears in Fig. 5.1. As is apparent, in terms of rumor prevention, attention must be directed to the two key variables most likely to be operating during the rumor generation stage: uncertainty and anxiety.

It goes without saying that it is no small task to attempt to eliminate the various questions and worries prevalent among a company's various publics at any particular time, especially given that change is the order of the day in the

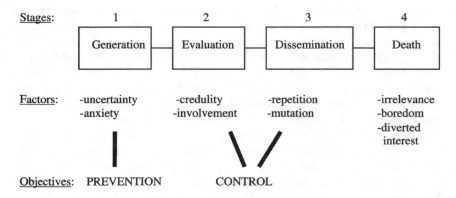

FIG. 5.1.   Stages of the rumor life cycle, critical factors, and company objectives.

contemporary marketplace. Mergers and takeovers are now commonplace events in most commercial industry sectors; scientific and technological advances continue to alter the manufacturing, production, and marketing of a wide range of consumer products; and the internationalization of most markets has added to the complexity of consumer choices even to the extent of obscuring the true origin of presumed domestic products (see Box 5.1). All of these developments serve to fuel speculation and fear, especially among rumor-prone individuals.

Although it is commonly assumed that innovation is the lifeblood of the marketplace, marketing professionals also are well aware that consumers dislike changes, but rather prefer the known, the familiar, and the expected, even when their lives can be made easier or more comfortable through innovation (Aaker, 1991). This basic marketing axiom helps explain the high failure rates of new products (estimates of which range from 40% to 90%, depending on the product category and industry; see Crawford, 1997), the tendency for consumers to develop strong loyalties to favored brands (Fournier, 1998), and the slow adoption rate for many ultimately successful new products and services (Holak, Lehmann, & Sultan, 1987). For example, the large-scale success of a fast-food hamburger chain like McDonald's is probably not due to the fact that hungry, loyal customers expect that they will be served a uniquely different gourmet meal during each visit, but is instead a function of the comfort that comes from knowing exactly what they will get—a quick, inexpensive, filling meal in a clean and efficient restaurant setting. For the most part, they do not expect, nor do they desire, surprises in that setting (such as a four-star, gourmet meal), but rather are attracted to the predictability of the experience.

The need for consistency in the consumer marketplace also helps explain why people often react vehemently when a long-standing product either is changed or discontinued. Such was the case in 1985 when the Coca-Cola Company decided to alter the original formulation of Coca-Cola, the company's primary brand, in favor of a sweeter variation (Hartley, 1998). Within 1 month of the introduction of "New Coke" the company was receiving more than 5,000 telephone calls a day, along with angry letters, from unhappy Coke drinkers who felt betrayed by the company and who demanded that the original Coke be brought back. Less than 3 months later, the company did just that, apologizing for changing the beloved traditional product and reintroducing it as Coca-Cola Classic. In a rapidly changing world, consumers like to have some constants to rely on, even if those constants are merely soft drinks, candy bars, or fast-food restaurants.

What all this means, basically, is that change in the marketplace is unsettling—in most change situations it is not clear whether currently received positive outcomes will continue to be forthcoming or whether undesired consequences will result. In such circumstances, it is not surprising that people become anxious, upset, and desirous of information that can reduce the

---

Box 5.1. What's In A Name?

Consumers take great comfort in having certain predictable and stable aspects to the marketplace, be it a favorite supermarket for grocery shopping, a traditional brand of breakfast cereal that reminds them of their childhood, or a preferred waiter in a local restaurant whom they can count on for outstanding service. The need for constancy is particularly strong in the contemporary shopping context, where the number of product and brand choices has proliferated in recent decades (Nilson, 1998) and changes occur at a pace unforeseen in previous decades. These developments have served to alter the face of business and the marketplace, which may appear more overwhelming and far less "knowable" to the typical shopper than ever before. The resulting uncertainty provides an atmosphere that is particularly prone to the development of rumors.

One form of uncertainty in the contemporary marketplace has to do with consumers' increasing lack of awareness of the true ownership of many companies and brands. Indeed, knowing the actual origin or identity of familiar products and brands is not as straightforward as it once was. This is seen in the growing number of brands that at one time were indisputably American but now are owned by European companies, including such well-known and long-standing American household names as Lucky Strikes, Amoco, Jeep, Holiday Inn, Burger King, Taster's Choice, and Brooks Brothers.

In actuality, every one of these products or names now belongs to European owners: Lucky Strikes are made by the London-based British American Tobacco, Amoco belongs to the British oil company BP, Jeep is a product of the German company Daimler-Chrysler, Holiday Inn is owned by the British hotel firm Six Continents, Burger King is owned by the British beverage corporation Diageo, Taster's Choice coffee now belongs to the brand portfolio of Nestle SA of Switzerland, and Brooks Brothers is part of the Italian conglomerate Retail Brand Alliance (Reid, 2002). This trend toward European investment in the American marketplace in large part reflects the strength and promise of the U.S. economy at the end of the 20th century. It seems reasonable to assume that with the loss of such domestically owned mainstays, consumers would be more likely to fall prey to a variety of conspiracy rumors (e.g., secret foreign control over the domestic economy) and contamination rumors (e.g., suspicions about the contents and safety of goods produced and manufactured by foreign companies).

---

uncertainty they are experiencing, regardless of how speculative that information may be. Fortunately, however, there are various marketing tools and practices that can be exploited to assist a firm's publics in coping with the inevitability of change and other conditions that are likely to lead to rumor-mongering. Collectively, these tools and practices can be classified under the more general marketing headings of public relations, relationship marketing, and ethically responsible marketing.

Public Relations and Rumor Prevention

As a basic tool of marketing communication, public relations represents one of the most effective means by which companies can garner trust and minimize the likelihood they will be targeted by false and malicious rumors. The meaning of public relations is somewhat self-evident, as apparent in typical definitions of the term (see Box 1.2). According to the (British) Institute of Public Relations, "Public relations practice is the planned and sustained effort to establish and maintain goodwill and mutual understanding between an organisation and its publics." This definition implies that public relations is an organized campaign or program implemented by a company; that is, it is comprised of a continuous series of activities that are not haphazardly selected.

By "publics," it is suggested that a company must manage a series of partnerships and interactions with a variety of organizational and consumer groups. The concept of stakeholders is often used to refer to these groups, which underlines the fact that companies and different groups exert a mutual influence on each other (Fill, 1995). Some of these stakeholder groups may be internal to the firm, such as employees or managerial coalitions, whereas others are apt to be external to the firm, including consumers, suppliers, distributors, buyers, shareholders, competitors, agencies, and the government. To develop effective public relations strategies, it is important to bear in mind that each of the organization's partner groups are likely to have varying objectives, motivations, and interests.

To a great extent, the overriding goal of public relations is to influence the behavior of groups of people in relation to each other (White & Mazur, 1995). According to Kotler et al. (1999), handling or heading off unfavorable rumors is one of the ways that a company can build good relations with its various publics. Although this is certainly true, this also is a two-way street, in the sense that a variety of public relations tools can be used effectively as a means to prevent rumors. That is, when a firm engages in activities designed to obtain favorable publicity, to build a strong and positive corporate image, and to strategically communicate with its various stakeholders, these activities not only serve to accomplish more general public relations objectives, but they also minimize the likelihood that false and potentially damaging rumors about the company will emerge or be believed. As suggested in Chapter 1, these goals can be achieved through the conversion of negative states, such as apathy, ignorance, and hostility, into more positive states, such as interest, knowledge, and sympathy (see Box 1.2). When consumers, for instance, become knowledgeable about a firm's policies and programs and sympathetic when it appears that the firm is being unfairly targeted, it is unlikely that they would view the spreading of rumors about the company as legitimate conduct. Described by marketing communications expert Chris Fill (1995) as a management process that provides visibility for a company, public relations allows the firm "to be properly identified, positioned, and understood by all of its stakeholders" (p. 387).

Another definition of public relations that is often cited is the so-called Mexican Statement, which was adopted at a world assembly of pubic relations associations in Mexico City in 1978: "Public relations practice is the art and social science of analysing trends, predicting their consequences, counselling organisations' leadership, and implementing planned programmes of action which will serve both the organisation's and the public interest" (Mexican Statement, 1978). This is an extremely insightful statement when it is read with rumor prevention and control in mind. It emphasizes the importance of understanding marketplace trends and their potential consequences (e.g., a growing concern among consumers about the safety of their food along with the concomitant potential for the emergence of contamination rumors), and recognizes the undeniable link between a company's reputation and its responsibility to the public interest (e.g., the firm's responsibility to respond to consumer anxieties by being forthcoming about its product manufacturing process).

Given the important functions that public relations can play for an organization, let us next consider some specific public relations tools and practices, along with some of their strengths and drawbacks with respect to rumor prevention. The particular combination of methods utilized typically depends on the needs, perspectives, and overall budget of a firm's marketing or public relations department. A variety of activities and practices can be carried out by a company as elements of a public relations program designed to promote goodwill, raise visibility, and enhance credibility. These include, but are not limited to, the following:

- *Product publicity and press relations.* Generally referred to as publicity, these methods involve the creation and placement of newsworthy information in the news media (e.g., via the use of news releases, press conferences, and publicity kits) to bring attention to the company and its products and services.
- *Event management and sponsorship.* The connection of a company, product, or brand name with a public event. In such cases, the manufacturer contributes toward part or all of the costs in return for the benefit of association (e.g., tobacco companies' association with the European Formula 1 race car circuit; JVC's sponsorship of the 2002 World Cup soccer tournament).
- *Public affairs.* Related to publicity and sponsorship, this form of public relations involves a firm's attempts to establish itself as a good neighbor in the business community by demonstrating corporate citizenship and sponsoring programs that promote social benefits (see Box 5.2).

> ### Box 5.2. Public Relations and La Caixa
>
> When it comes to public affairs and programs of social responsibility, few companies can match the exemplary standard set by La Caixa, Spain's largest financial institution and Europe's largest savings bank. Formed in July 1990 following a merger between Caja de Ahorros de Barcelona and Caja de Pensiones para la Vejez y de Ahorros de Cataluña y Baleares, La Caixa donates approximately 50% of its total annual profits to cultural, education, and civic programs throughout Spain. In 1992, for example, the budget for community projects totaled $72.4 million and steadily increased to more than $180 million in 2002. These donations are allotted to the following sorts of operations (Griffin, 1994; www.research.lacaixa.communicacions.com):
>
> - *Cultural programs*: Libraries, cultural centers, science museum, traveling science museums, exhibitions (art, photography, literature, and science), music programs (concerts, lectures, and music courses), poetry events.
> - *Educational programs*: Graduate fellowships, courses, educational activities for children.
> - *Social programs*: Recreation centers for the elderly, integration of immigrants and marginalized groups into society, competitions for nonprofit organizations working with these groups.
>
> Such socially responsible activity reinforces the image of La Caixa as a nonprofit, welfare-oriented institution, with the main purpose of encouraging savings and investment, while channeling its earnings back into the community. Apparently, much of this public relations effort has paid off and in no small part explains the company's enviable standing as the top financial institution in Spain.

- *Lobbying.* The involvement of firms within government through the development of relations with legislators and other government officials to influence legislation and regulations that could affect the firm's operations. The tobacco industry has extensively engaged in lobbying activities, as has the pharmaceutical industry, in attempts to influence legislation on new patent regulations and the information that must appear in promotional messages.
- *Corporate advertising.* A combination of advertising and public relations that involves advertising on behalf of the company in general rather than for its specific products or services. That is, instead of promoting the qualities of a product, the personality or values of the firm are presented to shape public opinion and foster identification with the firm. For example, the Philip Morris Company has engaged in an advertising campaign specifically detailing its position and policies regarding the need to prevent young people from having access to cigarettes (see Fig. 5.2).

Youth

At Philip Morris, we believe that adults have the right to choose whether to smoke or not.

Minors, on the other hand, should not smoke. Period.

We also believe that preventing minors from having access to cigarettes is the key to addressing this issue.

That's why we recently launched *Action Against Access*, one of the most comprehensive programs ever introduced to combat the issue of youth access to cigarettes.

Action Against Access is a series of tough initiatives that have as their ultimate goal making all cigarette sales face-to-face transactions so age can be verified in person.

We are confident that, when fully implemented, this program will make a difference.

Everyone has a role to play in preventing youth access: educators, lawmakers, parents, communities. And, of course, the tobacco industry.

At Philip Morris we will continue to take a leadership role so that minors do not have access to cigarettes.

PHILIP MORRIS U.S.A.

We want you to know where we stand.

Facts Matter | As part of *Action Against Access*, all Philip Morris cigarette packs and cartons in the United States will carry the following notice: "Underage sale prohibited."

FIG. 5.2. Philip Morris and public relations. This magazine advertisement represents an example of a Philip Morris corporate advertising campaign, which is intended to shape consumers's attitudes toward the tobacco manufacturer.

Although these activities represent the most common forms of public relations, we might consider virtually any corporate decision that becomes known to the public as capable of having an impact on a company's relationships with its various stakeholders, however indirectly. A case in point is the decision by the Philip Morris Company in November 2001 to change its corporate name to Altria Group LLC. (The new name is a derivative of the Latin word *altus* meaning "to reach higher.") As the biggest tobacco company in the world, in addition to being the owner of Kraft Foods, Inc. and the Miller Brewing Company, the decision makers at Philip Morris concluded that the name change would serve to differentiate the parent company from its tobacco units, which are involved in numerous lawsuits ("Philip Morris," 2001). The name Philip Morris is so strongly associated with tobacco products that it now serves as a brand equity liability among the growing number of consumers who object to corporations' involvement with tobacco and alcohol products. In this light, the name change makes good sense when one considers the potential public relations advantages it could bring to the company.

Strengths of Public Relations. In addition to the aforementioned functions of public relations in establishing goodwill and a positive relationship with a firm's stakeholders, there are other potential benefits inherent in this approach that are relevant to rumor prevention efforts. This is apparent if we focus on some of the specific aims of using corporate advertising. In a review of studies on the use of corporate advertising in the United States, Schumann, Hathcote, and West (1991) found that business executives tended to view the following goals as most important for a company that utilizes this form of public relations: enhancement of the company's reputation, support for its products and services, development of business interests, advocating of a position, and public communication of the company's social and environmental actions. In one way or another, these goals also can be achieved through use of the other forms of public relations described earlier.

I previously emphasized that rumors are especially likely to be generated during periods of transition and change, as people try to make sense of current and future events in situations where information flow is likely to be limited. Given the outcomes that might be satisfied through their use, it perhaps is not surprising that we recommend public relations activities as a potentially effective means of preventing and neutralizing rumors during change situations. For example, Fill (1995) suggested that corporate advertising can be useful as a defensive approach during the period of transition tied to a merger or takeover by convincing shareholders of the value of the organization and the need not to accept hostile offers. Further, corporate advertising can function to inform and advise about current policies as well as to shape the positioning of the "new" firm that results from the merger.

What is important to note with regard to these benefits is that public relations activities function to raise awareness and credibility with respect to a firm's activities, policies, and interests. By voluntarily serving to provide information to the public rather than to stifle it during periods marked by instability, the PR approach also goes a long way in reducing anxieties and concerns that might be prevalent among the firm's various publics. In part, it communicates the message that the company has nothing to hide and is willing to remain open and accessible to its stakeholders. Moreover, when a firm acquires a tarnished image as a result of any misunderstandings, perhaps due to poor communication on the part of the company or inaccurate information presented in the media, public relations often can be effective in serving as a corrective mechanism. For example, when financial analysts believe that a firm is underperforming despite the objective reality that performance is quite healthy, public relations can correct the misunderstanding and enhance corporate credibility and trust, thereby reducing the likelihood that the speculation will give rise to rampant, potentially damaging financial rumors.

Although much of this discussion can be seen as pertaining predominantly to the use of such public relations tools as publicity, press relations, and corporate advertising, we should not overlook the critical role that public affairs plays in the control of rumors. This is apparent if we reconsider the strategy of social responsibility utilized by La Caixa to foster community relations (see Box 5.2). Imagine how the company's stature and strong reputation in cultural, educational, and other community settings enables the firm to be well positioned to nip emerging rumors in the bud before they have the chance to fully develop and spread. Through the company's efficient communication and social programs, company officials have the ear of community leaders, who can serve as opinion leaders for further dispersing accurate information about the firm's policies and actions, along with correctives for situations in which there may be some misconceptions. Once social programs are in place, it should be easier to ask for the assistance of community leaders when a rumor problem has been identified.

Perhaps more important, because La Caixa has such strong ties to various social groups and has so effectively established an atmosphere of trust among them, members of the community can be expected to be more forthcoming in approaching company officials when they hear malicious idle talk targeting the firm, confident that a credible and open clarification will be provided. Strong social ties between the company and consumer groups might also make it easier to enlist community leaders as "rumor detectors" who can be asked to communicate to the company early signs that a rumor problem is imminent.

In a more general sense, there are other benefits to using public relations as a marketing tool. What makes a public relations message more credible than other forms of marketing communications is the apparent objectivity of the message, which typically is not perceived as having been issued by the company itself. For example, the marketing department at Nike might develop a press kit detailing its sponsorship of a basketball tournament for youngsters in poor local neighborhoods, which the company then distributes to local television stations. If decision makers at those stations decide to air a story about the tournament and Nike's sponsorship, viewers likely will perceive the story as having more credibility and as carrying more weight than had it been transmitted through a paid advertising medium clearly identifying Nike as the message sponsor (see Fig. 5.3 for a similar example).

Drawbacks to Public Relations. As is the case for other rumor control strategies, there are corresponding drawbacks and risks in the use of public relations as a prevention approach and, in this light, it is an approach that should never be used alone. It is true that public relations represents one of the least expensive means of marketing communication (e.g., relative to advertising, sales promotion, and personal selling), given that it does not require the purchase of television or radio airtime or space in print media. (This even is true of corporate advertising when the message is deemed by media owners as a public service announcement; in such cases, the owners offer space or time to present the information free of charge.) Nonetheless, a significant disadvantage to public relations is that it is difficult for the firm to manage the message that ultimately is transmitted, if it is transmitted at all, and the message may not be received by its audience in the intended way. These problems are most relevant when publicity and press relations are utilized because once the message is picked up by the media, the firm loses control over the way the intended communication will be presented. This can pose a real danger to a company that uses these forms of public relations to assist in the prevention of rumors. If the information distributed to the media is communicated inappropriately to a rumor-prone public or is treated in a nonserious manner, the rumor problem may only be exacerbated. For example, a critical piece of information may be left out of any broadcast to fit the limited time allotted to the story, thereby undermining the intended meaning of the message.

Sponsorship and event management entail another set of potential risks. The concerns here are linked to the possibility that the organization, cause, event, or person that the sponsoring firm associates with may itself become targeted by unfounded allegations. For example, if Nike sponsors the neighborhood basketball tournament mentioned in the preceding section, there could be carryover problems for the company if a rumor-related scandal develops with respect to the games (e.g., that organized crime figures have established a gambling ring or that some of the participants are dealing drugs). This is the same sort of problem that confronts companies that engage in promotion through a long-term, paid relationship with a celebrity endorser. As a case in point, the overwhelming popularity and success of professional golfer Tiger Woods has made him an extremely desirable (albeit expensive) spokesperson

Libération
Mercredi 16 octobre 1996, page 19

VOUS

Chez McDo dès le petit déj' Sucré, salé, et surtout pas cher, la chaîne mise sur le créneau matinal.

NOCE Vincent

Pour bien manger, mangez américain! La multinationale de restauration rapide McDonald's n'a décidément peur de rien, puisqu'elle pourrait reprendre à son compte ce paradoxe provocateur qui fera grincer des dents plus d'un Français. Depuis quelques jours en effet, tous les restaurants de la chaîne sont ouverts pour le petit déjeuner. Aucune concession n'a été faite à l'esprit français: la formule s'appelle "McMorning", et elle reprend l'exemple des petits déjeuners consistants à l'anglaise. Tous les produits sont anglo-saxons, et il faut apprendre à reconnaître un "muffin" (petit pain rond au goût un peu sucré) d'un "pancake" (variété de petite crêpe). Quant à la composition, elle est la même à Paris qu'à Londres, New York ou Hong-kong.

De 7 h 30 à 11 heures, les 500 "McDo" de France proposent donc, pour 17 F, le choix entre deux petits déjeuners (1): un salé, l'autre sucré. Avec un jus d'orange et café, thé ou chocolat, le client a le choix entre un ensemble oeuf-bacon-cheddar ou un muffin et deux pancakes, accompagnés de beurre, confiture et "sirop goût érable". Hier matin à Paris, on trouvait surtout des touristes pour apprécier ces plateaux d'un prix hypercompétitif, mais la chaîne doit lancer à partir de demain une campagne publicitaire nationale qui devrait donner plus d'ampleur à l'initiative. Les consommateurs des premiers jours paraissent plutôt satisfaits. Il est vrai qu'un effort a été fait sur le café. Les pancakes sont préparés à la demande, et, faible affluence aidant, le bacon est frais et craquant. Les formules ne sont pas obligatoires, et certains clients se contentent d'un café, ou préfèrent adjoindre un yaourt aux céréales (6,50 F) ou une salade de fruits (8,50 F) à un repas assez bourratif.

L'atmosphère est agréable, l'interdiction de fumer plutôt la règle que l'exception, les salles spacieuses et éclairées. Des quotidiens sont disponibles pour les clients, une jeune fille propose du café en plus à la ronde, un fond de musique classique ou de jazz contribue au calme ambiant. Certains lisent, quelques jeunes travaillent.

On est loin de l'atmosphère du bar du coin, et, du reste, les commentaires ne laissent aucun doute sur la déplorable image qu'entretiennent les cafés. "Ici, dit un étudiant de Censier, je suis sûr que le patron ne va pas me relancer toutes les cinq minutes en exigeant que je reprenne une consommation." "C'est propre, et je me suis dit que personne ne viendrait me draguer", assure une jeune femme, en face de la gare d'Austerlitz, entre deux trains. "Il est interdit de fumer, et pour moi c'est fondamental", précise un autre client. "On me laisse tranquille", enchérit une SDF voisine, qui fait aussi valoir l'argument du prix. "Beaucoup moins cher que les cafés d'à côté", lancent deux jeunes touristes bulgares, qui se sont livrés à une méticuleuse comparaison. Une litanie de reproches adressés en creux au bistrot traditionnel, dont il faut bien dire qu'il s'enfonce dans ses défauts. Certains hôteliers, qui facturent le petit déjeuner entre 30 et 100 F, risquent également de subir l'effet de cette concurrence.

FIG. 5.3. McDonald's and public relations in France. This article, which appeared in the French newspaper *Libération* describing McDonald's introduction of its "McMorning" breakfast meals in the French marketplace, signifies how a company can receive free promotion in the media through public relations efforts. Reprinted with permission of *Libération*.

for a number of consumer goods firms. However, if his image should become tainted by a negative rumor about his personal life, those firms could suffer serious collateral damage as a function of "guilt by association" (see Box 5.3).

Another consideration in using public relations as a rumor prevention mechanism involves the risk that comes from the growing public visibility that may result from public relations campaigns. This may sound contradictory at first, given that increased visibility tends to be a primary objective for such campaigns in the first place. However, the danger is related to the tendency for rumors to target highly visible firms or to jump from smaller, lesser known targets to bigger and better known ones. This is probably a risk that many large companies are willing to take, reasoning that awareness is an essential asset for building brand equity and profitability in a global marketplace. Nonetheless, it might be safer for firms to implement public relations campaigns that are relatively low key but likely to nurture relations with well-defined stakeholders, relying on other marketing communication strategies, such as advertising, to enhance brand equity.

Relationship Marketing

The success of the public relations methods described in the preceding section in preventing rumors is exceedingly difficult to assess. An analogy can be drawn to the ongoing war on international terrorism. Both before and after the September 11, 2001, terrorist attacks on the United States, other potentially devastating threats have been thwarted during the planning and preparation stages; nonetheless, these successes understandably have drawn far less attention than the attacks that eluded detection. However, when arrests are made and evidence of a planned attack is obtained, it is clear that something terrible has been averted. With regard to public relations as a rumor prevention strategy, it is virtually impossible to ascertain with certainty whether specific rumors have been forestalled. At best, this conclusion can only be drawn indirectly, as when a manager logically concludes, "Well, we haven't had any recent problems with rumors, so we must be doing something right. Maybe that 'something' is our public relations program."

In a similar sense, the same can be said about the next two prevention approaches to be described here: relationship marketing and ethically responsible marketing. Like public relations, if these other approaches counteract the generation of rumors, like public relations, they do so indirectly by increasing public confidence and trust in the company, reducing public anxieties, enhancing the firm's credibility, and so on—outcomes that are likely to influence the variables or conditions that have been implicated in the generation of rumors. With this in mind, let us continue our discussion of rumor prevention by turning to one of the fastest developing areas of marketing, which in recent years has come to be referred to as relationship marketing.

Box 5.3. Guilt by Association?

The fact that there are risks involved in a company's efforts to develop associations with other entities has been illustrated time and again in a variety of marketing circumstances. In one well-known case involving celebrity endorsement, Pepsi-Cola had to abandon its sponsorship of Michael Jackson after the singer was accused of child abuse. Other examples have resulted from the so-called brand extension strategy, which has been increasingly utilized by consumer goods firms.

Brand extension involves the practice of using a brand name established in one product class to enter another product class. For example, the French company Boucheron became established in the consumer marketplace as a maker of fine jewelry. Today, following several brand extension decisions, Boucheron also is associated with perfume, watches, prestige eyewear, and other luxury products. Similarly, whereas the American *marque* Jordache once was known only for its designer jeans, today the brand name also refers to any number of products, including footwear, umbrellas, clothing accessories, sunglasses, and watches. Extending the brand name has been the core of strategic growth for a large number of companies, especially in recent years.

Marketing professor David Aaker (1991) summarized the possible consequences of brand extension as "the good, the bad, and the ugly," suggesting that this marketing strategy can have both positive and negative outcomes for a firm. The major strength of this approach is that the brand name can positively contribute to the extension (by providing it with key associations) and the extension can positively contribute to the brand name (by reinforcing those associations). Moreover, the use of established brands is also a good way to achieve a quality perception (e.g., the name Hewlett-Packard lends its quality reputation to a large number of products under the Hewlett-Packard umbrella). Unfortunately, brand extensions may not pay off and do good for a company; to the contrary, these are the cases that Aaker referred to as the "bad" and the "ugly." It is possible that the brand name will not add value to the product or, worse, it could stimulate negative attribute associations. The BiC name did not work for perfume because the BiC associations with cheap and disposable plastic pens, cigarette lighters, and razors proved a handicap in the perfume category. Some marketing critics of the brand extension strategy also argue that extensions may cause the brand to acquire negative associations or serve to dilute the associations that are at the core of the brand image (e.g., Trout & Rivkin, 1996).

If we consider the relevance of these points with respect to a firm's decision to engage in sponsorship and event management activities to offset the emergence of rumors, we can recognize how important it is for the firm to consider some critical questions from the outset to avoid the potential dangers that the strategy could entail. Perhaps most important, the firm must determine whether the proposed sponsorship communicates or reinforces the image that the sponsoring organization would like to project and does not arouse unintended speculation among its stakeholders.

For example, in the realm of sports sponsorship, consumer research often is undertaken to examine the image of particular sports prior to selecting the most appropriate and influential ones for sponsorship. Proprietary research conducted by marketing consultants has revealed that Formula One, big boat sailing, basketball, and ice hockey are perceived by sports enthusiasts as more active sports, with the potential to create a more dynamic, exciting brand image (cf. Hastings & MacFadyen, 2000). Less active sports, such as darts, golf, cricket, snooker, tennis, and horseback riding are seen as more appropriate to reinforce existing brand imagery. Not surprisingly, the image of Formula One was described by respondents as international, glamorous, challenging, fast, furious, dangerous, living life to the full, and on the edge. In this light, for tobacco companies (such as the makers of Benson & Hedges) Formula One represents one of the least contentious sports for cigarette sponsorship because there exists a natural fit between the sport and the sponsor, with the former potentially bringing desirable image values to the brand, such as dynamic, macho, and international.

In conclusion, the key point here is that public relations activities such as sponsorship are not implemented haphazardly, but require careful planning and consideration. After all, if they do not satisfy their primary objectives—be it position enhancement, public service, or corporate relations—we can hardly expect them to do much good in offsetting rumors.

The concept of *relationship marketing* dates back to 1983 when Berry (1983) made the distinction between a marketing approach that is oriented toward the creation, maintenance, and enhancement of long-term relationships with customers, and *transaction marketing*, which viewed the customer in terms of short-term transaction objectives. In essence, relationship marketing is all about developing meaningful, value-laden relations with customers (and other stakeholders) over the long term and being less concerned about the quick payoff that comes from a one-time purchase (O'Connor & Galvin, 2001). In his book on the topic, Gordon (1997) described relationship marketing as an "ongoing process of identifying and creating new value with individual customers and then sharing the benefits from this over a lifetime of association" (p. 9).

The growing recent interest in relationship marketing has come about as more and more companies have come to recognize the importance of developing strong bonds and loyalties with consumers to maximize customer retention. As opposed to the "leaky bucket" theory of business, which holds that new customers will always be available to replace defecting current ones, it now is understood that retaining customers is a more efficient and cost-effective approach for assuring a company's success in the competitive contemporary marketplace. Indeed, long-term, loyal customers are profitable for a variety of reasons, including the fact that they tend to buy more and they sometimes pay more premium prices than other customers. In addition, they represent a source of referrals for new customers, they make it difficult for competitors to increase their market share, and having a happy and loyal customer base creates visibility and awareness for the brand, enabling the company to attract new customers (Aaker, 1991; O'Connor & Galvin, 2001).

Perhaps most important, current customers are cheaper and easier to hold onto when compared with the costs and efforts to recruit new ones, especially when existing customers are satisfied or loyal. This is because new customers not only will be expensive to contact, but they will need a substantial reason to risk leaving a company or brand that they already are happy with and that reason will be costly for the firm that attempts to attract them. Moreover, as argued earlier, people are comfortable with the familiar. This means that many existing loyals will usually stick with a favored company or brand unless they have a reason to switch (e.g., the company has not responded to their concerns).

Financial evidence attesting to the greater profitability of long-term customers has been demonstrated by Reichheld and Sasser (1990), who analyzed the actual lifetime value of customers across a variety of different industries. Their findings revealed that a 5% increase in customer retention resulted in 25% to 85% profit increases, depending on the industry considered. Nonetheless, customers are more difficult to retain than the preceding discussion might suggest. Reichheld (1996) later reported that American companies lose up to half of their customers in 5 years. Indeed, customers will leave, no matter how loyal they might be, if their problems, concerns, or complaints are not seriously addressed, their favored brands become too difficult to obtain through local channels, or their preferred firm breaks certain unwritten relationship rules (e.g., a breach of trust, failure to keep a promise, and neglect; Fournier, 1998). As you might have surmised, this is where relationship marketing becomes of interest to a business. The overriding objective in using this marketing approach is to deliver added value to customers to influence long-term satisfaction, which hopefully will translate into high levels of customer loyalty.

Although there are no hard and fast guidelines for how to develop stronger relationships with consumers or how to build true loyalty (see Box 5.4), a variety of marketing tactics can be employed with these goals in mind. Typically, however, a company that takes relationship marketing seriously is apt to devise a broad, all-encompassing program that is truly customer centered, such that each organizational decision focuses on how the experiences and satisfaction of the customer can be enhanced (O'Connor & Galvin, 2001). Several recommendations have been offered by marketing professionals as to what the components of such a program should consist of. For example, Kotler et al. (1999) suggested that a business can utilize any of three "customer value-building" approaches to create stronger customer relationships: (a) add financial benefits and loyalty rewards, such as frequent shopper programs, patron-

---
Box 5.4. Brand Loyalty

Although it is common to think of brand loyalty in terms of repeated purchase of a particular product, the concept represents more than that in the marketing literature. For true brand loyalty to exist, the repeat buying behavior has to be accompanied by an underlying positive attitude toward the brand; that is, a strong emotional attachment or emotional bond. This underlying attitude is akin to the sort of feelings one might have toward a person one cares about very much, such as a close friend or lover. Otherwise, the loyalty is likely to be superficial and perhaps more indicative of an unemotional habit than a deep commitment to a specific brand. More specifically, true brand loyals are characterized by an active (or involved) decision-making approach based on product features and quality, and are likely to view brand switching as risky (Knox, 1997).

These notions imply that there are two essential dimensions to strong brand loyalty: (a) brand support (as reflected by repeated purchasing behavior) and (b) brand commitment (as suggested by a strong emotional attachment). In this view, it is possible to distinguish between different levels of consumer attitudes toward preferred brands, depending on where consumers' reactions fall on the two dimensions. Aaker (1991) identified five different levels of brand loyalty, ranging from no loyalty to committed loyalty:

1. *No loyalty.* Nonloyal buyers will change brands, especially for price reasons. Such shoppers are indifferent to brands because they believe that most brands are alike.
2. *Satisfied customer.* At this level the buyer is not dissatisfied with the brand, but is not very loyal either. This is the habitual buyer who could be vulnerable to competitors.
3. *Satisfied plus switching costs.* This level characterizes the repeat buyer who thinks that changing the habitual brand would incur costs (in terms of time, money, or performance risks). Because of the perceived risks in switching to another brand, this customer would rather be safe than sorry.
4. *Strong loyalty.* Shoppers can be considered strong loyals if they value the brand and consider it a friend. This level describes habitual buyers who truly like the brand, perhaps because of vague, general reasons (e.g., it is perceived as having higher quality than other brands).
5. *Committed loyalty.* This is the highest level of loyalty, at which the customer is really devoted to the brand, takes pride in using it, recommends it to others, and believes that the brand is important to his or her self-image. A committed loyal would rather shop elsewhere than switch to an alternative product after learning that a favored brand is out of stock.

(continued)

Committed loyals might be so emotionally attached to a brand that they would go so far as to wear a tattoo with the brand logo or symbol or choose friends on the basis of whether or not they use the same brand. It usually is brand-loyal consumers who react most vehemently when products are changed (i.e., altered or no longer available), as when Coca-Cola replaced its leading brand with a new, sweeter version of the soft drink. In the United States this sort of fervent brand loyalty has been identified among large groups of visitors to the eBay online auction site, users of Apple Macintosh computers, purchasers of Ben & Jerry's ice cream, and Harley-Davidson motorcycle riders (Swartz, 2002).

age refunds, and upgrades to frequent customers; (b) add social benefits by individualizing and personalizing the company's products and services to better satisfy customer needs and wants; and (c) add structural ties by providing customers with special equipment or computer linkages that help them manage their orders or inventories.

Despite the proliferation of customer loyalty schemes, there are some questions about the effectiveness of this tool for retaining customers. Kotler et al. (1999) acknowledged that reward programs and other financial incentives can readily be imitated by competitors and thus may not be useful for differentiating one's business over the long term. Moreover, there is evidence that loyalty promotion programs such as frequent-flier schemes are inefficient in creating long-term loyalty but instead result in a "false loyalty" by functioning as little more than defensive measures in mature and highly competitive markets. Although loyalty schemes might make it hard for customers to defect (because they know they will be giving up something valuable), they may do little to establish those persons as committed loyals and strong advocates for the company and its products (Jones & Sasser, 1995; Miller, 1998; Sharp & Sharp, 1997). Nevertheless, many firms are fond of loyalty schemes because they represent an effective means to obtain personal information that can be used to develop a customer database.

Building true customer loyalty and retention first requires the identification of the key forces that are driving customer satisfaction, which are likely to vary significantly in different business sectors. Only then can management implement a specific plan for building value into their marketing efforts to retain customers over the long term. O'Connor and Galvin (2001) described how this might be accomplished in the context of a bank's customer service management. A required first step is for the business to conduct consumer research to identify key customers meriting relationship management and the factors that underlie a satisfying service encounter for them. Specific steps then can be taken to improve service staff interactions with customers, such as assuring (through training or computer support) that employees in the bank's call center have extensive understanding of the company's products so that they can explain product details to customers in need of assistance. Additionally, staff working at the bank's various branches should be committed to acquiring as much customer information as possible when new accounts are opened and to update key elements of information for long-standing clients. These represent efficient and inexpensive means for developing more complete and accurate customer profiles that can be used to determine how to better serve the bank's clientele.

Other procedures that could be implemented by the bank would be to design the customer service communication systems so that they are consistent and user-friendly (ATM, Internet site, telephone, etc.) and to have marketing managers utilize direct marketing efforts as a means of establishing an ongoing dialogue with customers, rather than as temporary promotions for specific products or services. As an example of building a relationship with a direct mail campaign, Pearson (1994) offered the case of Pepsi, which for years had developed marketing campaigns to generate the names of cola drinkers, who then could be targeted by short-term promotional appeals designed to motivate repeat purchases. An example was the "Summer Chill-Out" that was carried out in 1992. Recently, however, Pepsi's marketing department has concluded that a strategic commitment to direct marketing on a continuous basis would be more beneficial in maintaining longer term consumer relationships, which the company had been losing as soon as each isolated promotion ended.

Other straightforward guidelines for enhancing and maintaining loyalty have been suggested by marketing experts and, although they may seem obvious to the reader, it is easy to find examples of companies that violate them on a regular basis. Among his recommendations for enhancing a brand's equity through consumer loyalty, Aaker (1991) advised the following: (a) treat your customers with respect (i.e., avoid being rude, uncaring, and unresponsive), (b) stay close to customers (i.e., maintain regular contact; send production people to meet with customers who are using the product), (c) measure satisfaction to determine how customers feel and how products and services can be adjusted to suit their needs, and (d) provide extras, such as a few unexpected services, free gifts, and simple apologies when things go wrong.

Relationship Marketing and Trust. These various recommendations are crucial for increasing consumer satisfaction and loyalty levels, but we should not lose sight of our interest in their utility for indirectly preventing rumors. Toward that end, it is essential to introduce another concept that may be the most useful component of relationship marketing for rumor prevention efforts: consumer trust. Marketing research on business relationships has revealed that trust between partners can result in substantial benefits for the parties involved: It contributes to the level of commitment to the relationship, it serves to reduce perceived risks in an exchange situation (such as a purchase), it positively influences willingness to continue in the relationship and cooperate more closely, it can facilitate conflict resolution, and so on (e.g., Anderson & Weitz, 1989; Ganesan, 1994; Morgan & Hunt, 1994). An additional benefit that is particularly relevant to rumors is the reduction of uncertainty. Indeed, when it comes to relationships involving services (which are distinguished by their intangible nature), trust is essential in reducing uncertainty and vulnerability among users and potential users.

According to those who have studied the concept in the context of business relationships, trust operates as a key mediating variable that is central to all relational exchanges (Morgan & Hunt, 1994). Prior to evaluating its role in the prevention of rumors, it first is helpful to be clear about how this notion is conceptualized. In terms of its relevance to business relationships, trust has been defined as "a willingness to rely on an exchange partner in whom one has confidence" (Moorman, Zaltman, & Deshpandé, 1992, p. 314). As implied by this definition, trustworthy business exchange partners are characterized by confidence, honesty, and competence (Donney & Cannon, 1997; Ganesan, 1994). The element of confidence suggests that trust, which is based on the expectation that the partner will not behave opportunistically, is comprised of a cognitive component (i.e., confidence or belief in the reliability of the partner) as well as a behavioral component, reflecting confidence in the intentions, motivations, honesty, and benevolence of the partner (Ring & Van De Van, 1992). The degree of willingness to rely on another lies at the heart of the trust concept.

In addition to these notions regarding the basic nature of the trust concept, various authors have attempted to identify the key antecedents for trust and its likely outcomes. Although there is not consensus about the specific antecedent and outcome factors, the views suggest that a number of elements have the potential to build trust in business settings, including experience with the partner, shared values, honesty, explicit guarantees, communication, desire to continue the relationship, responsiveness, clarifying exchange parameters, and the like (e.g., Geyskens, Steenkamp, Scheer, & Kumar, 1996; Morgan & Hunt, 1994). In more practical terms, marketing managers can enhance trust through truth in advertising, ethical and fair selling practices, and by ensuring the integrity of product promotions, guarantees, and promises. Similarly, a variety of outcomes of trust may be anticipated, as previously mentioned, including commitment and loyalty, expansion of the relationship, cooperation, reduced uncertainty, interdependence, and higher levels of trust.

A recent assessment of trust in business relationships posits that trust is a dynamic aspect of an exchange between two parties and that it evolves between partners over time (Curran, Rosen, & Surprenant, 1998). Although this may seem rather obvious, previous attempts to identify the factors that give rise to trust have operationalized the concept as a static aspect of relationships;

that is, as something that either exists or does not exist between partners. Acknowledging its natural progression in relationships, Curran et al. (1998) proposed a four-stage model of trust (see Fig. 5.4) and argued that different trust antecedents may be relevant at each stage. According to this view, trust builds on a foundation of mutually satisfactory experiences between partners, while acknowledging that in some relationships the level of trust does not develop as deeply as in others. In other words, although a relationship can evolve through the four stages, the relationship may stall or fail at any stage as a function of the actions or needs of the partners.

In the first stage in the development of trust, the relationship between business partners is characterized as a riskless interaction, whereby the willingness to become vulnerable emerges. This is the stage in which trust really is not warranted or needed; rather, each party takes responsibility for their own interest, as in situations where there is an exchange of goods for money. During this first stage, one party may have complete control over the other, thereby eliminating any need for trust. The second stage is the leap of faith, which describes the relationship as having progressed from a riskless interaction to a trust-based one, as when the partner selling goods extends the buyer some credit, believing that the payment will be made at the specified time. Trust in this situation is limited by the uncertainty that exists due to the lack of prior relationship experience that could give either party confidence in the other. In our example, the seller is likely to harbor some doubts as to whether the buyer will, in fact, pay; however, by taking the leap of faith that the buyer will acknowledge the obligation on time, a basis for future trust has been established.

The ensuing stage is one in which trust may be conditional or given within limits, and must be validated on a regular basis. In other words, trust exists between the parties within clearly defined limits or parameters, actions are closely watched, and experience in the exchange process gradually is acquired. Although many business relationships do not progress past this third stage, some do move beyond conditional trust to a state of so-called transparent trust (Achrol, 1997), which is described by open and routine access to all information by all of the involved partners. Having achieved a sufficient level of experience with each other, the various protective barriers or limits between the partners can be eliminated and the fullest degree of trust can be achieved.

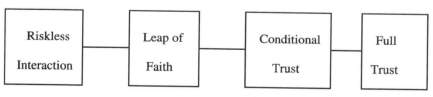

FIG. 5.4.   Stages in the development of trust. From Curran, Rosen, and Surprenant (1998). Reprinted with permission of James M. Curran and EMAC98.

Curran et al. (1998) expanded their notions concerning the evolution of trust by postulating that there are likely to be different antecedents and outcomes of trust at each of the four stages of their model. For example, for the riskless interaction stage, a preliminary basis for establishing a trusting relationship may stem from such factors as cost, reputation, advice of trusted others, need, and exposure to various sources of information that could signify the reliability of the partner. Possible consequences of trust at this initial stage include a willingness to become vulnerable, communication, knowledge of performance, and validation of input sources. Desire to reduce uncertainty and willingness to remain vulnerable are two important precursors to trust for both of the next two stages. To evolve to a state of full trust, Curran et al. identified as the key antecedents such factors as willingness to allow open access, strong conviction of the partner's trustworthiness, comfort and free communication, reduced need for performance verification, and sufficient "at risk" experience. With the establishment of full trust, business partners can anticipate increased reliability, efficiency, profitability, and a reduction of business transaction costs.

Trust and Its Implications for Rumor Prevention and Control.   Despite the importance of trust in reducing uncertainty and any associated anxieties in company–consumer relationships, there is a growing trend among consumers to be less trusting of business enterprises than in the past. For example, according to a USA Today/CNN/Gallup survey, nearly 50% of adults surveyed said that corporations can be trusted only a little or not at all to look out for the interests of their employees, as opposed to only 10% who thought that corporations can be trusted a great deal in this regard (Armour, 2002). In the same survey more than 40% of the respondents believed that top executives at American companies are only interested in looking out for themselves rather than the interests of their employees. Elsewhere, in a recent large-scale survey of American attitudes toward advertising, Shavitt, Lowrey, and Haefner (1998) found that although 44% of adult respondents claimed to like advertising in general, 52% believed that advertisements could not be trusted and 69% felt that they had been misled by advertising at least sometimes.

The rising levels of consumer distrust no doubt can be attributed to a variety of forces, including the prevalence of major scandals involving (previously) reputable companies (such as Enron, Worldcom, and Arthur Andersen) that have received extensive media coverage and have had widespread negative consequences for investors and employees; disapproval of multinational corporations and their aggressive marketing tactics; the prevalence of business scams, swindles, and unethical marketing practices (see Box 5.5); and the growing presence of large, anonymous companies (cf. Aditya, 2001; Klein, 1999; Langenderfer & Shimp, 2001). In such an environment, it is no wonder that marketplace rumors have thrived. The current business atmosphere in the United States was bleakly described in a recent *International Herald Tribune* article in the wake of yet an-

---

Box 5.5. Scams, Swindles, and Frauds

Collectively, the three terms that comprise the heading for this box are usually used interchangeably to refer to common examples of deceptive marketing practices. Although they may take a variety of forms, the typical scam offers consumers promises of money, prizes, or wealth and, once their confidence is gained and the targets are enticed to participate and pay, they end up losing their investment without ever receiving the promised reward. Among the most commonly reported scams are those that involve sweepstakes or prize promotions, advance fee loans, pyramid schemes, credit repair, and business opportunities. Elderly and low-income or fixed-income persons tend to be among the most common victims of such practices (AARP, 1994).

Deceptive marketing practices such as those described here represent a prevalent part of the global business landscape and exact a huge toll on individuals and society. In a recent assessment of consumer vulnerability to scams, Langenderfer and Shimp (2001) pessimistically concluded that "consumers are routinely victimized by deceptive marketers and unscrupulous con artists, and prevention efforts have largely failed" (p. 764). In partial support of this statement, the authors offered the following statistics:

- According to some estimates, scams cost American consumers over $100 billion per year.
- About 85% of all American consumers have been deceived or cheated in some manner.
- Telephone scammers are estimated to net over $40 billion a year in the United States.

Given these findings, it is no wonder that for many consumers, deception is viewed as an inherent element of contemporary marketing activities.

---

other major corporate scandal as follows (Pearlstein, 2002): "A major accounting firm convicted of obstructing justice. A top brokerage caught misleading clients. Chief executives falling like flies. Huge corporations tumbling into bankruptcy. Business pages that read like a crime blotter" (p. 11).

These developments serve to undermine efforts to reduce consumer uncertainty and anxiety through the establishment of trusting business relationships. Of course, there is not much that an individual firm can do about some of these external forces with the exception of recognizing that rumors will continue to represent a common aspect of the business landscape for the foreseeable future. This fact underlines the need for companies to establish a rumor control action plan for treating the eventual outbreak should it hit their establishment.

Certain implications can be drawn from the work on trust and relationship marketing with respect to how best to proceed in attempts to prevent and control rumors. The four-stage model of trust just described suggests that the common recommendation that businesses should be as forthcoming and open as possible with all information relevant to rumor (or potential rumor) content may be counterproductive in certain situations. Although we can presume that complete openness will serve to reduce levels of uncertainty and alleviate worries, this approach may not be well received if relationships with certain relevant business partners have not yet evolved to an advanced stage of trust. Belief or confidence in the information provided may be limited and the company's tactics may be viewed with a certain degree of skepticism (e.g., as an elaborate cover-up). A more reasonable approach would be to moderate the degree of openness according to the apparent levels of trust that characterize the firm's relationships with its different stakeholders. At the same time, the firm can take steps to develop trusting relationships through attempts to maximize the relevant antecedents for moving trust to a higher level.

Building Relationships With Other Stakeholders.   This consideration of relationship marketing has largely focused on its relevance to building loyalties and trust among consumer goods customers. Before leaving the topic, it is important to note that an efficient use of relationship marketing for dealing with rumors also requires the nurturing of relationships with other stakeholders. This includes direct intercompany relationships between buyers and suppliers, market channel relationships between manufacturers and retailers, relationships between service companies and individual service consumers, and so on. In this regard, establishing a favorable reputation in interorganizational contexts is necessary for achieving positive collaborations and cooperation (Anderson & Sørensen, 1998).

If a company's primary interest is in heading off developing rumors before they circulate among consumer groups, these additional relationships will be essential to create an efficient pipeline for early identification of a rumor problem. Suppliers, sellers, distributors, and the like often have closer and more frequent direct contacts with customers than do a firm's product and brand managers, so it is essential to maintain good relations with these marketing intermediaries. Consistent with this point, the survey of French consumer goods managers that I mentioned at the outset of this chapter revealed that respondents most frequently learned about rumors through word-of-mouth (face-to-face or telephone) communications from their various stakeholders (Kimmel & Audrain, 2002). As mentioned earlier, these stakeholders also can be utilized as partners in attempts to undermine the credibility of rumors once they begin to circulate.

Ethically Responsible Marketing

In Part I we discussed the possibility that some marketplace rumors get started as a result of negative word-of-mouth stemming from consumers who harbor

certain grievances against a company (or business in general) and want to exact some degree of revenge. As Malheiro, Farhangmehr, and Soares (2002) recently conjectured, when consumers evaluate a firm as having acted
unethically, they might be moved to punish that firm. Indeed, when businesses engage in unethical or otherwise irresponsible conduct, it is not surprising that people might be stimulated to try to hurt those firms, especially if
these individuals feel that their lives somehow have been adversely affected by
a company's actions (Friedman, 1999; Shaw & Duff, 2002). In light of highly
publicized recent scandals involving corporate misconduct, perhaps best ex-
emplified by the 2002 Enron debacle, the motivation to transmit negative
falsehoods about business enterprises may be stronger than ever.

Despite numerous headline-grabbing examples of business fraud, insider
trading, misleading accounting and the like during the early 2000s, perhaps
none captured public attention as much as the collapse of Enron, which at the
time represented the largest bankruptcy in U.S. history. The collapse led to
thousands of employees losing their 401(k) retirement plans linked to the energy company's stock and seriously damaged the reputation of Enron's audit-
ing firm, Arthur Andersen, when it was learned that Andersen officials
destroyed thousands of sensitive Enron documents. A series of governmental
probes following in the wake of the scandal revealed a far-reaching web of unethical business practices and misconduct, including Enron's establishment of
numerous partnerships set up to keep debt off its accounts, and the company's
failure to pay income taxes for several years preceding the collapse.

In fact, such business scandals are nothing new—corporate misconduct has
been a part of every period of financial boom for centuries, when dramatically
rising profits and stock prices provide something of a smoke screen for underlying financial problems (Pearlstein, 2002). What is different in contemporary
times, however, is the enormous sums of money involved, the apparent au-
dacity of the corporate misbehavior, and the media frenzy that has followed
each scandal with extensive coverage. In addition to widely publicized cases of
corporate scandal, critical attention in the mass media to such practices as deceptive advertising, bait-and-switch selling tactics, the invasion of consumer
privacy, deceptive pricing, and selling under the guise of marketing research
(so-called sugging) also has begun to seriously tarnish the image and reputation of legitimate marketing practitioners (Aditya, 2001; Schlossberg, 1992).
Further, the emergence of new communication and data processing technologies offers marketers ever more efficient means of deceiving their prospects
and targets.

The resulting picture suggests a contemporary business culture bereft of
professional ethical standards and a progressive erosion of public confidence
in the business community. In such a context, the marketplace becomes less
predictable and consequently more worrisome as companies begin to operate
according to their own private agendas and unwritten codes—in short, just

the sort of environment likely to give birth to rumors. In Enron's case, for example, numerous rumors emerged about the company as the scandal unfolded, including initial speculation that the company was about to issue profit warnings, stories implicating Democratic politicians and the Clinton administration in the scandal, rumors that Enron controlled more than 30% of North American pulp and paper inventories, and stories linking the war against terrorism to the company.

A possible solution to slow the proliferation of rumors tied to business corruption and wrongdoing is for companies to implement and follow a more ethical marketing approach. In what may be the only good side to this new wave of corporate misconduct, calls for ethical integrity, social responsibility, and a more forthcoming approach to corporate communication have grown louder and an increasing number of firms have begun to establish more rigorous standards for ethical business practices in response (see Box 5.6). Indeed, the promotion of ethical conduct has become increasingly important to many

---

Box 5.6. Ethics and Corporate Communications in the Post-Enron Era

A recent press release by the New York Times Job Market research team illustrates just how much of an impact the Enron scandal has had in the business environment with respect to a growing demand for ethical responsibility and a more open corporate communication structure ("In Wake of Enron," 2002). The New York Times Job Market is a service that facilitates the hiring process for employers by reaching top job prospects through an efficient advertising approach and also issues original research reports on employment trends in the New York City metropolitan area. The aforementioned press release announced that certain characteristics have become more desirable for hiring managers and job seekers in their search for employees and organizations, respectively, since the Enron scandal unfolded.

Characteristic	Hiring Managers	Job Seekers
Employee ability to access management with concerns or questions	62%	46%
Organizational ethics	58%	38%
Organizational policies and rules of conduct	56%	41%
Individual candidate's ethics	55%	38%
Consistent internal communication to employees	52%	50%

According to the same report, although 57% of job seekers claimed that they had not been affected by the Enron scandal, 42% revealed that they believed that the Enron revelations had caused them to become more cynical about the corporate workplace.

firms and corporate codes of conduct have been implemented by a number of companies in North America and Europe.

Additionally, professional codes of marketing ethics have been implemented by various marketing associations and societies (e.g., Council for Marketing and Opinion Research, 1999; Council of American Survey Research Organizations, 1995). The code of ethics adopted by the American Marketing Association (AMA, 2001) represents a good example of professional self-regulation. In its opening statement, the AMA code emphasizes the overriding ethical responsibilities of each marketing professional: "Marketers must accept responsibility for the consequences of their activities and make every effort to ensure that their decisions, recommendations and actions function to identify, serve and satisfy all relevant publics: customers, organizations and society." This statement is followed by generally-stated standards falling under the areas of "honesty and fairness," "rights and duties of parties in the marketing exchange process," and "organizational relationships." The standards for honesty and fairness in marketing practice in part state that the ethical marketer upholds and advances the integrity and dignity of the marketing profession by "being honest in serving consumers, clients, employees, suppliers, distributors, and the public." Subsections pertaining to the marketing exchange process cover the areas of product development and management, promotions, distribution, pricing, and marketing research. This set of principles recently has been supplemented by an American Marketing Association Code of Ethics for Marketing on the Internet. Although only a small step toward restoring public confidence in the marketplace and business environment, these ethical advances represent a positive development in efforts to ultimately reduce marketplace rumors.

Professional ethics codes have been criticized along a number of fronts in marketing and related areas, including the complaints that such codes include standards that are overly general, unrealistic, or simply ignored by professional practitioners and researchers. One way that companies can overcome some of these complaints is by more fully involving consumers and other stakeholders as participants in ethics research and in the development of ethical review policies (Malheiro et al., 2002). Such an approach also should serve to further enhance a firm's relationships with its various partners in the exchange process. Finally, it might be added that corporate ethics codes should be developed with a consideration of relationship building in mind. Because a company's business partners, such as retail sales personnel, distributors, suppliers, wholesalers, and other organizations must do business with other firms, it is essential to maintain trusting relationships with these intermediaries to establish a positive reputation of the company as fair, ethical, and trustworthy. Attempts to plant rumors about competitors, for example, should be clearly prohibited by corporate ethics codes. Not only does a company run the risk that its corporate name will ultimately replace the intended rumor target (as previously discussed), but it would serve to undermine its relationships with other stakeholders once word gets out about its rumor-planting actions.

SPECIFIC STEPS FOR PREVENTING RUMORS

To this point we have considered some rather generalized approaches that a firm may follow in order to reduce the likelihood that it will be struck by a rumor-related crisis. The proactive approaches described above are intended to satisfy broad objectives that should help reduce the sorts of uncertainties and fears that tend to promote the emergence of rumors. These objectives include the creation of positive and more trusting relations with the company's publics, enhancement of the company's image and reputation among its various stakeholders, and the development of a corporate culture that is more ethical and people-centered than self-centered and profit-oriented.

In addition to these general approaches, some specific methods for rumor prevention have been recommended by various authors (e.g., Bernstein, 2000; Esposito & Rosnow, 1983; Fearn-Banks, 1996). These methods, summarized below, represent relatively inexpensive, practical recommendations for averting a rumor crisis through the maintenance of open channels of communication and careful monitoring of a rumor's early progress.

Create a Rumor Hotline

When consumers and other stakeholders are confronted by worrisome uncertainties about a company's business practices and operations, it helps to know that they can go directly to the source to have their questions answered or concerns addressed. The most effective means for assisting people in this process is the establishment of a rumor hotline. In the past, a "hotline" meant one thing—a telephone number that could be dialed so that both anonymous and "for the record" means of reporting or asking about something one had heard could be responded to directly by a company representative. Today, of course, the rumor hotline need not be limited solely to the telephone. It may involve the provision of voice mail, fax numbers, e-mail addresses, and Internet site-based forms for reporting rumors. Whichever method is utilized, it should be possible for personal identification to remain optional if the individual prefers to receive a personalized response.

Company representatives who are selected to manage rumor hotlines need to be chosen with care, trained fully, and kept regularly informed about the firm's policies, practices, and any planned changes. As a first line of defense in the fight against rumors, they will provide a human "voice" for the company and may ultimately function as the sole spokespersons with whom certain individuals will have contact or exposure. Possible responses to consumer questions might be carefully scripted to avoid the provision of inaccurate, incomplete, or misleading information that could serve to worsen the situation by adding to the conditions that stimulate rumor generation. It is also essential that the availability of rumor hotlines be adequately publicized through channels that are likely to reach rumor-sensitive publics, opinion leaders, and marketing intermediaries (e.g., salespeople and distributors). All such publicity should clearly inform those persons who choose to retain their anonymity how they will receive their answers (e.g., through Web pages, company newsletters, or bulletin boards; Bernstein, 2000).

Rumor hotlines tend to be good investments for companies because they can fulfill multiple functions. They represent one of the most efficient means for companies to first identify that they are being targeted by unfounded speculation or emerging rumors because some individuals immediately will be moved to contact a company that they have heard something upsetting about, particularly if they are current or past users of the company's products or services. They do so either to complain that the company should change its policies or practices (e.g., "You should stop putting worms in your hamburgers!") or to seek confirmation about the credibility of what they had heard (e.g., "Is it really true what they say about your putting worms in your hamburgers?").

In addition to identifying that there is a potential rumor crisis in the making, hotlines represent a practical mechanism for providing information that may serve to reduce anger or fear among the company's publics. Moreover, a set of frequently asked questions (FAQs) for the firm's Internet site can be developed based on content or themes that tend to be repeatedly received from rumor hotline users (see Box 5.7). Finally, hotlines provide a means by which the firm can begin to develop a database for monitoring the location and extent of rumor activity.

Maintain Rumor Vigilance Through Personnel Training Efforts

Given that marketplace rumors have grown more numerous in recent decades, they should now be considered the norm rather than the exception. Marketing managers and other company personnel should expect to encounter harmful rumors at any time and must remain vigilant to that possibility. Toward that end, periodic rumor-sensitivity training sessions and workshops can be carried out among various levels of the company's hierarchy or special rumor seminars might be scheduled.

These activities can be organized and conducted by rumor specialists who would explain how rumors may be detected (including early warning signs), the sorts of psychological and contextual factors that provoke rumors, and effective means for coping with rumors. Case studies involving other similar companies that have experienced rumor-related problems can be analyzed and open discussions focusing on rumors that could damage one's own company can be organized (Fearn-Banks, 1996). The training sessions also should

Box 5.7. Frequently Asked Questions (FAQs)

A growing number of Internet newsgroups and Web sites now offer listings of FAQs, which reflect the kinds of information or clarifications that people seek about a particular piece of ambiguous or troubling information. FAQs and accompanying authoritative answers are usually accepted as the last word on their particular topics. These items are useful from the perspective of rumor prevention because they can serve as an effective method for identifying likely rumor content areas, as well as offering a means to reduce public uncertainties through the provision of much-needed authoritative information.

As an example, I recently conducted a study on rumors related to electricity for the French national electric company (EDF). One of the company's overriding objectives was to identify the kinds of concerns and fears prevalent among the French consuming public relative to electromagnetic fields (EMFs) emanating from outdoor power plants. Company representatives conjectured that these misconceptions and fears could provide the basis for electricity-related rumors that ultimately could harm the company and exacerbate public anxieties. As a result of our search of numerous Web sites related to electricity, it was obvious that there were widespread concerns about EMFs among the consuming public. A majority of the FAQs found at those sites had to do with risks attributed to outdoor EMF sources as opposed to those emanating from domestic appliances. For example:

- How big is the cancer risk associated with living next to a power line? What is the risk of cancer in general? What is the risk of childhood leukemia?
- How close do you have to be to a power line to be considered exposed to power-frequency magnetic fields?
- If exposure to power-frequency magnetic fields does not explain the residential and occupations studies that show increased cancer incidence, what other factors could?
- What sort of power-frequency fields are common in residences and workplaces?
- What is the difference between the electromagnetic (EM) energy associated with power lines and other forms of EM energy such as microwaves or X-rays?
- Is there any evidence that power-frequency fields cause any human health hazards, such as miscarriages, birth defects, or Alzheimer's disease?

The electricity company intended to use these FAQs as the basis for developing materials for better informing consumers about the facts concerning EMFs (e.g., by distributing brochures responding to the kinds of questions appearing on the consulted Web sites).

provide an opportunity for participants to reveal whether they have heard any rumors recently about the firm or have detected any signs suggesting that this could be a problem in the foreseeable future.

Maintain Rumor Vigilance by Monitoring Rumor Effects

A variety of changes in the marketplace vis-à-vis one's products and services might represent early signs of a rumor problem and should be regularly monitored with that possibility in mind. Possible measures to track include variations in sales volume and market standing or sudden shifts in levels of customer complaints, Web site visits, brand switching, and turnover rates in the sales force. Although it is true that changes in these areas could be a function of any number of business and economic factors (e.g., competitors' actions, new product introductions, modifications in the company's current products, elimination of offerings from the company's product line), it is important to be vigilant to the fact that they may represent early effects of negative word-of-mouth and false rumors.

Designate Rumor Monitoring and Control Officers

Another readily implementable method for early rumor detection and monitoring is to appoint certain company personnel as rumor control officers (RCOs; Bernstein, 2000). RCOs would have the role of keeping an ear to the ground in an effort to detect early signs of potential rumors and identify whether emerging rumors represent a serious threat. It is important that designates for this position are persons in the organization with whom employees and other groups close to the company are comfortable speaking and who have a reputation as being credible and trustworthy.

Because a company's employees often prefer to restrict confidential discussions to others who are close to their "rank," this is another important consideration in selecting the most appropriate persons for any rumor monitoring positions. As Bernstein (2000) suggested, the astute human resources director will usually know who these people are and thus would be the appropriate person to make the designation. The firm's various audiences would then be informed that when they hear what they think could be a potentially damaging rumor they can confidentially approach an RCO, who will have the authority to research the facts and get back to them with a response.

Communicate the Facts Through Word-of-Mouth Networks

This step essentially can be seen as another aspect to the functions of the RCOs, involving a form of rumor "back-tracking." That is, to the extent possible, those persons who report rumors can be asked to provide information about their source. The source then can be approached in a nonthreatening, nonpunitive way to detail from whom they received the information. This back-tracking procedure can be repeated until the original source of the misleading information is identified or the trail runs cold. At every step of this process, each person contacted can be provided with the true facts and asked to communicate them throughout their word-of-mouth network, especially to persons who are spreading false or inaccurate information. In so doing, rumor spreaders will have been converted into fact spreaders.

If contacted individuals are unable to recall how they received the speculative information, focus group discussions might be employed, assuming that the persons concerned are comfortable with this. The focus group approach involves interviewing a small group of relevant participants (typically between 10 and 12) at the same time in the form of a loosely structured, informal discussion. In such group interviews, a comment by one participant frequently serves to jog the memory of others and it is common for useful information relevant to the problem to emerge spontaneously once group participants get caught up in the discussion.

A couple of points discussed earlier in Part I suggest some potential limitations to the back-tracking approach. This includes the likely difficulties that will be encountered when trying to trace a rumor (or indicators of developing rumors) back to its original source. As previously suggested, this is an endeavor that is often doomed to failure. It should be recognized, however, that the communication of facts through word-of-mouth networks does not necessitate that the actual originator of the rumor be revealed. The key is to tap into active word-of-mouth networks to influence network hubs and other prominent word-of-mouth participants. Marketing research oriented to the identification of consumer referral networks could be helpful in this regard (see Fig. 4.6; Reingen & Kernan, 1986).

When using the back-tracking approach, the media are often implicated as message sources. This need not be considered a problem, but rather as an opportunity. Once given the true facts about the situation, journalists and media owners can be encouraged to transmit this information to their audiences to help ward off the emergence of rumors that could have potentially damaging consequences for the company and the rumormongering public.

Anticipate the Role of the Media

Whether or not the media are involved in the generation of a marketplace rumor, it is almost inevitable that journalists will pick up on the story and report it once the rumor begins to circulate and a crisis begins to develop for the targeted company. Consistent with the growing cynicism about big business and marketing, there is a tendency for the public to react with a kind of morbid fascination when a large corporation is in trouble. Media owners are aware that stories about corporations in crisis sell newspapers and boost ratings. As Fearn-Banks (1996) pointed out:

The media gives the public what it wants to know rather than what it needs to know …The public is perceived to enjoy watching, reading about, uncovering, and hanging organizations, companies, and individuals that *might* have done harm to people, or even worse, to animals. (p. 64)

This being the case, in addition to the other measures described here for preventing rumors, it is important for company representatives to anticipate what the media will want to know should a rumor-related crisis begin to take shape. A planned strategy for enlisting the media as partners in the fight against false rumors at the outset of a crisis could be helpful in undercutting the possibility that the media will simply add to the problem once the situation begins to get out of control.

Treat All Early Signs of Rumors Seriously

As discussed in Box 3.5, even the most ridiculous stories have the potential to evolve into rumor crises. In this light, all early signs of rumors should be treated seriously. Many companies have followed the strategy of ignoring emerging rumors because it was believed that the falseness of the rumor content would be as self-evident to their publics as it was to company officials. This was the initial reaction of Leonard Marsh, the president of Snapple when, in 1992, rumors began to circulate that the company had ties to the KKK and supported the prolife group Operation Rescue. By the time Marsh recognized that Snapple might have a rumor crisis on its hands, he commented, "The rumors are so ridiculous we thought they would go away, but they didn't. It reached the point it was getting out of hand and we had to address it" ("Snapple Dragoon," 2000).

To facilitate this rumor prevention step, RCOs can also be assigned the task of maintaining sensitivity to any company policy changes, marketing actions, and other business practices that could be misinterpreted or picked up on as potential rumor-causing issues. When appropriate, they then can issue rumor warnings to the company's management through office memos, faxes, or e-mails, indicating that care must be taken because this sort of thing could cause rumors (cf. DiFonzo, Bordia, & Rosnow, 1994).

CONCLUSION

It has often been noted that prevention represents the most effective cure for a crisis (e.g., Fearn-Banks, 1996). Bearing that in mind, I have suggested a number of general approaches that a company may follow to help offset the emergence of a crisis linked to marketplace rumors, including the implementation of ongoing public relations programs, the careful management of relationships with business partners and other stakeholders, and the establishment of an ethical corporate culture. In addition to these general approaches that emphasize the utility of positive and socially responsible business practices in rumor prevention, I also have described some specific measures for anticipating rumors and for monitoring their early course. These measures essentially are based on the recognition that rumors may strike at any time and that companies must remain vigilant to that possibility and be prepared to launch an immediate response before the situation gets out of hand.

Rumor prevention represents a difficult and imprecise objective, one that in some respects poses a more daunting challenge than efforts to fight rumors already in widespread circulation. In the latter case, the enemy is known—the extent of its threat and its potential for damage can be estimated, and it often is possible to determine on which fronts a fight can best be mounted and the tactics most likely to beat it. In the case of rumor prevention, however, the enemy is unknown and it may appear at any time from unknown directions. Moreover, even the best efforts at prevention will not meet with success all of the time. Companies that have done an excellent job following the general recommendations offered here at times have been targeted and have suffered the effects of malicious rumors. In the following chapter we turn our attention to what companies can do to cope with marketplace rumors that have moved beyond the birth stage of the rumor life cycle.

CHAPTER SIX

Managing Commercial Rumors: Strategies and Tactics for Neutralizing Rumors

"Talk!"

When I asked Joshua Jampol, a freelance journalist and specialist in crisis management, what he would suggest that companies do to control rumors, the extent of his response was summed up in that one-word quote. He was not being facetious in offering this curt suggestion, but rather wanted to convey what he thought was one of the worst strategies that can be applied to fight rumors, which is silence. Indeed, there are numerous examples in the business world in which managers have simply dug their companies into deeper and deeper holes by offering a "no comment" response to questions pertaining to the credibility of rumors or to requests for information that could have helped mitigate a rumor crisis.

For the most part, a refusal to talk, whether it be to journalists, customers, marketing intermediaries, shareholders, or other concerned parties, conveys the message that the company has something to hide and adds to uncertainty, or sometimes merely serves to confirm the fears underlying the requests for information. This is not to suggest that a "no comment" response might not be appropriate in certain situations, especially when the true facts or sought-after details are unavailable even to company spokespersons or when there are legal barriers that preclude a public response. Therein lies a critical point to bear in mind with regard to rumor control, one similar to other caveats previously issued: There are no hard and fast rules or guidelines for fighting rumors that can guarantee success in all situations. Although there are likely to be similarities from case to case, and some tactics that are more likely to meet with success than others, the antecedents and circumstances surrounding each marketplace rumor will be different enough to warrant a unique rumor control plan. Any number of additional factors could influence the appropriateness and likely success of a specific strategy, including the type of organization targeted, the publics that are most affected, the potential for damage, the channels through which the rumor is being spread, the extent of credibility of the rumor content, the organization's past history with crisis situations, and so on. The difficulty in finding the right approach is reflected in the comment of one public relations executive who suggested that the attempt to control a rumor is "like trying to package fog" (Levy, 1985, p. vi).

This chapter provides a survey and critical assessment of the various strategies and tactics that business enterprises can use to fight rumors, drawing heavily on ideas taken from the areas of crisis management and attitude change, as well as from specific cases in which consumer goods companies have done battle, both successfully and unsuccessfully, with malicious rumors. As it turns out, not all rumors need to be fought; in fact, in certain cases, idle speculation about a company and its offerings may be beneficial to the firm involved.

GATHERING THE FACTS

From the outset, once it becomes evident that rumor prevention efforts have not completely succeeded and that idle, malicious talk about the company has begun to enter public discourse, the company must act. This does not mean that the firm should blindly unleash a barrage of rumor-fighting attacks because, without knowing the nature and extent of the problem as fully as possible, that strategy will be like flailing away in the dark. Thus, the initial response to marketplace rumors requires a determination and analysis of the rumor problem, focusing on such questions as the following:

- What are people saying? Does the content of their exchange constitute rumor?
- Who are the people involved in the transmission of the rumor?
- Through which media are the rumor being spread?
- Does the rumor pose a threat to the company?
- What is the extent of information spread and where is it geographically centered?
- What are the likely underlying motives for the rumor?
- Is the situation likely to get worse or does it appear the rumor will go away on its own?

Of course, some of these questions will be easier to assess then others, depending on the situation. Moreover, it will be counterproductive to abstain from initiating a rumor-control effort before all questions are fully answered. Valuable time will have been lost and it is inevitable that needed information will be unavailable to provide complete clarity regarding specific aspects of the situation. The key is to gather as much information about these kinds of questions as quickly as possible to be able to move on to develop a rumor-control plan. If we consider again some of the companies that have been targeted by false rumors in the past, the significance of a timely response is more than evident. Recall, for instance, how an immediate assessment and response on the part of company officials in the Diet Pepsi tampering hoax case (see chap. 4) effectively served to avoid a potential crisis involving reports about syringes in the company's soft-drink cans. As soon as it was determined that the false rumor had begun to spread nationally, an effective antirumor campaign was launched and within little more than 1 week the false stories were extinguished. By contrast, although P&G took initial outbreaks of rumors about the company seriously, the extent of the problem and the groups involved in its spread were not satisfactorily ascertained and it was several months before a full-blown effort to quell the rumors was launched. The result? P&G has had to cope with further outbreaks of the Satan rumors to this day (see chap. 1).

If we return again to our model of the rumor life cycle, we can find some of the more pertinent reasons for initiating an immediate response to rumors, once they become evident (see Fig. 5.1). As explained in Part I of this book, the generation and widespread dissemination of a rumor depends very much on the credibility of the rumor's content. The two factors in Fig. 5.1 that are most relevant during the rumor dissemination stage—repetition and mutation—relate to rumor credibility in the sense that the more a rumor is repeated, the more believable it is likely to appear and the more it will mutate into a form that conforms more readily to personal beliefs and expectations. The quicker the rumor is attacked, the less likely such processes will transpire.

Information Gathering

Consistent with the kinds of questions already presented with respect to analyzing the rumor problem, Esposito and Rosnow (1983) suggested that information gathering is comprised of three steps, the first of which involves an assessment of the extent of rumor circulation. According to Esposito and Rosnow, this can be determined by informally contacting customers and other pertinent stakeholders, such as retailers, distributors, and franchise managers, and by unobtrusively questioning them about what they may have heard about the subject matter of the rumor. This task should be carried out in a rather low-key manner, providing as few details about the rumor as possible to avoid arousing concern and running the risk of stimulating unwarranted speculation among contacted individuals. Another possibility is to conduct a random telephone survey of the public to determine what people have heard and how they received the message, whether or not they passed the message on to others, and whether there are regional or local differences within the sample.

Along with Esposito and Rosnow's (1983) suggestions, relevant information regarding the extent of rumor circulation can be obtained from company hotlines and interactive Internet sites that have been put in place as elements of the sorts of rumor prevention measures described in the preceding chapter. That is, assuming concerned individuals directly contact the company to obtain clarification about an unconfirmed story they hear, company representatives can exploit the opportunity by acquiring descriptive information from the caller or Internet user, including demographic characteristics (age, area of residence, etc.), how they heard about the story, number of persons with whom they discussed it, and so on. The back-tracking method (see chap. 5) also can be utilized in an attempt to ascertain whether rumor transmission networks have begun to evolve. Through these approaches it should be possible to determine regional boundaries of the problem and characteristics of the rumormongering public.

An evaluation of the extent of rumor circulation might also take into account whether other companies, including competitors, have been targeted by the same rumor or others like it (Koenig, 1985). Along these lines, it may be determined that the rumor started elsewhere and then moved to target your company or that the rumor is spreading throughout the industry and targeting several companies at the same time. Finally, in light of the rapidity with which messages can be transmitted via the Internet and other media, an assessment of the extent of rumor circulation should be an ongoing effort rather than a one-time measurement. A rumor that is localized today could expand into a nationwide scandal within days.

In addition to assessing the extent of the rumor's spread, a second step in the information gathering stage is to collect as many facts as possible about the rumor and people's reactions to it (Esposito & Rosnow, 1983). This would include attempts to determine the extent of belief in the rumor content and concerns about it, reported changes in consumer behavior (e.g., purchases of the company's products, calls for a product boycott), specific wording of the allegations and target, variations in the rumor content across different publics, and apparent reasons underlying the rumor's existence. To a great extent, this step can be carried out hand in hand with the first, by relying on informal discussions with stakeholders, questioning hotline callers, and commissioning surveys or focus groups to assess public response to the rumor.

These fact-collection activities enable company officials to clearly define the problem and identify whether or not a crisis is at hand. It may be determined, for instance, that an apparently malicious rumor that has come to the attention of company representatives is perceived as nothing more than a harmless joke by those who are passing it along. Although temporarily amusing, it is likely that the joke will soon be forgotten, especially if its premises lack credibility and do not arouse undue fear. On the other hand, it may be the case that a rumor that has begun to enter widespread circulation is based on a certain degree of truth. Many rumors bear some element of truth; if they did not, there is little likelihood that they would pose much of a problem for the firm in the first place. Either of these possible scenarios would imply a different course of action for the company. The humorous rumor that nobody seems to be taking very seriously in most cases will not merit a response from the company, whereas the partially true rumor is more likely to require some sort of immediate action, even if the response merely consists of confirming the part of the rumor that is true. The more complete the information gathering, the better positioned the firm will be to disseminate accurate information, correct misunderstandings, mount a counterrumor campaign, and so on.

The third step in the information gathering phase, according to Esposito and Rosnow (1983), consists of attempts to ascertain the source of uncertainty and anxiety. A determination of the psychological forces that are fueling the rumor is essential if the company's efforts to allay public apprehensions and arousal concerning the rumor content are to prove successful. Again, this step requires that persons involved in the transmission of the rumor be directly questioned to effectively gauge their level of concern, involvement with the rumor content, and likely behavioral response. Face-to-face individual interviews and focus groups, which enable the interviewer to probe for underlying feelings, motives, and beliefs, are recommended for these purposes.

Preparing a Public Response

Whether or not the information gathering phase ultimately suggests that a current rumor poses a potentially damaging threat to the firm and is beginning to gain momentum, a contingency plan should be put into place so that quick action can be taken to confront the rumor, should that prove necessary. Such a plan should take into consideration the intended target audiences for public statements or an information campaign, the facts necessary for developing antirumor communications and news releases, the appropriate media for reaching intended publics, budgeting considerations, and the selection of a spokesperson and rumor management team. Although highly dependent on what is learned about the nature of the rumor as the facts are acquired, the preliminary formulation of statements that eventually can be issued to the public and the media should be drafted. Even if the rumor dies out on its own before a formal response is required, this effort will not be in vain because it could prove useful if rumors target the company again at a later date.

Once rumors begin to gain widespread circulation beyond a localized setting, it becomes essential to enlist the mass media in efforts to stem the crisis. This ensures that the broadest possible audience is reached, but is also intended to reduce the possibility that the media will serve as an adversary by reporting on the rumor as fact and making matters worse. Thus, the firm's rumor contingency plan should emphasize what will need to be communicated to the media and how that message should be presented. In her book on crisis communication, Fearn-Banks (1996) offered some useful advice for preparing to face the media by suggesting the kinds of questions journalists are likely to ask during a crisis. These include inquiries along the lines of the following: What is going on? What is the extent of the damage and is there a danger of future harm? Why did it happen? Who is responsible? What is being done about it? When will it be over? Were there any warning signs leading up to the problem? By preparing in advance how these questions will be handled, company officials will be in a far better position to cope with an eventual rumor crisis.

DETERMINING THE EXTENT OF THE CRISIS

To more effectively develop strategies for coping with potentially damaging rumors, it is helpful to have some degree of understanding about corporate crises and crisis management. If a rumor situation represents a crisis for the company, it is important that it be recognized as such. As discussed in Part I, not all rumors or rumor situations are alike. Although company officials may learn that there are various falsehoods circulating about the firm and its products, often such talk is impotent; that is, the situation poses little potential for damaging the reputation of the company or negatively influencing consumer behavior. Such rumors can be handled in a rather low-key manner, perhaps through the management of a public relations campaign over the long term. Labeling the situation as a crisis, however, implies that the rumor poses certain dangers for the firm and should be dealt with quickly and forcefully. In this light, however, what exactly do we mean by crisis?

In the context of the contemporary business world, a *crisis* refers to a pressurized situation faced by an organization as a result of sudden change that cannot be coped with effectively through the use of normal, routine procedures (Armstrong, 1990; Booth, 1993). Corporate crises have become dramatically more frequent in recent years as a result of several factors linked to the modern age in which we live, including the emergence of electronic media, which have facilitated the rapid and widespread dissemination of information within minutes of an occurring event and crises engendered by human error and disasters associated with rapidly advancing technology (Berge, 1991). Other factors accounting for the recent proliferation of business-related crises include the rise of consumer action groups (e.g., Greenpeace, culture jammers, world trade protest groups), the changing meteorological climate that is responsible for causing natural disasters in certain parts of the world, and the changing economic environment (e.g., vitalization and competition from the developing world and the impact on some Western industries; scandals linked to unethical accounting schemes; cf. Fill, 1995; Klein, 1999). The risks that bad situations may spiral out of control for companies are much greater than ever before; in fact, one estimate maintains that one in three companies that undergoes a major crisis never recovers to its preincident trading levels, if it survives at all (cf. Yeshin, 1998).

These recent developments have brought about a growing recognition of the significant role that crisis management can play for the contemporary organization and have led many companies to review the manner in which they anticipate and respond to crisis situations. It is now generally assumed that companies that plan for disaster are in a much better position to experience more favorable outcomes; however, even the best crisis planning will do little good if the plan is not effectively implemented. With these points in mind, Fill (1995) noted:

> Crisis planning is about putting into position those elements that can effect speedy outcomes to the disaster sequence. When a crisis strikes, it is the application of contingency-based tactics, by all those concerned with the event, that will determine the strength of the outcome. (p. 404)

Because the timing and precise nature of corporate crises cannot be known in advance, preparation for a crisis is at best an imprecise science; however, the process of anticipation is the most frequently cited key to successful coping efforts. In terms of planning for crises caused by rumors, contingency plans along the lines of those detailed earlier (see the section "Preparing a Public Response") are essential. A critical element of contingency plans is the identification of all areas of potential risk, including a consideration of worst-case scenarios during times of corporate change, along with actions that can be taken to respond to each risk (Yeshin, 1998). Such preplanning can serve to assure management that procedures are in place for rapidly responding to an unfolding crisis, and the confidence that comes from knowing that diminishes the likelihood that the crisis will cause panic within the organization, which could only serve to undermine the effectiveness of the coping strategies. It also helps to stay cognizant of the types of rumor crises that have befallen other organizations, with an eye to the management actions that proved effective or ineffective in each situation. Clearly established chains of responsibility within the organization for responding to a crisis—including the identification of a spokesperson, individuals who will be assigned the duties of preparing press releases, persons who will respond to consumer inquiries, and so on— also must be assured and communicated to all company personnel.

Types of Corporate Crises

Corporate crises can be distinguished in a variety of ways. For example, Pearson and Mitroff (1993) suggested that there are six fundamental forms of crises, identified by their primary causes:

- *Megadamage*. Caused by environmental accidents.
- *External economic attacks*. Associated with extortion, bribery, hostile take-overs, and boycotts.
- *External information attacks*. Attributed to breach of copyright, information loss, counterfeiting.
- *Breaks*. Caused by recalls, product or factory defects, computer breakdowns, poor security.
- *Perceptual*. Damage to reputation.
- *Psychological*. Terrorism, executive kidnappings, sexual harassment, rumors.

Although Pearson and Mitroff aptly classified rumor-based crises as psychological, it is likely that rumors will circulate in the context of the other forms of crisis, thereby serving to add fuel to the severity of the situation. In those cases, although the situation may not be identified as a rumor crisis, rumor control efforts will doubtless have to be included in the overall crisis management plan.

Another approach to identifying the different forms that corporate crises might take was offered by Fill (1995). In his view, organizational crises can be described according to two key variables: (a) degree to which management has control over the origin or cause of the crisis and (b) the potential impact of the crisis on the organization (see Fig. 6.1). Earthquakes or hostile takeovers represent examples of crises attributed to causes that are outside management's control, whereas a crisis associated with poor trading results is within management's control. These crises fall on opposite ends of the horizontal axis in Fig. 6.1. The vertical axis, which denotes the scale of impact the crisis can inflict, suggests that although all crises are potentially damaging, some are more containable than others (e.g., in a geographical sense). According to Fill, crises linked to product tampering and environmental pollution can have a tremendous impact on the organization. Of course, rumors may be associated with any of the crises appearing in the four quadrants of Fig. 6.1.

Crisis Phases

Despite the fact that most crises are by definition unexpected and sudden events, discernible phases characterizing the period during which a crisis unfolds can be identified (see Fig. 6.2). The *scanning* or *signal detection phase* describes the initial period of a crisis during which early warning signals can be detected (Fill, 1995; Yeshin, 1998). By scanning the environment, alert managers should be able to detect early signs of significant change that could suggest an emerging problem situation. For example, this could consist of regularly checking for a drop in product sales or a marked slowdown in sales increases, as well as a careful monitoring of employee absenteeism and tardiness rates, product returns, and unusual occurrences in the general business

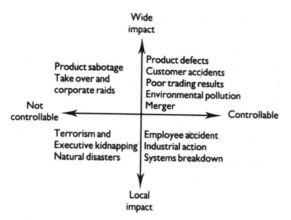

FIG. 6.1. Organizational matrix of crisis management. From Fill (1995). Reprinted with permission of Pearson Education Limited.

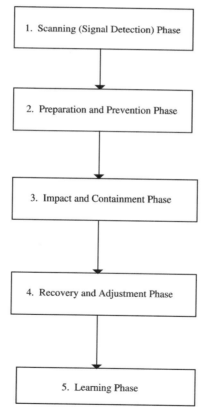

FIG. 6.2. Organizational crisis phases. Adapted from Fill (1995) and Yeshin (1998).

environment. As previously noted with respect to the early stages of rumor generation, many early signals of an emerging crisis not only are ignored by management but sometimes are actively avoided (Pearson & Mitroff, 1993).

The next phase through which a crisis passes can be described as that of *preparation and prevention*. This involves the preimpact period that is marked by an increase of activity as the organization anticipates and prepares for the crisis once its nature and direction have been determined (Fill, 1995). In essence, the first active steps in dealing with a crisis consist of efforts to prevent it from breaking out at all or, given that this often is not possible, defusing it as much as possible and readying one's forces to be able to cope once the crisis event begins to unfold. Much of the preparation during this phase should consist of training and deploying crisis teams and informing significant stakeholders about what they can expect.

The *impact and containment phase* characterizes the period during which the crisis erupts and the crisis management plan is put into action in attempts to limit the damage as much as possible. This typically consists of efforts to contain the spread of the crisis by localizing it and preventing it from contaminating other parts of the organization or affecting other stakeholders, as when a company takes steps to contain an oil spill.

The next crisis phase is that of *recovery and readjustment*. Once the significant impact of the crisis has transpired, the firm must take steps to regroup, in terms of both short-term and long-term readjustment. Of critical importance during this stage is the necessity to satisfy the needs of stakeholders, such as assuring them that there will not be an interruption in their receiving products or services. During this stage consumers typically look for assurances that the company is recovering and operating effectively, that it will be around for the long term, that product warranties will be honored, and so on.

For example, once the immediate shock of the September 11, 2001, terrorist attacks in the United States had passed, firms that were most directly affected by the events, such as financial companies and others with offices that were destroyed, needed to inform their clients and the general public that they were still around and open for business (O'Connell, 2001). Much product-related marketing was cut back during that period because advertising and other forms of promotion likely would have been viewed as in bad taste during a time of national grief. Instead, many companies used the opportunity to engage in public relations activities by disseminating humanitarian messages that offered condolences and support. One advertisement, for instance, that ran in major newspapers during early October 2001, showed the image of fashion designer Ralph Lauren clad in a sweater bearing the image of the American flag. The accompanying text was presented as if it were a personal message from the designer commending Americans for their fortitude and describing the creation of the American Heroes Fund of the Polo Ralph Lauren Foundation "to honor the heroic efforts of those who lost their lives and to benefit their survivors."

As Fill (1995) noted, much of the success of a company's recovery in the wake of a crisis depends on how effectively it manages the likely fallout during this phase, such as governmental investigations, criminal liability actions, public demonstrations, court cases, and media probing. The successful management of public perceptions will go a long way toward restoring the company's precrisis position. This requires an approach to the crisis fallout that appears consistent and reasonable, perhaps one that positions the firm as a victim of circumstances that could not be avoided rather than as a villain responsible for whatever disastrous chain of events had taken place. A strong corporate image and reputation as a credible and trustworthy company will play a significant role in determining the success and rate of the postcrisis readjustment.

A final *learning phase* consists of a process of drawing insights from the crisis experience so as to develop more adequate and complete contingency plans for dealing with future such events. Despite the fact that this step often is avoided by firms preferring not to open old wounds (Pearson & Mitroff, 1993), postcrisis meetings and analyses by managers to determine what they did right, what they did wrong, and what they could improve for next time will better prepare the firm to cope with future crises.

Crisis Management and Rumors

The various phases described in the preceding section suggest that a crisis management plan should involve the structuring of a series of actions that must be implemented before, during, and after the crisis occurs. Effective crisis management action plans tend to be characterized by these four key components (Yeshin, 1998):

- *Speed.* The effective handling of a crisis requires an immediate response to the crisis situation.
- *Accuracy.* The response to the crisis must be based on verified information rather than speculation and "gut" feelings.
- *Credibility.* Whoever is selected to speak for the organization must have high perceived believability and trustworthiness; the fewer retractions of previously delivered information, the more likely company officials will be perceived as credible.
- *Consistency.* All official spokespersons during the crisis should speak with a common voice; that is, differing views and interpretations must be avoided and positions adopted must be adhered to.

A consideration of these points within the context of crises linked to the spread of false rumors suggests some important recommendations with regard to rumor control action plans (see also Box 6.1). As emphasized at various junctures in this volume, it is of utmost importance to respond to rumors as

---

Box 6.1. Handling a Rumor Crisis: Recommendations From Crisis Management

---

Several specific recommendations for handling potentially disastrous events have been offered by crisis management experts and these have obvious relevance to the ways in which company officials can attempt to cope with crises associated with marketplace rumors (Richardson & Richardson, 1992; Wisenblit, 1989; Yeshin, 1998).

1. Identify specific senior-level personnel whose responsibility it will be to deal with events as they occur. Designate and train specific individuals who should be contacted during the crisis and emphasize the accessibility of these persons.
2. Identify potential crisis areas and situations in advance; develop strategies for avoiding their occurrence and programs for dealing with them should they come to pass.
3. Identify the audiences that would be affected by the crisis.
4. Formalize the action plan and ensure that it is communicated throughout the organization.
5. Devise effective communication channels. Take the initiative by maintaining close relationships and ongoing contact with the media.
6. Provide only information that is based on fact; avoid speculation and guesswork. Defer questions until the facts are available but explain why the questions cannot be answered right away.
7. Anticipate the questions in advance and keep responses simple to avoid the impression that the company is building a "smoke screen."
8. Monitor all media coverage of the crisis.
9. Maintain good internal communications within the organization so that personnel will not be moved to rely on external sources for news and explanations.
10. Analyze the crisis and the effectiveness of the company's response to it once the critical situation has passed.

---

quickly as possible, before the situation gets out of control. The fact that rapidity of response is stressed in the crisis management literature simply underscores the point. Although it is essential that any active response be undertaken only after a sufficient amount of information gathering has been completed, it must be remembered that time is of the essence.

Whichever type of response ultimately is chosen—forceful denials or refutations, information dissemination, open town meetings, and so on—the information used to counter a rumor in general circulation must be based on the truth. If it is not and the inaccuracies are revealed, this will seriously undermine the company's credibility in its efforts to quell the rumor. In addition, credibility can be strongly enhanced through the careful selection of company officials who are assigned the responsibility to handle the rumor-fighting effort and speak to the firm's various publics. Because credibility also depends on the provision of consistent information, only one spokesperson or a small team of spokespersons working closely in concert should be given the responsibility to speak on behalf of the company. This circumvents the possibility that the public will receive mixed (and sometimes contradictory) messages from various company representatives, each trying to battle the rumor in a different way. Overall, the key components of effective crisis management—speed, accuracy, credibility, and consistency—clearly are essential to rumor control.

STRATEGIES AND TACTICS OF RUMOR CONTROL

Having now completed our overview of crises and crisis management, we can next focus our discussion more specifically on a consideration of rumor-control strategies (i.e., the basic approaches chosen to manage rumors) and tactics (i.e., the specific actions undertaken to implement the control strategies). To guide us through this discussion it is useful to think of the steps that can be carried out during three key stages of a rumor crisis situation: the alert phase, the evaluation phase, and the action and media campaign phase. This three-phase model, originally suggested by Koenig (1985), represents a somewhat simplified version of the five crisis phases we described earlier and correspond closely to our model of the rumor life cycle (see Fig. 6.3).

Rumor Control Steps During the Alert Phase

The rumor alert phase begins when company officials learn of a rumor for the first time. Without delay, attempts should be made to locate the rumor's

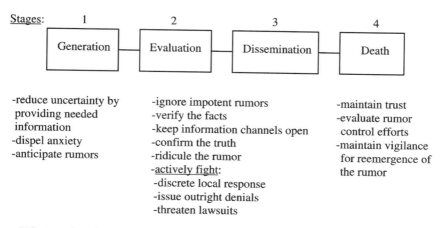

FIG. 6.3. Sample strategies for preventing and neutralizing rumors.

spread and to determine the specific nature of the allegation and target. At the same time, attention should be paid to the two rumor processes described in Chapter 3, rumor convergence (i.e., whether other rumors are targeting the firm) and divergence (i.e., whether other companies are presently affected by similar rumors). If a rumor is targeting several companies at the same time (divergence), this reflects an underlying problem that a single firm alone may not be able to eliminate. Although a firm may be able to dissociate itself from the rumor temporarily, there is the possibility that it will become a target again if the rumor remains active in other contexts. In such cases, the best strategy might be for several companies in the market sector to join forces to attempt to control the situation.

Moreover, as explained in early chapters, once a business organization has become a target for one rumor, the likelihood that others will begin to converge on the company is increased. Thus, as soon as it is evident that a rumor has begun to circulate about the company, it is important to stay vigilant to the possibility that other rumors may emerge as well, which could turn out to be equally troubling. Recall that McDonald's chose to ignore the worm rumor when that falsehood was targeting a competitor (Wendy's) because resources already were being allocated to fight Satan-related rumors. Before long, the worm rumor had jumped from Wendy's to McDonald's.

Also during the alert phase, immediate steps should be taken to ascertain the extent and location of the rumor's diffusion. This can be accomplished through the use of the sorts of approaches described previously—the questioning of hotline and Internet users, along with discussions among distributors, franchise managers, competitors, salespeople, and other persons who have direct contact with the public. If time permits, consumer studies can be carried out, including the direct questioning of consumers in shopping contexts (so-called mall intercepts), focus group discussions, and more formal in-depth interviews with persons who already have been exposed to the rumor. Care must be taken to avoid repeating the rumor during this phase to the greatest extent possible, to reduce the likelihood of bringing the story to the attention of a wider audience.

It may be too early to develop an information or fact sheet for distribution during the alert phase, especially in cases when the actual nature of the rumor content is still somewhat ambiguous or incomplete, but it would be a good idea to have something that consumers who participate in these surveys or interviews can take home with them. For example, if it is apparent that a contamination rumor has begun to circulate about one of a food processor's dessert products, a brochure detailing quality control in the manufacturing process, testimonials regarding the reputation of the firm and its concern for consumer well-being, or a free sample of another product in the company's line should help to put the enterprise in a more positive light and reduce rumor credibility. Even at this early stage, one objective in addition to the interest in accumulating information about the rumor is to convey this message: "We have nothing to hide; your interests are our interests."

Rumor Control Steps During the Evaluation Phase

It is during this period that monitoring of the early impact of the rumor should be undertaken. This includes a check on whether sales have been adversely affected, monitoring of the level of customer inquiries or complaints, a focus on whether the media has picked up and reported the story yet, and a consideration of the morale of company personnel. The long-term survival potential of the rumor should be estimated along with any corresponding risks its longevity would bring. Another important element to assess, perhaps through a mail or telephone marketing survey, is the degree and extent of belief in all or part of the rumor (see Box 6.2).

At this stage, in addition to the rumor's apparent direct impact on profits, efforts should be made to assess how the company is being perceived by the

---

Box 6.2. Examples of Measures For Evaluating Rumor Effects

Attempts to measure the impact of rumors during the evaluation phase of a rumor control plan can be fraught with difficulty. Much of the evidence will be indirect at best and a judgment must be made about the extent to which it is the rumor that is responsible for the apparent effects rather than other unacknowledged market forces. Additionally, information must be gathered delicately, so as not to bring it to the attention of a wider audience, and ethically, in conformance with ethical research standards. In addition to the examples provided in this chapter, marketing professor Oliviane Brodin (1995) has offered the following examples of measures for diagnosing the effects of a rumor:

1. Indirect measurement of the effects on attitude toward the brand targeted by the rumor (e.g., comparison of groups exposed vs. nonexposed to the rumor).
2. Measure memorization of the rumor.
3. Conduct behavioral observations:
   - Search for information.
   - Purchase behavior.
   - Vandalism, complaints, and so on.
4. Obtain indirect measures of belief in the rumor (e.g., perceived importance of the rumor's contents).
5. Obtain measures of likelihood to transmit the rumor and reasons for the rumor's diffusion.
6. Measure directly stated effects (e.g., purchase and usage intentions).
7. Obtain direct measures of belief in the rumor.

public during the growing crisis. Along these lines, Koenig (1985) offered two questions that bear particular attention: (a) "Is the corporation in danger of appearing to be an inept, impotent, and passive victim of the rumor problem?" and (b) " How much is management's image affected by the way things are going?" (p. 172). Of course, answers to these kinds of questions will be difficult to acquire and somewhat subjective, given that they will be interpreted by company officials, who have a vested interest in their firm's competitive position. Nonetheless, insight might be gained by enlisting the services of opinion leaders and market mavens who have strong ties to consumer networks, Internet chat groups and bulletin boards can be tracked for comments about the company (e.g., through the emerging methodology of "netnography"; see Kozinets, 1998), and journalists who cover the business beat might be contacted and tactfully questioned.

Although these monitoring efforts will not serve to control the rumor per se, they are essential for any judgments that will need to be made about what steps should be taken next. For example, if it appears that there are high levels of belief in the rumor, active efforts will have to be made to refute it. If the firm's image has been tarnished by the rumor and efforts to quell it, any rumor control actions will have to be supplemented by a public relations effort.

Rumor Control Steps During the Action and Media Campaign Phase

Despite the importance of acting quickly when a rumor emerges, care also must be taken to avoid an overly hasty response. To be sure, rumors proliferate in the contemporary marketplace and it is the rare organization that remains immune to their bite. However, many of these rumors turn out to be harmless, or at worst, temporary nuisances. A rumor that spreads like wildfire overnight on the Internet might fizzle out the next day as interest is diverted elsewhere. Some rumors hang around—they remain listed on Internet sites, they are discussed from time to time at cocktail parties, they enter the litany of amusing or titillating stories from the world of business—but do little harm to the target. On the contrary, they keep awareness levels high for the firm and may indirectly reflect positively on its capacity for survival in the competitive marketplace even though targeted by malicious chit-chat. It is these sorts of rumors that warrant a "do nothing" response (see also the later section "To Respond or Not to Respond?").

The decision to ignore an impotent rumor is least risky in situations where the rumor is unlikely to persist. This might be the case for which events negate (or perhaps confirm) the rumor's basic assertions. For example, a deadline might pass that was to mark the closure of a shop, the resignation or replacement of a CEO, or the discontinuation of a product, without the rumored event having occurred. Or, conversely, in other cases the event actually may come to pass. In either case, the (confirmed or unconfirmed) rumor should cease to be relevant. Thus, if it seems possible that "waiting out" a rumor that is likely to become irrelevant on its own will not be damaging, the do nothing approach would appear to be the appropriate short-term remedy. The risk is that if too much time is allowed to elapse before the level of credibility becomes apparent, the situation might change—deadlines might be pushed back, the rumor might evolve into something potentially more harmful, or it might stimulate the emergence of additional rumors.

In a case described by Fearn-Banks (1996), Gerber Products chose to wait before responding to a story that a grocery store customer had found a fragment of glass in one of its baby food products. A potential crisis was averted when Gerber's test labs could find no traces of glass in the allegedly affected jar and when the store could not provide the fragment supposedly found by the customer. Because the rumor's credibility was suspect, Gerber's decision to allow the rumor to self-destruct on its own appears to have been well-chosen. In most alleged product tampering cases, however, the potential damage can be so great that companies choose to take more immediate and forceful action (see Box 6.3).

Developing the Rumor Action Plan: Preliminary Steps

Once the required background work has been done in terms of evaluating the rumor and its potential for harm, it may be apparent that the story will not die out on its own and requires a more active response. The nature of the action taken, however, will depend on various considerations, including the extent of spread and the potential for wider diffusion (local, regional, or national), believability of the rumor (credible or noncredible), veracity of the rumor (based on truth or untrue), the likely impact of issuing a denial (effective, ineffective, or counterproductive), and the ability to reach the appropriate target audiences with the rumor control message (active rumor transmitters, vulnerable individuals; see Fig. 6.4).

Prior to selecting a specific course of action, company officials who have been assigned to serve as the rumor management team must assemble all of the facts and present them clearly and accurately to coworkers and superiors (Koenig, 1985). This is a necessary step to increase the likelihood that the entire organization understands the nature of the problem, the tasks at hand for coping with it, and the need to work toward a solution in a unified manner. Details can be provided to employees via a company newsletter (or similar medium) along with suggestions as to what to say about the problem if approached by persons external to the organization, including friends, neighbors, relatives, and the press. To inform superiors, the recommended approach is to formally present the problem and the team's proposed action plan in a face-to-face meeting where feedback and support can be solicited.

Box 6.3. The Tylenol Crisis

Johnson & Johnson's successful handling of the well-known Tylenol product tampering scare represents a model example of the crisis management efforts that can be undertaken when a firm's worst fears are realized. Over the course of a dramatic few days beginning on September 29, 1982, seven people in the Chicago area died from cyanide poisoning after using Johnson & Johnson's benchmark pain-killer product, Extra-Strength Tylenol capsules. Nonetheless, the company managed to avert disaster through a combination of quickly implemented marketing measures.

From the very first day, the poisoning scare was the leading story reported in print and broadcast news reports and marketing experts were predicting that the Tylenol brand, which represented 17% of the company's net income in 1981, would never recover (Rehak, 2002). However, this is one time the experts got it wrong. Within 2 months of the onset of the crisis, a modified Tylenol was back on the store shelves in a new tamperproof packaging and within 1 year its market share of the $1.2 billion analgesic market was nearly back to its precrisis level. With the stakes so high, and facing an unprecedented crisis in the history of consumer goods marketing, it is informative to consider how Johnson & Johnson managed to rebound so quickly.

According to company officials, at the heart of their handling of the crisis was a firm commitment to placing consumers before profits at any cost, consistent with a strategic management credo written during the 1940s by the son of the company's founder. The credo describes a commitment to a decentralized management approach, ethical principles, and an emphasis on managing the business for the long term (Johnson & Johnson, 1982). This credo set the tone for the immediate key business decisions that were made both during the Tylenol crisis and in its aftermath, summarized here:

1. Recognizing the potential scope and gravity of the situation, the first step implemented by the company was to quickly get the U.S. FDA involved. It was assumed that the successful management of the case would require close involvement between government and industry.
2. More than 31 million bottles of Tylenol capsules were recalled from shelves in all of the U.S. states in which the product was distributed. The media were informed so that they could warn consumers and all Tylenol advertising was suspended. (Prior to 1982, product recalls were virtually never carried out by consumer goods firms.)
3. Warnings about the tainted capsules were sent out to the medical community through more than 450,000 mailgrams.
4. Special telephone hotlines were set up to respond to anxious consumers and the medical profession.
5. Consumer surveys were initiated by Johnson & Johnson's advertising and public relations firms to assess consumer perceptions and reactions.

(continued)

6. Production of Tylenol capsules was halted on October 1.
7. A reward of $100,000 was offered for information leading to the apprehension of the perpetrators of the adulterated batches of the capsules.
8. Tylenol capsules were reintroduced in November in a triple-seal tamper-resistant package, which began to appear on retail shelves the following month. As a result, Johnson & Johnson represented the first company to respond to new FDA regulations requiring tamper-resistant packaging.
9. In an effort to entice consumers back to the brand and to restore their faith in the company, Johnson & Johnson distributed free $2.50 coupons good toward the purchase of any Tylenol product. The coupons originally were made available to callers of a toll-free telephone number and later were included in high-circulation newspapers.
10. More than 2,250 company sales representatives made a total of nearly 1 million presentations by the end of 1982 to physicians and others in the medical community in support of the Tylenol reintroduction. Despite the fact that the Tylenol capsules were part of the over-the-counter analgesic sector, it was recognized that more than 70% of all Tylenol users had received a recommendation to use the brand from their physicians.
11. On October 24, the company ran a television announcement featuring one of their medical directors who talked about Tylenol's 20-year history, offered to replace capsules with tablets, and asked the public to maintain their trust in Johnson & Johnson.
12. Following another Tylenol poisoning episode in February 1986 and a much smaller recall of the product than during the original tampering crisis, Johnson & Johnson discontinued the manufacture and sale of all its over-the-counter medicines in capsule form. At the same time, the company offered at its expense to replace nearly 15 million packages of its capsule products in homes and retail stores with an easier to swallow, tamper-resistant caplet. A free trial coupon for a package of the new Tylenol caplets was distributed (see illustration). Together, these later efforts resulted in an estimated cost of $150 million for the company (McFadden, 1986).

Additional activities undertaken by Johnson & Johnson during the Tylenol comeback in the aftermath of the original crisis included visits by the company's corporate relations department to Congressional offices to support efforts toward preventing future product tampering incidents; personal appearances and interviews involving company executives through a variety of national media outlets; distribution of videotaped special reports to employees, retirees, and the mass media detailing the company's response to the crisis; and replies to all letters received from consumers asking about the tampering incidents.

(continued)

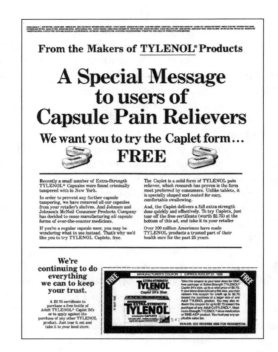

From the Makers of **TYLENOL®** Products

A Special Message to users of Capsule Pain Relievers

We want you to try the Caplet form...

FREE

Recently a small number of Extra-Strength TYLENOL® Capsules were found criminally tampered with in New York.

In order to prevent any further capsule tampering, we have removed all our capsules from your retailer's shelves. And Johnson and Johnson's McNeil Consumer Products Company has decided to cease manufacturing *all* capsule forms of over-the-counter medicines.

If you're a regular capsule user, you may be wondering what to use instead. That's why we'd like you to try TYLENOL Caplets, free.

The Caplet is a solid form of TYLENOL pain reliever, which research has proven is the form most preferred by consumers. Unlike tablets, it is specially shaped and coated for easy, comfortable swallowing.

And, the Caplet delivers a fall extra strength dose quickly and effectively. To try Caplets, just tear off the free certificate (worth $2.75) at the bottom of this ad, and take it to your retailer

Over 100 million Americans have made TYLENOL products a trusted part of their health care for the past 25 years.

We're continuing to do everything we can to keep your trust.

A $2.75 certificate to purchase a free bottle of Adult TYLENOL® Caplet 24's or to apply against the purchase of any other TYLENOL product. Just tear it out and take it to your local store.

The quick decision to pull Tylenol off the market and the company's straightforward approach in dealing with the media and the public are widely considered to be the most instrumental components of the successful outcome to the Tylenol story. In a recent recounting of the crisis, it was concluded that "Tylenol made a hero of Johnson & Johnson" (Rehak, 2002, p. 15).

Consistent with information obtained during the previous phases, a decision must be made about whether the rumor should be treated at the local or national level. If the former, officials must remain alert to the possibility that the rumor could spread quickly beyond the local area. Demographic characteristics of the focal population and appropriate media outlets for reaching persons in the targeted geographical areas also should be determined.

Determining the Appropriate Action.   Once the decision is made to counter the rumor in an active fashion, the specific form of action must be chosen. Whatever means ultimately is decided on, the tasks at hand for implementing the strategy will require the development of pertinent messages and the selection of appropriate media outlets. Although perhaps the most obvious means of fighting a rumor is to strongly deny it, Figure 6.4 suggests that outright refutation is not the only possible course of action. The rumor control decision tree depicted in Fig. 6.4 is somewhat of an oversimplification be-

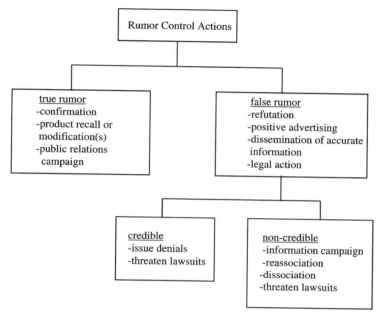

FIG. 6.4.   Rumor control decision tree. Adapted from Brodin (1995). Reprinted with permmission of Oliviane Brodin and *Décisions Marketing*.

cause many rumors have both credible and noncredible aspects and the various actions appearing in the different boxes in reality often are combined in an overall rumor action plan. Nonetheless, the decision tree is useful in helping recognize the situations in which certain tactics might be more effective than others.

As is evident in the figure, an initial consideration pertains to the extent to which the rumor is false or based, at least in part, on truth. A true and potentially harmful rumor should be confirmed as quickly as feasible (or at least that part of the rumor that is true should be identified). Because of the public's thirst for information and the media's relentless pursuit of newsworthy stories, in most cases the truth eventually will come out. From a public relations standpoint, it serves to benefit the organization if the confirmation and accompanying details come from company officials rather than from having the facts exposed and interpreted by an external source.

Damage can be minimized if the admission about a truthful rumor is accompanied by a clearly planned agenda for dealing with the situation. For example, if the rumor pertains to an allegedly contaminated food product, the company should clarify the extent of the problem and describe the blueprint for rectifying any damages that were entailed and for resolving the situation (such as a product recall, new factory safety procedures, etc.). If the rumor deals with personnel issues, such as the removal of a CEO, elimination of jobs, or relocation of a factory to another town, it may not be in the best interest of the organization to confirm the story immediately for a variety of reasons (e.g., ongoing negotiations). In such cases, company officials could acknowledge that "there are some stories going around" and that "it is true that there are internal discussions to that effect." It then should be explained why further statements cannot be issued at the current time and that additional announcements will be forthcoming as soon as the issues are decided or the situation resolved. Such an approach may not sate public concerns and the need for clarification, but it should at least slow down the rumor more effectively than a curt "no comment" response.

In most cases, a more challenging situation will involve the control of false rumors. People often choose to believe what they want to believe, no matter how much evidence there is to the contrary. Thus, the design of messages for countering untrue rumors must be undertaken with great care and foresight. Different strategies can be used to undermine false allegations, either alone or in combination, including the issuance of denials, threats of legal action, enlisting the aid of community leaders and other respected spokespersons, taking actions that are inconsistent with the rumor allegations, and the dissemination of accurate information that is contradictory to the content of the rumor. Which course of action will prove to be most effective cannot be ascertained with certainty beforehand, although the more complete the information gathering and analysis during the previous rumor-control stages, the more likely the strategy will meet its objectives.

Consistent with Fig. 6.4, the success of specific actions for dealing with a false rumor will depend on the degree of credibility the rumor bears for a specific audience. When rumors are unlikely to be viewed as credible by particular groups among the firm's stakeholders or when a rumor's credibility appears to be based on a weak foundation, the straightforward strategy of disseminating clear and accurate information is recommended. Assuming that this is done effectively through the development of believable and positive messages that can reach hotbeds of rumor activity, a body of evidence can be built that strongly implies that the rumor is untrue (Fearn-Banks, 1996). With this approach, there typically is no need to mention the rumor at all; in fact, doing so may serve to negate the influence potential of the rumor-control messages.

As part of McDonald's overall strategy for countering the worm rumor, promotional kits sent to franchise owners and a subsequent advertising campaign emphasized the high quality of ingredients used in their hamburgers and included the phrase "Nothing but 100% pure United States Government-inspected ground beef." A letter attributed to the U.S. Secretary of Agriculture was posted by the franchise owners claiming that "hamburger produced by these [McDonald's] establishments is wholesome, properly identified, and in compliance with standards prescribed by Food Safety and Quality Service regulations." At no time was the word *worm* used to counter the rumor in advertisements directed to the public; instead, it was stressed that the fast-food restaurant chain added "no protein additives" to its food. Additionally, public relations statements directed to other company stakeholders noted how from a financial position putting red worms in the hamburgers would be unaffordable, given that red worms were more than five times more expensive than hamburger meat. From a cognitive perspective, such messages were intended to be inconsistent with the rumor allegations that worms were added to boost the protein content of the hamburgers.

During the 1993 product tampering hoax that struck the Pepsi-Cola Company, which claimed that syringes and hypodermic needles were found in cans of the company's leading soft-drinks Pepsi and Diet Pepsi (see chap. 2), a speedy informational response helped to reduce credibility levels so effectively that a potential public relations catastrophe was quickly averted. When initial tampering claims came to the attention of the company, a local response was initiated whereby executives from Pepsi's main bottler were made available to the media. However, once it appeared that the story was spreading and that tampering claims were emerging in other regions of the country, a crisis team of 12 company executives was activated immediately.

The one person designated to serve as spokesperson, Pepsi-Cola North America President and CEO Craig Weatherup, readily accepted invitations to appear on several network TV newscasts. The crisis management team had assembled video footage showing Pepsi's canning process and making it clear how it would be virtually impossible to insert a foreign object into one of the cans before it was sealed. This footage was aired repeatedly during Weatherup's TV appearances and later during further news reports about the story. The company's strategy in being forthright with information and accessible to the public was essential in this case because anxiety levels were very high and a media frenzy was evident from the outset. According to Weatherup, within hours of the tampering scare there were so many satellite trucks and helicopters filled with television crews landing at a helicopter pad near Pepsi's headquarters that it "looked like a moon landing" ("The Right Moves," 1993, p. 36). Pepsi also was fortunate to have received the support of the U.S. FDA Commissioner David Kessler, who advised consumers to pour their canned soft drinks into a glass before consuming the beverage and warned of stiff criminal penalties for making false complaints (Magiera, 1993).

The importance of having highly trustworthy and expert sources communicate information to strike at the credibility of a rumor cannot be overemphasized. Numerous studies in the field of attitude change have consistently revealed that the two key characteristics of persuasive communicators are trustworthiness (i.e., how honest and objective the source appears to the audience) and expertise (i.e., how knowledgeable the source is with respect to the content area of the message; cf. Perloff, 1993). In the Pepsi case the management team chose Weatherup to serve as spokesperson because of his straightforward, articulate style and his expertise in the intricacies of the canning operations. In his six TV appearances, Weatherup displayed a calm and convincing earnestness that was well received by the media, customers, and other stakeholders. Moreover, the assistance of an established, objective agency like the FDA added credibility to the company's campaign. That credibility was a central issue in this case is reflected in the comments of a marketing consultant at the time: "What we're dealing with is what does the American consumer come to believe. One reason this was spinning out of control is that particular image [a syringe popping out of a can of Pepsi]" (Magiera, 1993, p. 46).

Consistent with our earlier point that rumor control efforts should also involve a consideration of the postrumor (or death) stage, Pepsi ran an advertisement in more than 200 local newspapers shortly after talk about the syringes had died out thanking consumers for their support during the crisis. The headline of the print ad read "Pepsi is pleased to announce … nothing." The ad's text emphasized how "those stories about Diet Pepsi were a hoax. Plain and simple, not true." Nowhere in the message was the nature of the hoax mentioned, only that "it's over" and that there was "nothing more to say." Such a message provided closure to the situation and reduced the likelihood that there would be lingering doubts that the story had yet to play itself out. It also reinforced the image that the company cared about its consumers and had their safety and welfare in mind.

It might be recalled that P&G also relied heavily on an approach that attacked the apparent veracity of the Satan rumors when they first targeted the company during the early 1980s (see chap. 1). As I described, once the seriousness of the rumor campaign had become apparent, P&G enlisted the assistance of fundamentalist church leaders to get the message out to their parishioners and also provided evidence that belied the claim that a company owner had appeared on a popular TV program to admit his relationship with the devil. For example, it was revealed that the program did not even air on the date that the owner had allegedly appeared. In another vein, the company pointed out the logical absurdities of having an owner reveal the conspiracy to a nationwide audience—that nothing would be gained in doing so—and how the decision to remove the company logo from products did not conform to the claim that the company was working for Satan.

To increase the likelihood of success, the dissemination of accurate information in an attempt to fight rumors should not be carried out haphazardly, but should be based on a formalized plan. One systematic approach, proposed by Esposito and Rosnow (1983), is summarized in Box 6.4. The information dissemination plan (IDP) represents a simple framework for disseminating the facts to the media and the public once the decision is made to issue the information. According to its authors, the extent to which any combination of the specific methods should be employed will depend on the severity of the rumor and the size of the targeted audience.

In addition to the dissemination of accurate information, other basic tactics for dealing with noncredible rumors can be drawn from information processing theory, and are represented in the decision tree as positive advertising, dissociation, and reassociation. Information processing theory, which is described in fuller detail in Chapter 2, posits that the cognitive processes of storage and retrieval influence what (and how) we think about objects we encounter in our everyday lives. That is, incoming information is stored in active

---

Box 6.4. The Information Dissemination Plan

From Esposito and Rosnow (1983).

Public Relations Campaign

Options:
1. Send correspondence listing the facts to concerned publics (religious groups, parent–teacher groups, retailers, etc.).

2. Schedule public appearances by public relations personnel or corporate executives.

3. Enlist a trusted individual (a respected public official, consumer advocate, or expert scientist) to speak on your behalf.

4. If all else fails, call a press conference to publicize the facts.

Mass Media Campaign

Options:
1. Send the facts to newspaper editors and TV and radio station owners. They may publish or broadcast the information outright or draft an editorial on your behalf.

2. Publish a letter from a trustworthy source (e.g., the president of the company, the product developer, a public health official) as part of your print advertising. (For an example, see Box 6.6.)

3. Alter product advertising to restore consumer confidence in your product and company.

Publish Research Findings

If a research investigation was conducted to test some aspect of your product during the information gathering phase, you can increase the credibility of the findings by having them published in a reputable scientific journal or endorsed by a government or health agency. The findings then can be cited in any advertising or public relations messages.

memory where it stimulates the retrieval of previously processed object-relevant thoughts. The more times specific attributes are associated with an object (so-called rehearsal), the more likely those attributes will be stored as object-relevant thoughts in long-term memory. In the context of rumors, this suggests that repeated reception of a rumor involving the association between an object (such as McDonald's hamburgers) and a negative attribute (such as red worms) will result in a less favorable evaluation of the object (McDonald's or McDonald's hamburgers) than if the rumor had not been received. This is because when consumers think about the product or company, their thoughts will activate the negative attribute stored in memory, even if the rumor is not believed (i.e., noncredible).

Using these notions as a springboard, Tybout et al. (1981) devised an ingenious laboratory experiment to compare three different strategies for combatting rumors: refutation, storage strategy, and retrieval strategy (the latter two are referred to as dissociation and reassociation in Fig. 6.4). The *refutation approach* is based on the application of basic persuasion methods that are intended to contradict the rumor by claiming that it is not true (i.e., denial of its veracity). The *storage strategy* involves the attempt to associate the negative attribute described by the rumor (worms) to another object that is more positively evaluated (such as a delicious gourmet sauce that happens to include worms in its recipe). Even though the attribute may still be associated with the object, this approach should result in a more favorable evaluation of the object. The *retrieval strategy* involves encouraging people to think about the more positive associations to the object that they previously have stored in memory to dilute the effects of the negative attribute created by the rumor. This strategy is more relevant to consumers who have had good experiences with the company or brand prior to receiving the rumor. Both the dissociation and reassociation strategies can be seen as forms of the so-called positive advertising approach for coping with rumors, whereby the attempt is to weaken the rumor impact by stimulating favorable thoughts about the rumor target or the attribute claimed by the rumor (cf. Kapferer, 1990).

To compare these three rumor-control actions, Tybout et al. (1981) ostensibly informed their research participants that the study involved the evaluation of violent TV programs and that they were to watch a videotape and subsequently evaluate both the program and the products advertised during commercials that were interspersed throughout. Three of the 12 commercials shown during the videotape presentation were for McDonald's. Following the third McDonald's ad, an experimental confederate who appeared to be another participant but was secretly assisting the researchers, planted the worm rumor by stating, "You know these McDonald's commercials remind me of that rumor about worms and McDonald's—you know, that McDonald's uses worm meat in their hamburgers." For some participants, refutation was introduced by having the experimenter immediately contradict the confederate's rumor statement by saying the story was untrue, referring to the arguments that worms are too expensive and that an FDA study found that McDonald's uses 100% pure beef.

As a means of implementing the retrieval approach, some participants were asked to respond to a series of questions after they had evaluated the TV program, but before they evaluated eating at McDonald's. The questions pertained to their recent visits to McDonald's in an effort to stimulate the retrieval of (presumably more positive) object-relevant thoughts that were unrelated to the rumor. The storage strategy was effected by having the experimenter respond to the confederate's comment by mentioning a well-known French restaurant that serves a delicious sauce made from worms. All participants were asked at the end of the experiment to rate McDonald's on a variety of dimensions, including quality of food and their likelihood of eating at McDonald's.

The results of Tybout et al.'s (1981) study were consistent with information processing theory. Because it was presumed that the refutation strategy would serve to increase rehearsal of the rumor and strengthen the negative association in memory, the researchers predicted that this approach would adversely affect how people felt about the object. In other words, even if they accepted the claim that the rumor was false, the very fact that it came to mind whenever they thought about the target (McDonald's) would be offputting enough to negatively affect their evaluation of the target. This is exactly what occurred: When compared with the ratings of participants who had not heard the worm rumor, participants in the refutation condition rated eating at McDonald's less favorably. By contrast, both the retrieval and storage strategies resulted in more favorable evaluations of eating at McDonald's as compared with ratings obtained from participants who heard the rumor but were not exposed to either of the strategy manipulations (see Fig. 6.5). These strategies effectively served to transform the rumored negative attribute into something that was no longer perceived as so bad (earthworms can be a delicacy) or else led them to think more favorable thoughts about eating at the restaurant (e.g., "I remember the good times I had last summer at McDonald's with my friends.").

In a more recent study, Misra (1992) utilized a research manipulation similar to that employed by Tybout et al. (1981) to shed light on a cognitive phenomenon known as the *perseverance process*. This refers to the process whereby false perceptions and beliefs continue long after they have been discredited by a credible source. This tendency has been of serious concern to behavioral scientists who employ deceptive manipulations in their research investigations (cf. Kimmel, 2003). For example, it has been shown that false perceptions created by deceptive feedback following experimental tasks may become cognitively detached from the evidence that created them; as a result, even after the basis for the perceptions is disconfirmed (via a debriefing that occurs at the end of the investigation), individuals may tend to cling to the original beliefs (Ross, Lepper, & Hubbard, 1975).

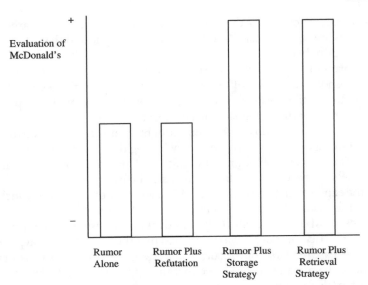

FIG. 6.5. The effect of refutation, retrieval, and storage strategies on rumor impact. From Tybout, Calder, and Sternthal (1981). Reprinted with permission from *Journal of Marketing Research*, published by the American Marketing Association, A. M. Tybout, B. J. Calder, & B. Sternthal, 1981, vol. 18, p. 77.

Although Misra's (1992) experiment did not pertain to rumor per se, his findings are relevant to our assessment of rumor-control actions in that they cast doubt on the efficacy of the refutational approach. Participants first answered a set of questions pertaining to fast-food restaurants and then were asked if they had heard a rumor that McDonald's was putting worms in its hamburgers and whether they believed it. They then either received no debriefing (i.e., they were not told whether the rumor was true or false), a *conventional debriefing* (in which they were informed that the rumor was not true), or an *explicit debriefing* (which added to the conventional debriefing feedback a formal discussion of the perseverance phenomenon). All participants then rated their preference for McDonald's on several attitude scales. The results revealed that those persons who had not been debriefed, as well as those who received a conventional debriefing, rated McDonald's significantly less favorably than those who received the explicit debriefing or had not been told the rumor (i.e., the control group). If we regard the conventional debriefing as not unlike a standard rumor denial, it is apparent that denials alone may not be sufficient to eliminate the persistence of beliefs attributed to noncredible rumors. We further consider the implications of these studies for developing effective denials in the following section.

Before leaving our survey of strategies for coping with noncredible rumors, it should be noted that other strategies could be added to our discussion, such as creating a counterrumor and spreading disinformation or ridiculing the rumor (cf. Kapferer, 1990). We have alluded to the limitations of these sorts of approaches in previous chapters and they entail too many risks to be recommended across a wide number of rumor situations.

Rebutting Credible Rumors.   Although rumor rebuttals comprise "the most straightforward and aggressive strategy" for coping with credible rumors (Koller, 1992, p. 168), as pointed out in the preceding section, it is an approach that is fraught with potential risks and its effectiveness is far from assured. Reflecting these problems, Kapferer (1990) referred to the strategy of denying rumors as a "perilous art." Despite potential drawbacks, rebuttals can be effective in offsetting marketplace rumors, particularly when they are developed and communicated with intelligence and care (see Box 6.5).

A primary concern with this approach, of course, is that the act of denying a rumor may have the counterproductive effect of bringing the false allegations to the attention of a wider audience than would have been the case had the denial not been made. There also is the risk that it will increase audience awareness of the company–rumor link for persons who may have heard the rumor but were uncertain as to the target. As the results of the studies described in the preceding section indicate, the more the rumor is repeated (e.g., through rebuttals), the stronger the link between the target and the allegations becomes.

Kapferer (1990) identified some additional handicaps associated with denials, the foremost being that they are expected and, as a result, not considered very seriously. In fact, in a period of rampant corporate misconduct and widespread litigation, it is almost automatic that an aggrieved party will respond, as Kapferer suggested, by saying "I am innocent." However, an "I did it" response would certainly capture attention more effectively. In short, one reason that denials may not be seriously heeded is that in a majority of cases the denials tend to be more discreet and less newsworthy than the hot news provided by a fresh, titillating rumor. In Kapferer's words, "Denials are cold, almost kill-joy information. They defuse the imagination, plunging us back into the banality of reality" (p. 235).

Despite these points, in many cases denials have to be made. It is true that on the one hand, a denial is expected. An expected typical reaction from a wary public is likely to be "Of course they are going to deny it. If they admit it, they will be in worse trouble than they are already." On the other hand, to sit back while potentially damaging allegations are eroding the firm's reputation would no doubt induce a reaction such as, "Well, they haven't denied it, so it must be true." However, what may appear to be a no-win situation can be circumvented, as suggested earlier, by acting swiftly and forcefully in attempting to undermine the rumor. In fact, there are three basic aspects that must be considered when formulating a rebuttal response: when to deny, who is to issue the denial, and what should be communicated in the denial.

Box 6.5. Example of an Antirumor Print Advertisement

RUMORS

ru•mors / 'rü-mers / n 1. general talk not based on definite knowledge; 2. mere gossip; hearsay; 3. an unconfirmed story
(Webster's Dictionary)

Dear Neighbors and Customers:

JASPER'S RESTAURANT IS NOT GOING OUT OF BUSINESS!
As Mark Twain once said "the rumors of my death are greatly exaggerated."

Although we initially chose to ignore these rumors, we believe that the time to address the issue is now!

THE FACTS ARE:

WE ARE NOT CLOSING
"As the accounting firm for Jasper's Restaurant we would like to state that the business is very much alive and well."
— Larry Kaminitz, David Uhlfelder — Kaminitz, Uhlfelder & Permison PA

WE ARE NOT FILING FOR BANKRUPTCY
"I have been Jasper's attorney for six(6) years and the owners are solid businessmen. No discussion of bankruptcy has ever, ever taken place."
— David Rodman Cohan, Esq.

WE ARE NOT C.O.D. WITH ANY OF OUR VENDORS
"We, the below listed vendors, are proud to serve Jasper's Restaurant in Baltimore. They are a valued customer in good standing, enjoying a full line of credit with our organization":

- Adams Burch
- Catons Plumbing
- Myland Farms
- Ellis Coffee
- Kraft Food Service
- H & S Bakery
- Keany Produce
- Maryland Hotel Supply
- Burns Chemical
- Smelkinson / Sysco
- Metropolitan Poultry & Seafood
- Acme Paper
- Geller Lighting
- Bakery De France
- Instantwhip
- Shenandoah Pride Dairy
- Daval Ice Cream
- Complete Cleaning Services
- Quality Brands

WE ARE NOT SELLING THE BUSINESS
(unless it's an offer we can't refuse!)

WE ARE Booking Banquets well into 1994 and 1995, often with repeat customers who were thrilled with their previous affairs with us.

"The only thing better than the food or prices is the service!"
— William Stanley and Diana Scheinberg Stanley

"No restaurant, reception hall or other fancy catering hall could have outdone you!"
— Dr. Kenneth L. Glick

"There were so many comments on how good the food was!"
— Fred Weiss

"The food was delicious . . . The room looked Fabulous!"
— Sandi Shane

"Everyone applauded the decor, the food and service!"
— Chip Silverman

"The Hors Douevres were excellent and the meal magnificent!"
— Alvin A. Wolf

"The best place in Baltimore for a business luncheon."
— Mike Gimbel

WHAT WE WILL DO:
Although these rumors have not effected our business, some of our banquet clients have, understandably, voiced concern. As proof of our financial stability and long term commitment to our customers and as a sign of good faith, for the next 12 months Jasper's is establishing a "Banquet Deposit" escrow account with our accounting firm of Kaminitz Uhlfelder & Permison. Upon your request we will place your deposit in this account until the date of your event.

WHAT WE ASK OF YOU:
From you, our neighbors, we appeal to your sense of fair play in helping us put an end to these totally unfounded and untrue rumors by not participating in them.

There is really no effective way to combat rumors totally. We debated long and hard as to whether to even address them at all in public. There will always be a few people who will insist on continuing them, no matter what we say or what the facts are, but for the majority of you, we hope this information will put an end to your concern.

Visit us soon for good food, good friends, good times . . . We'll be here for a long, long time.

Very Truly Yours,

Leslie, Jay & Fred Rosenthal
(A family business)

Jasper's

If it is true that denials are expected, then they should be made as soon as possible; to delay could convey the impression that the company is not being completely forthright. This is not unlike a situation in which a person is attempting to draw out a liar. For example, suppose a woman suspects her husband of having an affair. Late one afternoon, she asks him whether he had lunch today. This is a question that normally would not require much deliberation—a quick "yes" or "no" would be expected in response. If he hesitates in responding (e.g., "I'll get back to you on that one, honey."), the wife might suspect that he is thinking up a more plausible answer to mask what he was really up to at lunch.

An important consideration related to the timing of the rebuttal has to do with the extent to which members of the target audience have prior knowledge of the rumor before they are exposed to the denial. It appears that when people first learn about the rumor from the denial, the denial is less apt to be effective than if they had learned about the accusation first, and then were exposed to the rebuttal. This was originally suggested by a study in which participants judged a defendant as more guilty when he denied having committed a crime before he was accused compared with other participants who first learned about the accusation and later were confronted with the rebuttal (Yandell, 1979). This finding was interpreted by the study's author in terms of attribution theory (see chap. 2). Consistent with this theory, when a direct accusation has been made, an observer is likely to perceive that there is a sufficient external cause for the subsequent rebuttal (i.e., it is the result of a defensive response to an untrue accusation). By contrast, when a rebuttal is made in the absence of a direct accusation, an observer may attribute the rebuttal to an internal quality of the person, such as existing guilt (i.e., the rebuttal is a kind of hushing-up machination).

In a series of studies pertaining to marketplace rumors and rebuttals German social psychologist Michael Koller (1993) reported similar results regarding the role of participants' knowledge of an existing rumor prior to the issuing of a rebuttal. However, Koller's research revealed that other variables also play a role in people's reactions to rumor denials, such as the extent to which the rumor is of high personal relevance to audience members and the credibility of the source of the accusation. Overall, the evidence suggests that rebuttals are more likely to be successful (in terms of evaluations of the rebuttal and of the target) when the following conditions are met: (a) the observer has learned about the rumor previously from a low-credibility source, and (b) the rumored accusation is of low impact for the observer (i.e., it does not affect him or her personally).

In another study, Koller (1992) found that whereas rebuttals plus prior knowledge reduced belief in a rumor, a positive advertising strategy was superior to the rebuttal approach when it came to reducing an individual's susceptibility to subsequent rumors about the target. This study involved an actual rumor about the Stroh Brewery Company which, during the early 1980s in the U.S. Midwest, was alleged to be illegally financing political candidates. Rumor knowledge was manipulated through the use of questionnaires that either included or did not include fictitious newspaper articles describing Stroh's rumor problems. The type of corporate response to the rumors also was manipulated, such that some individuals were exposed to the actual rebuttal ad placed by Stroh in 1983 in the *Chicago Tribune* (see Box 6.6), whereas others were exposed to a positive ad that made no mention of the rumor but instead detailed Stroh's commitment to public programs. The results of the study revealed that when people had prior knowledge of the initial rumor the positive advertising strategy was more effective than that of the rumor rebuttal in lowering people's susceptibility to subsequent rumors.

According to Koller (1992), the results of the Stroh study can best be explained by information processing notions in that the positive advertising may have endowed Stroh with positive features while weakening the Stroh–rumor association. Moreover, the rebuttal may have activated individuals' recollec-

---

Box 6.6. The Stroh Brewery Company Rebuttal

From Koenig (1985, p. 61).

STROH OFFERS $25,000 TO STOP RUMORS!

There are rumors in the Illinois and Indiana areas that The Stroh Brewery Company is making contributions to presidential candidates. These rumors are not true. **They are completely, totally false!**

The Stroh Brewery Company **does not** contribute to any political candidates' campaigns. We cannot. It is against the law for us to do so. Even if it were legal, we would not. We are in the business of selling our products nationally to consumers of legal drinking age. Our customers represent all political parties. We would not, and never will, anger any of our customers by supporting any candidate for office at any level of government!

However, we **do** contribute to certain non-partisan programs such as the current Statue of Liberty renovation effort. We were one of the first major corporate contributors to this nation-wide civic endeavor.

We believe that the rumors claiming The Stroh Brewery Company helps finance presidential campaigns are out-and-out attempts to slander The Stroh Brewery Company.

We saw that we had no choice but to speak to you, the public, on this issue. We want you to know the facts. It's unfortunate that we have been put in this position, but we will not turn away from an issue that affects us as an American corporation and affects you as the American consumer.

We are ready to take **all** legal and judicial actions against the person or persons responsible for beginning this rumor. We will pay a **$25,000 reward** to the first person who identifies to us the person or persons who began this rumor, where such identification leads to successful legal action by The Stroh Brewery Company. If you have information, please contact the Investigative Research Agency, Inc., at: (312) 745-1111

The Stroh Brewery Company, America's third largest brewer, is a private company solely owned and operated by the Stroh family. The Stroh family began brewing beer in Germany in the 1700s. The Stroh Brewery Company has brewed beer in America since 1850 when Bernhard Stroh settled in Detroit. The Stroh Brewery Company has always been, and plans to remain, family owned.

THE STROH BREWERY COMPANY

tion of the initial rumor ("Wasn't there something wrong about this company?"), thereby increasing their susceptibility to subsequent rumors. Taken together, however, these studies suggest that decisions regarding the rebuttal strategy should take into account how widespread a rumor is at the time. In Koller's view:

> If the rumor is relatively *well known* among the public, the best strategy seems to be to promote positive features of the target, thereby dissociating the target from the rumor. In case a rumor is *not yet widespread*, but the realistic danger exists that the rumor is evolving and is likely to [receive] a high degree of publicity, a firm, convincing rebuttal strategy seems appropriate, thereby literally "inoculating" the public to forthcoming allegations. (p. 185)

Turning next to the question of who is to deliver the rebuttal, as previously discussed, spokespersons who are selected to represent the company in handling a rumor should be credible, confident, and effective communicators. This particularly holds true for persons selected to issue rumor rebuttals, although different spokespersons will be appropriate depending on the severity of the situation. If the rumor has reached crisis proportions, having a lower level company official will belie the seriousness of the problem. On the other hand, if the rumor is relatively low key and has limited circulation, the lower level official would be a better choice to serve as spokesperson than an executive officer whose presence could arouse greater concerns than are justified.

In addition to denying quickly, it is important to determine which points to refute. As Koenig (1985) noted, if a spokesperson denies more than is in the original allegation, the response could trigger additional associations or residuals that could serve to worsen the situation. Koenig also recommended that denials should convey the impression that the allegations not only are untrue but also unjust; that is, even if the financial health of the business is not suffering, the rumor is not fair marketplace practice. Although there may not be complete agreement about what to say in rumor rebuttals, most experts agree that the rumor itself should be explicitly repeated as few times as possible, if at all.

Designing Effective Rebuttals: Structuring the Message.   At the heart of most successful denials are strong, persuasive arguments that effectively serve to negate the allegations contained in the rumor. Marketing communicators tend to focus on three aspects of message structure when developing persuasive communications and each has relevance to the formulation of rumor rebuttals: (a) conclusion drawing, (b) one-sided versus two-sided messages, and (c) the order of presentation of the arguments or information (cf. Fill, 1995; Perloff, 1993).

Conclusion drawing deals with the question of how to formulate an appropriate ending to a persuasive communication. There are two possibilities, both of which can be said to have merit in particular situations. The first is to utilize an implicit, subtle approach by allowing the audience to draw its own conclusion from the message content. This would be illustrated by an antirumor message that simply presents details intended to undermine the rumor's allegations and then concludes with the statement, "Now that you know the facts, decide for yourself who to believe—the company that has your interests at heart or those persons who choose to spread falsehoods and slander our good reputation in the business community."

Had Stroh chosen to counter the rumor about illegal political contributions by designing a positive advertising message that emphasized its commitment to public programs, this would have reflected the implicit conclusion-drawing approach. Instead, as Box 6.6 makes clear, Stroh incorporated an explicit conclusion in its message by claiming, "These rumors are not true. They are completely, totally false." In other words, the explicit approach involves having the message itself draw a firm conclusion for the audience. The explicit approach also was utilized in the construction of the Jasper's Restaurant rumor rebuttal (see Box 6.5) in which the listed facts are followed by the admonishment to "[help] us put an end to these totally unfounded and untrue rumors by not participating in them."

Another example of the explicit approach is found in a print advertisement issued during the 1970s by Hunt-Wesson Foods, Inc. to dispel rumors that the company was owned by a businessman who had been accused of criminal misconduct. The clever message depicted a variation of the famous Norman Rockwell painting shown in Fig. 4.2. The last person to receive the rumor in the serial chain is identified as a Hunt-Wesson home economist, whose comments comprise the only text in the ad:

> So many rumors travel through the grapevine you can't always tell what's true and what's not. There's one rumor going around that I'd like to set straight right now: You may have heard that Hunt-Wesson Foods is owned by a man from Texas, named Hunt. It's not so. Hunt-Wesson Foods is located in California. Always has been .... We have nothing, not a thing, to do with any other Hunt. That's the truth. Won't you tell your neighbor and help set the record straight?

It should be clear that nearly all rumor rebuttals, by definition, reflect the explicit approach to conclusion drawing. Nonetheless, this implicit–explicit distinction is important because it suggests the situations in which a rebuttal would be more (or less) warranted than a positive advertising message (based on the implicit approach). Indeed, the effectiveness of the specific conclusion-drawing strategy has been shown to depend on several variables in the persuasion situation, one of which pertains to the complexity of the issue. When the message is difficult to comprehend and the receiver may not be motivated to draw the appropriate conclusion, it is more effective to draw the conclusion explicitly, otherwise the main point of the message might be missed. Attempts to actively counter rumors involving intricate details about health care products and personal finance services might require detailed and complex arguments that could be difficult for audience members to understand. In light of the point made earlier—that rebuttals tend to be more banal and less interesting than the rumors themselves—we might imagine that few people would be motivated to take the time to try to process and understand such complex messages. This would argue for a clear, concise, and explicitly worded rebuttal of the form used by Stroh and Hunt-Wesson, especially if the message is communicated through a medium that would make it difficult for people to process the message at their own rate, such as television or radio.

Specific characteristics of the audience, however, would suggest the appropriateness of an implicitly worded positive advertisement in lieu of explicit rebuttals. One such characteristic is the educational (or intelligence) level of the audience. Better educated audiences usually prefer to draw their own conclusions; to do so for them might lead them to view the message as an insult to their intelligence or cause them to feel undue pressure to conform with the recommended position. Further, message recipients who are highly involved in the issue usually desire to make up their own minds and may reject the conclusion or resent having it drawn for them.

A second issue pertaining to message structure is whether to use one-sided or two-sided messages. In the context of antirumor communications, this distinction to a large extent involves the issue of whether the rumor should be mentioned in the message. We previously have discussed some of the risks that are entailed when the rumor is repeated, but the one-sided versus two-sided issue also brings to bear some additional considerations. A *one-sided message* only gives arguments in favor of the persuader's position on an issue, as when a firm transmits a communication that argues against the veracity of a rumor without directly mentioning the rumor or its allegations. This was the strategy utilized in the McDonald's anti-worm rumor advertising campaign, which described the high quality of the hamburger meat without ever mentioning worms. By contrast, a *two-sided message* provides arguments for both sides of the issue and then specifically argues for one of the positions. This would be the case in which the rumored allegations are presented along with the arguments intended to refute them. This strategy was incorporated into the design of the Jasper's restaurant message (see Box 6.5).

Beyond the risks entailed by mentioning the rumor and possibly bringing it to the attention of those who were not yet aware of it, there are other considerations that would argue in favor of one or the other of these approaches (cf. Fill, 1995; Perloff, 1993). In general, the preponderance of research evidence indicates that the one-sided message is recommended when the audience initially favors the position offered in the message (e.g., the rumor is untrue), is not aware that an alternative position could be taken (e.g., they have not heard the rumor), or when the audience consists of persons who are not well educated (e.g., hearing both sides of the issue could confuse them). Two-sided messages tend to be more effective when the intended receivers initially disagree with the position presented in the message and are fairly well educated.

Given these tendencies, it is not surprising that many antirumor messages take the form of two-sided messages, by presenting both the allegations brought forth by the rumor and the refutational arguments (as is the case in the Jasper's, Stroh, and Hunt-Wesson ads). By the time a firm chooses to create and run messages that take the form of print or broadcast communications, a majority of people in the target audience are likely to have heard the rumor and have received at least some information about the allegations. The two-sided refutation would improve credibility in this situation and giving both sides when people tend to agree with the allegations indicates that the message source respects the recipients' intelligence. That is, the implied message—"We think you are smart enough to know that there are two sides to any issue and we are going to give you both sides, even though we think one is better"—is likely to be disarming and well received by the audience.

The third issue related to message structure pertains to the order in which message arguments are presented. This nature of this issue depends on whether a one-sided or a two-sided message is to be used. When only one side is presented, a decision must be made about how the strong and weak arguments are to be ordered. When a two-sided message is used, the consideration has to do with which side to present first (as in a criminal trial or political debate). Because it would be difficult to imagine an antirumor rebuttal that ends with a declaration of the rumor (or its allegations), our discussion of ordering focuses only on the one-sided message case. Three basic ordering structures can be used: the anticlimax order (i.e., starting with strong arguments and ending with the weaker ones), the climax order (i.e., beginning with weaker arguments and ending with the stronger ones), and the pyramidal order (i.e., putting the strongest arguments in the middle).

Both the anticlimax and the climax orders of presentation have been shown to induce attitude change, whereas the pyramidal order tends to be least effective, with little evidence that it facilitates comprehension or attitude change. Which structure to utilize may depend on the nature of the medium through which the message is to be communicated. In print contexts, audience members often will not attend to the entire message, unless they are highly involved. We might conclude from this that if audience members are likely to have low involvement with the issue, the strongest arguments should be presented at the beginning in an anticlimax fashion.

In a face-to-face situation, however, where one has a captive and involved audience (as when a company official meets with community members), the climax order is recommended because it allows the speaker to build up to a powerful and convincing close.

It has been suggested that rumor rebuttals should be relatively short, which would imply that the message should simply exclude any weak arguments for one's position and rely solely on the most cogent points. The logic behind this recommendation is that people tend to remember "sound bytes" and that a lengthy and verbose rebuttal will be unconvincing and perceived as a cover-up (DiFonzo et al., 1994). Although these are good points, this view is somewhat oversimplified in light of recent research revealing that the length of a persuasive message will have differential effectiveness depending on the target audience's level of involvement with the message (Friedrich, Fetherstonhaugh, Casey, & Gallagher, 1996). It appears that adding weaker arguments to strong ones tends to suppress or dilute the overall persuasiveness of the message for highly involved message recipients, who are likely to pay very close attention to the message content. For these persons, the weaker arguments will reduce the overall persuasiveness of the message because they will be integrated with the stronger ones and will tend to elicit counterarguing and unfavorable thoughts.

On the other hand, for low-involvement recipients who, by nature of their low level of interest, are unlikely to carefully process the message, adding weak arguments makes it appear that there are more arguments favoring the stated position and less counterarguing is likely to be stimulated. In other words, one can conclude that the more arguments comprising the rumor rebuttal, the better, but if some are weak, the message should be targeted to low-involved recipients only.

In sum, it is clear that the successful implementation of the rebuttal approach for refuting credible rumors is no simple task given the diversity of factors that must be considered (see Table 6.1). The challenge is in being able to gather sufficient information that would enable the proper identification and analysis of the target audience quickly enough so that the rebuttal approach can be launched before the situation gets out of control. Once again, when it comes to countering rumors, speed is essential and this is no more true than in the case of denials.

THE MEDIA AND OTHER MECHANISMS FOR RUMOR CONTROL

We have considered the various roles played by the media in the rumor process at various junctures in this book, particularly in terms of pointing out how the media can exacerbate the rumor problem for businesses through the spread of unconfirmed stories. However, it is clear that few rumor action plans could be carried out effectively without the cooperation and assistance of the media, given the size and widespread dispersion of many rumor audiences in today's business environment. The development of adversarial relationships between corporations and the mass media serves few if any interests when it comes to rumor control. Broadcast and print media represent the very

TABLE 6.1

Rumor Denials

Denial Elements	Recommended Conditions for Effectiveness
Source	Credible: expertise, trustworthiness, sympathetic, confident, independent
	Hierarchical status in the organization matches the level of the rumor situation (e.g., high-level company official denies rumors with high potential for damage)
Diffusion	Rapid, after the allegation has been received by a significant number of the target audience
	Low profile (if limited to specifically targeted group; directed at opinion leaders)
	High profile; repeated over time (if widespread, diffused through mailings, news conferences and reports, rumor hotlines, etc., to all stakeholders, including consumers, distributors, personnel in contact with customers, etc.)
Contents	Only deny what is necessary (i.e., pertaining explicitly to the allegations) Repeat the rumor as few times as possible
	Develop and structure arguments according to target audience awareness of the allegations, involvement, and educational level
	Provide evidence, where possible, to counter each allegation
	Avoid all forms of ambiguity that could serve to reinforce the rumor (e.g., by using irony or esoteric humor)
	Attribute diffusion of the rumor to nonloyal motives and attempts to damage the company's good reputation

Note. Adapted from Brodin (1995). Reprinted with permission of Oliviane Brodin and *Décisions Marketing.*

outlets that company officials will have to turn to if and when a rumor crisis strikes their firm; journalists are ideally committed to reporting the truth and will require access to company spokespersons, and consumers increasingly are demanding to be accurately informed, especially during times of crisis.

Working With the Media

As discussed earlier in this chapter (see the section "Preparing a Public Response"), the groundwork for enlisting the assistance of the media should be laid out during the prerumor stage as the facts are gathered. More specifically, public relations expert Otto Lerbinger (1997) recommended the following steps to increase the likelihood of receiving cooperation from the media (adapted here to apply to rumor crises):

1. Establish contacts with local newspapers and radio and television news divisions. Encourage television and radio station owners, publishers, editors, and news directors to become actively involved in the general planning process and to develop their own rumor crisis action plans.

2. Because a rumor crisis can strike at any time, determine audience listening and viewing preferences from such sources as Nielsen and Arbitron surveys so that the most effective media can be deployed during the crisis (e.g., certain minority groups might be best reached through foreign-language stations).

3. Considering that the mass media alone will not be able to reach various segments of the affected population and given the significant influence of word-of-mouth communication, it is important to encourage the media to establish and maintain contacts with opinion leaders. They also should be willing to assist the firm in recruiting opinion leaders to alert other segments of the community during a crisis.

4. Be prepared for the differing demands and interests of local, regional, national, and international media. For example, local media will be most interested in providing practical information to residents in the area, such as the status of local product recalls, the availability and safety of specific products, plant or store shutdowns, and so on. By contrast, national and international media will focus on information of a broader interest, such as extent of the rumor's spread, its impact on business affairs and the stock market, probability of government intervention, and the like.

5. Be prepared to respond to the differential needs and requirements of various types of mass media. Local radio news teams, for instance, typically will be the first to contact the firm and likely will ask to interview a company representative right away. Television stations will require visual as well as verbal reports (usually in the form of brief sound bytes), whereas print media are more concerned with providing in-depth analyses and graphics. These variations should be factored into the precrisis planning phases.

The following recommendations can be added to Lerbinger's list:

6. Media representatives can be invited to participate in any rumor workshops or seminars that are organized by the firm and one or two volunteers can be asked to serve on the company's rumor management team.

7. Television station owners should be willing to provide ready and free access to airtime for a company spokesperson in the event of a potentially damaging rumor outbreak.

8. Company personnel who are likely to come into contact with news representatives during a rumor crisis should receive training to successfully handle media interviews and press conferences. As is evident during crisis situations, how clearly and confidently a spokesperson presents the information is as important (perhaps more so) as the information itself in allaying public doubts and anxieties.

9. All those who speak on behalf of the company should take care to say nothing off the record (Jefkins & Yadin, 1998).

Rumor Control in the Electronic Age

With the emergence of the Internet and other electronic technologies that enable the instantaneous spread of information, rumor control has become more of a challenge than ever before. According to a July 2002 estimate, more than 3,800 new Web sites are created each day, more than 600,000 pages of HTML files are added daily to existing sites, and more than 250,000 new messages are posted to Usenet newsgroups (CyberAlert, 2002). Monitoring this overwhelming amount of information for accuracy has become a daunting, time-consuming, and expensive task for companies, even with the aid of public search engines such as Yahoo!, Google, and AltaVista. Nonetheless, although new forms of communication technologies have sped up the means by which falsehoods can be transmitted to vast audiences, they also can be used by rumor targets to rapidly disseminate rebuttals, corrections, clarifications, and evidence. This can be done by establishing and maintaining up-to-date, clear, and user-friendly company Web sites specifically for disseminating corporate news, FAQs, and copies of antirumor materials that are disseminated through other media.

Those individuals who maintain general or business-oriented Web sites pertaining to rumors, gossip, and urban legends (e.g., snopes.com) should be contacted and, as Lerbinger (1997) suggested for more traditional media, invited to participate in developing a rumor action plan. Such Web sites (identified from a periodic search of the Internet) should be regularly monitored and checked for any inaccuracies pertaining to the company as well as rumors targeting other companies in similar business domains. This task has become easier with the emergence of companies, such as eWatch, Inc., that scour Internet chat rooms, discussion forums, and other sites on behalf of their clients to detect any rumors or innuendoes in circulation that could damage corporate reputations and stock prices (Richtel, 1999; see Box 6.7). These services represent the new generation of more traditional so-called clipping services that monitored corporations' appearances in conventional news media.

To be sure, there are growing calls from the general public for efforts to help stem the spread of rumors on the Internet and through news wire services. Some news services, such as Bloomberg News, now require that their

---

Box 6.7. The Mrs. Fields Cookie Rumor

Following the not-guilty verdict in the murder trial of O.J. Simpson in October 1995, Mrs. Fields Cookies was rumored to have supplied free cookies to a victory party at the former American football star's home. The rumor originated on a broadcast of the televised news magazine show *Hard Copy*, which later recanted the story, and was repeated on CNN. Less than 10 minutes after the rumor was aired, a boycott of the cookie company was being organized on the Internet by an anti-Simpson Web site. The rumor quickly circulated on the Internet, leading to a single-digit drop in sales despite the company's quick actions to circumvent the rumor's spread (Bulik, 2000).

One innovative measure taken by Mrs. Fields to put a stop to the false rumor was to hire the Internet scouring company eWatch to search for online discussion groups where the rumor was appearing. Once located, corrective messages describing the false nature of the O.J. Simpson story were posted and, shortly thereafter, Mrs. Fields's cookie sales returned to normal.

The Internet searches originally conducted by eWatch involved manual monitoring of discussion groups and chat sites, but this method has more recently been supplanted by an approach utilizing automated *spiders*, which are search tools that scour sites for key words and phrases (Richtel, 1999). Humans then screen out the results to eliminate less fruitful leads prior to submitting a report to eWatch clients.

---

reporters confirm out-of-the-ordinary information from press releases before using it, to avoid the possibility that hoaxes like that involving Emulex will be reported (Berenson, 2000; see chap. 1). In addition, some public relations firms are now arguing for press release wire services to institute uniform security standards to lessen the risk that unfounded stories will enter the news pipeline. As for the Internet, the consequences of the dissemination of rumors over that medium, as noted in previous chapters, can be dramatic. The issue of policing the Internet and perhaps restricting the right to free speech is a contentious one and we do not purport to be able to resolve the thorny issues here. This is a challenge that governments, free speech activists, business leaders, and everyday Internet users will have to grapple with in the near future.

Press Conferences and News Releases

The press conference represents one of the most potentially effective weapons in a company's arsenal for confronting a rumor head on. This approach to getting the truth out through the media, if utilized, should be carried out as quickly as possible once the essential facts of the rumor crisis have been clarified and verified. A *press (or news) conference* involves an invitation to journalists to meet with a company spokesperson or officials at a specified time and place to receive an announcement, which is then discussed. This is a more direct approach than scheduling an *availability*, in which persons are made available to the media to respond to questions (Fearn-Banks, 1996). Even if the purpose of the conference is to explain why the firm can offer only a "no comment" response to the rumor crisis at the time, the very fact that there is a willingness to meet with the press, to admit the firm is aware of public concerns over the situation, and to demonstrate a genuine interest in being as forthcoming and honest as possible all serve to enhance the company's reputation during a difficult period.

Press conferences often are called on short notice to circumvent the likelihood that the news will be leaked to the media. Once details have been leaked, the interpretation and presentation of what is going on will no longer be under the control of the company concerned. Another kind of press event that can be very effective for countering contamination rumors is to invite journalists to a *facility visit*, which involves a visit inside a company facility, such as a factory, to demonstrate or describe production, packaging, or distribution processes. Whichever sort of press event is developed, there are essentially two keys to success: The event must have news value and it must be well-organized (Jefkins & Yadin, 1998).

The press conference typically is accompanied by a corporate news release, which essentially puts into print the critical information that is to be disseminated during the face-to-face meeting with the media. News releases are regularly used by companies to enhance their image and to establish good relations with the press and, accordingly, they are not limited to crisis situations. Jefkins and Yadin (1998), however, argued that nothing in public relations is carried out less effectively than the writing of news releases. In their view, a well-written news release tells the story the same way a journalist might have written it for a newspaper article, having been given the same information. Thus, the release should be written in a journalistic style, set out in manuscript style (as opposed to letter style), and appropriate to the specific news outlets to which it will be sent. Additional recommendations for writing a news release are presented in Box 6.8.

Rumor Control Centers

Although perhaps not the most obvious approach for fighting rumors from the perspective of marketplace hearsay, the independently run rumor control center can serve as a kind of objective intermediary linking companies and consumers. Such centers represent a long-standing institutionalized means of rumor control that evolved in the United States from the rumor clinics of World War II (Rosnow & Fine, 1976). In more recent periods, rumor control centers in one form or another have functioned during crisis and noncrisis situations, as a response to social disorders in Northern Ireland, in the aftermath

---

Box 6.8. Writing a News Release: The Seven-Point Formula

The news release can be used either to offset the emergence of rumors (by providing details, for example, about new products or business relationships) or to fight rumors that are presently in circulation (by countering the allegations with accurate information, clarifications, and denials).

Public relations expert Frank Jefkins argued that a well-written news release should be modeled after an informative newspaper article. In his widely-known seven-point formula, Jefkins identified the essential points to consider when checking data to be included in a news release (Jefkins & Yadin, 1998, p. 84):

1. *Subject.* What is the story about?
2. *Organization.* What is the name of the organization?
3. *Location.* Where is the organization located?
4. *Advantages.* What is new? What are the benefits?
5. *Applications.* What are the uses? Who are the users?
6. *Details.* What are the sizes, colors, prices, performance figures, or other details?
7. *Source.* Is this different from location (e.g., location might be where the work is done; source will be the head office address)?

---

of the 1979 accident at the Three Mile Island nuclear reactor in Pennsylvania, as a preventive social control mechanism operated by the U.S. Anti-Defamation League, and as a federation of nearly 500 Citizen Advice Bureaus in England that function during noncrisis periods to disseminate information to the public (Ponting, 1973).

The key function of the typical rumor control center is to respond to public concerns and questions, most commonly via the telephone and Internet, by providing accurate, verified information intended to offset the spread of falsehoods. A majority of centers exist as "intermittent" organizations that remain in a state characterized by minimum activity until the demands of the situation warrant full operation. Whereas most centers tend to limit their external relations to police departments, community relations agencies, the mass media, and local government offices, the centers represent a significant resource for a response to corporate rumors. Company officials would do well to maintain good relations with the operators of local and national rumor control centers and to recognize them as an important conduit for the provision of information to the general public during times of rumor crises. In-house centers also could be established, with the function of maintaining a quick-response unit for the corporate crisis management team when a rumor-related situation emerges. For specific recommendations about how to develop and run a rumor control center, see Rosnow and Fine (1976).

Legal Action

Often a last resort when other strategies for rumor control fail, a company may bring legal action to bear against those persons who are implicated in the generation or subsequent spread of malicious falsehoods. Lawsuits also may be undertaken against media sources responsible for presenting false stories about a company. In most cases in which this approach has been utilized, a settlement is reached before the case ever is brought to trial, with the responsible party issuing an apology or retraction and promising not to engage in any further rumor spreading. We described in Chapter 1 how P&G ultimately resorted to legal action to fight the Satan rumors that were targeting the company. As the P&G case revealed, the mere threat of lawsuits against rumor perpetrators can be an effective deterrent against the further spread of unfounded allegations against a company.

By the time a legal response is considered seriously, the rumor has likely already done some damage to the firm's profits and reputation and it will probably be too late to successfully identify the individual or groups responsible for originating the story. Some companies go so far as to hire detectives to try to track down a rumor's source. This move was undertaken by Snapple in 1992 as part of its successful all-out offensive to counter rumors that the company was supporting prolife causes (such as Operation Rescue), the KKK, and antigay groups (Franklin, 1998). Once the seriousness of the rumor campaigns became evident to Snapple officials the company began answering each and every letter (even supportive ones) it received from consumers with a statement of its neutral position toward the issues at the heart of the rumors. Affidavits were sent to that effect to other stakeholders, including distributors, retailers, and relevant political groups.

In response to anti-Snapple fliers that began to circulate at the peak of the rumor crisis, Snapple sent out its own counterfliers. It was at this point that a private detective was hired. Not surprisingly, the original source of the Operation Rescue rumor never was identified, although one person was found who appeared to be at the center of several rumor networks through which the rumor was particularly widespread. As in most cases of this nature, Snapple asked the person to desist from further rumormongering, which he did, thereby averting any formal legal steps.

To Respond or Not to Respond?

In some circumstances, idle speculation can have beneficial consequences for a firm. This largely pertains to cases in which active attempts are made to stimulate positive word-of-mouth about the company's products and services. In Chapter 4 I described the potential values that can be accrued through the favorable discussions that characterize some informal consumer interactions.

Rather than discouraging this sort of idle talk, it would be to the company's benefit to outwardly encourage such activity. The risk, of course, is that the informal nature of positive small talk may turn sour and what started out as positive content may ultimately be converted into negative rumormongering (e.g., when a disgruntled former customer enters the scene). In some cases, periodic contacts with brand loyals and opinion leaders can provide the opportunity for monitoring the course of word-of-mouth.

One marketing strategy that may be employed to stimulate favorable buzz is to preannounce new products some time before they are introduced on the consumer market. This is a frequently used strategy in communication industries, where the rate of innovation remains very fast and the level of competition can be fierce. In 1995, for example, several firms announced the DVD digital video disc standard, a full 3 years before its market introduction. Similarly, Microsoft revealed its Windows 95 computer operating system 2½ years before launch, and preannouncements of new video game consoles are common. Such preannouncements have been found to have a significant positive impact on the long-term sales of a new product (such as videocassette players) as well as contingent products that can be used with the preannounced product (such as video games and videocassettes). However, it also appears that when raised expectations attributed to preannouncements are not met once the new product appears on the market, the percentage of adopters in the population tends to be lower (le Nagard & Manceau, 1999). This suggests that, despite its obvious potential benefits, positive buzz can have negative effects when a company cannot coordinate its offerings to match raised consumer expectations.

CONCLUSION

A number of different methods can be implemented to actively fight both credible and noncredible marketplace rumors during each phase of the rumor life cycle. Given that each approach tends to have certain limitations, any one method will likely prove insufficient to offset potentially harmful allegations. Accordingly, for a rumor-control action plan ultimately to prove successful in undermining a rumor campaign, it should incorporate a combination of different approaches, and the targeted firm should be willing to implement the campaign forcefully and quickly. Recognizing that some rumors may in fact be true (or partly so) suggests that efforts in such cases should be directed to fixing the problem that gave rise to speculation and attempting to restore the company's good name through public relations measures. For false rumors, different strategies for countering the potentially damaging allegations must be based on the level of credibility of the rumors and characteristics of the audiences involved in their spread.

As Esposito and Rosnow (1983) cautioned, "it is important not to paint an overly optimistic picture of what can be accomplished in combatting rumors" (p. 49). The more direct offensive strategies described in this chapter—from outright rumor denials to legal action, all have the potential to convert a rumor crisis into a news story about a malicious, potentially damaging, false rumor. This conversion process often signals the death knell for even the most troubling marketplace rumors.

CHAPTER SEVEN

Managing the Organizational Grapevine

The choice is yours. You can be fearful of the grapevine, or you can strategically manage it. The grapevine will always exist. Is your organization capitalizing on it, or being victimized by it?

—Elizabeth Sharp-Henricks

Now that we have completed our consideration of marketplace rumors and the means for controlling them, we turn our attention in this final chapter to the management of rumors that circulate within the organization. In Chapter 2 we referred to such hearsay as internal rumors, or rumors that are of interest primarily to persons who are involved in some way with organizational operations, such as production, sales, and distribution. These are the sorts of rumors that comprise a large part of the scuttlebutt that flows through the grapevine, the unofficial, informal system of communication that functions within organizations in addition to official information networks.

As previously pointed out, the grapevine can have a variety of beneficial consequences for a firm, particularly during periods of change when much-needed information is at a premium and tensions are running high among the workforce (see Box 7.1). At such times, the grapevine's primary appeal is apparent in its usefulness for organizational sense making. In other circumstances, the grapevine can foster employee motivation and satisfaction, and it can encourage commitment to the organization and its corporate objectives. It is not surprising, then, that the spread of rumors through the grapevine, whether they pertain to possible impending takeovers, confidential personal matters, personnel changes, or gossip and scandal is not only openly acknowledged by many senior managers, but also encouraged, at least in the sense that the organization's informal system of communication is allowed to survive. The grapevine provides a fast and efficient means of distributing news, and also serves as a means by which management can

---

Box 7.1. Grapevine Functions

It is quite understandable that the organizational grapevine is often taken for granted. Its informal nature tends to belie the important role it can play in work settings. Some of the particular functions of the organizational grapevine are described here, along with examples of illustrative grapevine remarks (Cole, 1985).

1. The grapevine functions as a tool that enables the workforce to deal more effectively with uncertainty. "Is it true some of our benefits are going to be eliminated?" "Are they really considering moving our unit from Paris to Lyons?"
2. The grapevine can serve to reduce some of the anxiety associated with uncertainty and change by creating a forum for discussion and revealing that others share similar fears. "I thought I was the only one who was afraid they were going to transfer us once the merger goes through. It makes me feel better to know I'm not alone worrying about such things!"
3. The grapevine operates as a validator by which people can assess the credibility of an assertion or claim. The question "Say, did you hear …?" may induce the response, "Yes, and what's more …"
4. The grapevine can provide an outlet for negative thoughts or feelings about the organization. "This place expects too much from us for the money they are willing to pay us." "It's the manager's responsibility, so why doesn't she do it?"
5. The grapevine provides certain emotional gratifications that can raise levels of group cohesiveness and job satisfaction. By providing opportunities for socializing, it can serve to reduce some of the stresses that can undermine job performance and satisfaction. Unfortunately, however, the grapevine can function as a distraction from job tasks and efficient time management. "Boy, if we didn't have the chance to have our little discussions about last night's television shows or ball games, I wouldn't be able to handle this place! Whoops, is it really 11 a.m. already? Now, I'll never finish that work before lunchtime."

---

indirectly disseminate certain views that it may not want to communicate officially (Bennett, 1994).

Unfortunately, although it is true that much of the information that flows informally among a company's workforce turns out to be accurate (see chap. 1), the grapevine can also misrepresent reality. It can give rise to malicious, harmful rumors that distort information, create resentment, exaggerate the details of a situation, and work against the achievement of management plans and objectives. When the grapevine functions to these effects, active attempts are often made by management to suppress it. However, this is not always the best strategy because although the immediate problem may be temporarily controlled, this will likely be done at the risk of seriously damaging the overall well-being of the company.

The quotation appearing at the head of this chapter, which was taken from a description of an online continuing education seminar for financial professionals (www.passonline.com), acknowledges the positive and negative potential impact of the grapevine and maintains that it can be successfully managed for the good of the organization. To a great extent, this chapter is intended to elaborate on these same themes. More specifically, this chapter provides a number of recommendations for managing the informal communication system so that its beneficial effects are maximized and harmful rumors are neutralized or prevented from occurring. Because of these two sides to the grapevine, I emphasize approaches that are oriented toward the elimination of potentially damaging rumors, but not the informal communication system through which they travel. In fact, it is virtually impossible to completely shut down the informal flow of information in an organization. If suppressed in one context, it is likely to reemerge in another context or in a different form. This point also was emphasized by Mishra (1990), who observed, "The grapevine cannot be abolished, rubbed out, hidden under a basket, chopped down, tied up, or stopped … Organizations cannot 'fire' the grapevine because they did not hire it. It is simply there" (p. 6).

MANAGING INTERNAL VERSUS EXTERNAL RUMORS: SIMILARITIES AND DIFFERENCES

Given various similarities with respect to the underlying dynamics and functions of external marketplace rumors and internal organizational scuttlebutt, one is apt to find commonalities among the management approaches used to control both kinds of hearsay. Nonetheless, there are some significant differences, which I also intend to clarify in this section.

One of the outstanding similarities between marketplace and organizational rumors is observed in the rapidity with which they spread. Given the rather primitive connotations associated with the origins of the term *grapevine* (i.e., the stringing of telephone wires across battlefields) and the common image of organizational small talk as something limited to water cooler or lunchroom chatter, one might think that organizational rumors circulate at a snail's pace. This could not be further from the truth. In fact, the development in recent years of electronic transmissions of information by fax and e-mail have greatly facilitated the speed with which the grapevine functions, just as emerging communication technologies have added to the alacrity with which marketplace rumors are spread. From a rumor management perspective, this highlights the importance of taking steps immediately to counter the spread of false rumors through the grapevine before they become unwieldy and cause damage to the organization. Recent evidence, however, suggests that few companies have clear policies for dealing with the grapevine and that managers typically do not take an active role in managing or controlling informal communication networks (Crampton, Hodge, & Mishra, 1998).

Efforts to manage the internal grapevine require a certain degree of preparedness, as I similarly emphasized with regard to the external rumor mill. Company officials should obtain a good understanding of how the firm's grapevine operates, which members of the workforce are especially influential in the network, and the sorts of situations that are likely to stimulate grapevine activity. This implies that some management representatives should be capable of tuning into the grapevine without intruding on the communication network's normal functioning or having some other means of gaining awareness that the grapevine is stirring or becoming uncommonly active.

One means of carrying out the information gathering required for gaining an understanding of the organization's informal communication system is for management to develop good relations with the key communicators (or "bridgers") who are most active within that system. The approximately 10% of employees who play this role, by nature of their extensive connections, are sometimes referred to as liaison individuals (Rowan, 1979). This is a good term to describe the potential for having these individuals serve as links between the organization's decision makers and the rest of the workforce. Liaisons can provide insight into current concerns and information needs while obtaining accurate information that they can then feed back into the informal communication network.

These points also allow us to draw another useful parallel between the grapevine and external consumer networks. In Chapter 4 I described the important role that opinion leaders and network hubs play in the circulation of word-of-mouth and suggested that if company officials could identify such persons, they then would be in a better position to understand the forces giving rise to marketplace rumors and the means by which they are spread. Just as marketing researchers may conduct interviews with consumers and other corporate stakeholders to gain insight into the word-of-mouth communication process, so too, managers can attempt to obtain insight about the grapevine. This can be achieved during meetings with individual employees, by engaging the cooperation of liaisons, through exit interviews with outgoing personnel who are leaving the firm, and by holding discussions with "deadenders" who choose not to transmit grapevine rumors.

Despite these parallels, however, it also is important to point out some differences between the communication networks that function within the organization and those in the external marketplace. Rumors that circulate outside the firm are likely to reach and affect far greater numbers of individuals than grapevine rumors, and these persons may have little in common with each other. Whether they participate in the rumor process as transmitters or receivers, there will be extensive variability in the level of involvement among them. For some, such as consumers who are loyal purchasers of a brand that is targeted by malicious speculation, personal involvement will be high, whereas for others, the rumor may simply be seen as providing grist for casual conversation. These characteristics are less likely to hold for grapevine rumors, which travel through networks of individuals whose involvement no doubt will be high (by nature of their membership in the organization) and among persons who are apt to be more familiar to one another.

Moreover, organizational rumors are more self-contained than marketplace hearsay. This perhaps is less true today than it was in the past, given that mass media coverage of the successes and foibles of the corporate executives of major companies has been elevated to a a level once reserved for pop stars and major sports personalities. Although speculation about internal corporate affairs now is likely to interest a wider audience than before, the majority of internal rumors are still largely reserved for members of the workforce (as would be the case, for example, regarding speculation about which colleague will be assigned the next account involving an important client). Further, because of the (implicit or explicit) organizational hierarchy that characterizes the structure of most companies, the spread of specific rumors is likely to be less diffuse than is the case in the marketplace. Instead, one is likely to find patterns of communication that are characterized by either an upward, downward, or lateral flow of information. Rumors and their effects can be more readily tracked when they flow through narrowly defined organizational pathways (as compared, for example, to the patterning depicted in Fig. 4.5).

Communication Networks

Figure 7.1 depicts some examples of the kinds of communication networks that characterize the nature of interpersonal exchanges underlying the execution of specific work-related tasks in organizations. These networks affect employee access to information, with some persons occupying more central positions than others. Job effectiveness is likely to be influenced by the nature of the network and the complexity of the task involved. For example, performance on simple tasks tends to be optimized in the Y-structured communication network, less so in the chain, and least in a circle arrangement (Porter & Roberts, 1975). A wheel structure also is efficient for the carrying out of simple tasks, although individuals who occupy the ends of each spoke are apt to be dissatisfied as a function of simply receiving orders. By contrast, the circle network produces high performance and satisfaction for complex tasks, especially those that undergo changes in task requirements, because the structure allows for direct interactions among all participants.

It seems reasonable to assume that these varying network organizations are likely to influence the nature and extent to which individual members of

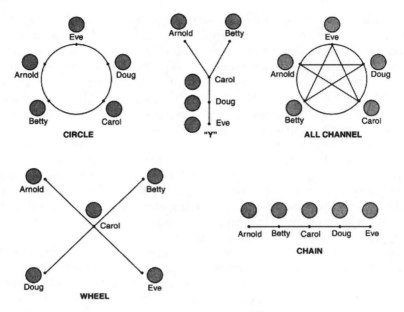

FIG. 7.1. Organizational communication networks. From Tosi, Rizzo, and Carroll (1994). Reprinted with permission of Blackwell Publishers Ltd.

the workforce participate in the grapevine. Those who occupy isolated positions in their task-oriented communication networks may be highly motivated to receive information that is otherwise inaccessible to them, unless they feel alienated by their position and choose not to participate in the grapevine at all. On the other hand, persons in central positions are more apt to be perceived as credible sources of valued information and may be more likely to recognize the influence potential of the grapevine. Managers should understand that it is these centrally placed individuals who may be especially prone to put their own personal "spin" on official communications when discussing them informally with others. Overall, the more restrictive the formal networks of communication, the more people will be induced to participate in the exchange of information through informal channels. Informal networks are likely to be less rigid than formal ones, but nonetheless not as open as external marketplace exchanges.

Communication Distortion

As is the case with marketplace rumors, distortions during the transmission process also are likely to occur when informal communications are transmitted within organizations. In addition to the expected mutations in the message that occur as it is transferred from one person to another (see chap. 4), in the organizational setting some communication distortions will have their origins in the nature of the company's hierarchical structure and differential status levels.

For example, in some organizations the formal chains of command may include so many levels from the top to the bottom that it will take longer for messages to reach intended final audiences and the probability is high that the intended message will be distorted in transit (Bennett, 1994). Should a communication have its origin at a higher echelon of the organizational hierarchy (e.g., a senior manager who informally transmits a message to a middle-level manager as a sort of trial balloon to test employee reactions to a proposed procedural or structural change), the meaning could readily evolve into something quite unintended. A message along the lines of "Word from the top is that they're thinking of redesigning the packaging plant" could ultimately become "They're going to eliminate some of our jobs" once the message reaches the company's packers.

Another way that communication distortion occurs in organizations is linked to the differential status level of the participants in the exchange. Porter and Roberts (1976) reported several findings linking status and power differences to the likelihood that errors or omissions will occur as a message is transmitted. For example, distortion in a communication that flows from lower to higher status persons increases as the status difference between the participants involved grows larger (as when a subordinate is interacting with a manager). Moreover, distortions as messages are passed up or down the organizational hierarchy are largely inevitable because individuals will tend to communicate (consciously or unconsciously) what they perceive to be in their own best interests. Thus, members of the workforce will be selective in what they choose to pass on to others. Managers will adapt messages to induce better performance from their subordinates, whereas the latter will shape their messages to obtain more rewards. In this respect, information in a structured setting such as the workplace functions as a valuable commodity. People can use it to obtain selfish or unselfish ends: to strengthen good relations with their coworkers, to mislead a rival for a promotion, to get one's project approved, to motivate performance in the work group, and so on.

There are other sorts of communication problems that can emerge in organizational contexts that are not particularly relevant to marketplace rumor processes. One has to do with the possibility that in organizations some individuals assume that others have been informed of certain issues when in fact they have not (Bennett, 1994). This might account for why some employees become dead-enders—they avoid repeating rumors that they have received from colleagues because, due to their position in the communication network, they assume that to repeat it would risk being redundant.

Additionally, people may transmit less than they know or not all that is necessary to keep coworkers sufficiently informed. This is especially the case in light of the demanding nature of many jobs and the new technologies that have emerged for information exchange. These days, more and more workers complain of not having sufficient time during a typical work week to attend to all the incoming information that is sent their way via telephone messages, courier, faxes, e-mails, and memos. To counter the possibility that our messages will be screened out (i.e., e-mails deleted, telephone messages not returned, memos left unread) we may choose to shorten the intended communication and wait to fill in the missing details in other ways. Returning to our earlier example, the "word from the top" might more accurately be "they're thinking of redesigning the packaging plant to be able to expand the production process and hire more people." That message, if sent in full, would be far less likely to evolve into one suggesting employee layoffs than if only the first part of the message was communicated.

MANAGEMENT OF THE GRAPEVINE: SOME BASIC RECOMMENDATIONS

It should be obvious that some of the communication processes associated with the spread of false, misleading, or distorted information through the organizational grapevine are unavoidable. In many cases, there is little that can be done to eliminate potentially damaging rumors that emerge in such an informal communication system, short of attempting to shut it down completely. However, efforts to suppress the grapevine, as previously suggested, not only are likely to fail, but will also eliminate an important channel through which members of the workforce can vent work-related stress, translate job tasks and company policies into more understandable language, nurture group cohesiveness, and the like.

Because of the informal nature of the grapevine, attempts to control the diffusion of rumors in organizations pose some of the same difficulties for managers as attempts to manage consumer word-of-mouth communications. Typically, there are no simple mechanisms for tracing the origins of the message or for controlling the spread of falsehoods. There are, however, several recommendations that can be offered for the effective management of the grapevine to reduce the likelihood that damaging rumors will emerge. Although these ideas are rather straightforward, it is far easier to recommend them than to effectively implement them in practice. Nonetheless, just as Joshua Jampol admonished that consumer goods officials should talk rather than remain silent to control marketplace rumors, so too does that suggestion apply to the management of rumors that flow through the organizational grapevine. This implies that in addition to providing employees with clear, accurate, and complete information, corporate managers should themselves become active participants in the grapevine.

As Mishra (1990) noted, many lower level and middle managers already actively participate in the grapevine. These individuals hold central positions in the network, serving as intermediaries between higher management and lower level employees by blocking and filtering out messages that flow between these two groups. Overall, however, managers have three options to select from in terms of their level of participation—they can ignore the grapevine and not participate in it at all, they can participate only when it serves a useful purpose (e.g., the need to obtain feedback relative to an ongoing issue), or they can become full, active participants.

Preventing Rumors Through Grapevine Management Efforts

Nothing we have said to this point would suggest that efforts should be made to suppress the grapevine to eliminate any problems linked to rumors, yet this is exactly what some company officials attempt to do. That this approach is ill-conceived from the outset is echoed in another statement taken from Sharp-Henricks's grapevine seminar description:

> In 1995 a high-tech firm in Colorado Springs, Colorado was experiencing some large-scale changes. Typical. But this company chose to distribute a memo indicating that "spreading rumors" would be grounds for immediate termination. This shows a fundamental lack of understanding of the grapevine, employee needs, and managers' ability to successfully use this informal system.

The threatening approach described by Sharp-Henricks is likely to create resentment throughout the workforce and would probably not succeed anyway, if only for practical reasons. As I explained in earlier chapters, rumors are elusive and ever-changing entities and much speculation that would fit common definitions of the term are not perceived as rumors by those who are actively engaged in its spread. Moreover, telling people to "stop spreading rumors" probably would do little more than fuel further speculation.

Rather than choosing to ignore or suppress the grapevine, managers can attempt to implement strategies that enable this communication vehicle to be used to the advantage of all parties concerned. Because grapevine activity tends to flourish during critical periods marked by uncertainty, it is especially important that as much timely information as possible be provided through formal communication channels with respect to key issues and decisions that are likely to have an impact on members of the workforce. Timeliness in the presentation of needed information is essential; just as described with respect to the marketplace, the longer a rumor circulates in the workplace, the more difficult it will be to effectively counter it with accurate facts. Formal communication channels must be maintained in an open fashion, providing people with the opportunity to obtain rapid clarifications following announcements, responses to questions about impending changes, and whatever else they may need to know to reduce the sorts of uncertainties and anxieties that give rise to rumors. With these points in mind, I offer the following guidelines for rumor prevention via management of the grapevine, largely adapted from a list developed by LRI Management Services, Inc. (www.lrims.com), a consulting firm that specializes in employee relations:

1. Do not ignore the grapevine. It is important for managers to recognize that information transmitted through informal channels may be perceived as more credible than official facts and thus may play a more influential role in determining organizational behavior. Moreover, the grapevine should be viewed as a channel through which potential problems in the workplace and employee concerns can be identified. Indeed, rather than ignoring this rich source of employee feedback, managers should exploit the grapevine for the purpose of enhancing management efforts.

2. Inform all key communicators within the organization about short-term and long-term prospective changes. These people include managers, supervisors, human resources personnel, team leaders, and active grapevine participants. All impending decisions regarding work procedures, company policies, or personnel should be announced as early as possible so that members of the workforce (at every level) have the opportunity to ask questions and any misperceptions can be corrected. At the same time, such announcements must be made with corresponding efforts to eliminate as many communication barriers as possible to avoid distortions and misunderstandings (see Box 7.2).

3. Regularly keep workers informed through as many communication vehicles as possible, including memoranda, news updates, regularly scheduled staff meetings, daily briefings, fliers, e-mailings, company newsletters, and other publications (see Box 7.3).

4. Clearly state the reason for change in the message communicated to employees. It is not enough simply to announce the change or to provide a detailed description of the nature of the change; to do so will naturally invite speculation. Care should be taken to maintain consistency in the messages disseminated through different media channels.

5. Educate employees about the reasons for not announcing news of business plans that have not yet been finalized. Workers need to appreciate that the premature release of information can impede negotiations with outside parties (as in the case of an acquisition or divestiture), affect investors' decisions, and cause customer relations problems.

6. Potentially threatening news should be communicated sensitively, recognizing the emotional underpinnings that give rise to rumors, and early enough so that employees can take steps to reduce the negative impact of a managerial decision that could affect their status in the company (e.g., ample time to search for another job).

Box 7.2. Communication Barriers

Effective communication within organizations requires the smooth flow of information through both formal and informal networks. A variety of obstacles, referred to as communication barriers, can impede the communication process, including the following examples (Bennett, 1994; Robbins, 1997):

1. *Message distortion.* When messages must be transmitted across extensive chains of command consisting of many levels, there is a high probability that content will be lost or distorted as the message moves from the sender to the ultimate destinations.

2. *Information overload.* As described in the text, the quantity of information has expanded to such a level in the contemporary organization that much is discarded or ignored. The decision about which messages to attend to and which to ignore (e.g., telephone message or letter?) is often arbitrary.

3. *Filtering.* This is the process by which a message source purposely manipulates information so that it will be more favorably received. For example, an employee may withhold certain information about some problems with an ongoing project when discussing the project with a boss. Consistent with the message distortion barrier (see Item 1), the more vertical levels in the organization's hierarchy, the greater the likelihood that information filtering will occur.

4. *Selective perception.* During the communication process, there is a natural tendency for a message receiver to selectively attend to and interpret messages consistent with one's needs, motivations, previous experiences, background, and other personal characteristics. Because of this selective perception process, there is no guarantee that a message will be decoded as intended by the sender. In short, people respond to objective reality in their own personal, subjective ways.

5. *Semantic imprecision.* Unclear, ambiguous, and vague terminology and grammar can serve as prime communication barriers. Office memos and other organizational media channels typically are not the places to try to impress people with one's command of the language; more likely, the intent is to make sure that people receive necessary information and that key points are stated clearly and concisely so that they are understood in the intended way.

6. *Suitability of messages for particular audiences.* As a corollary to the preceding points, messages must be designed with their intended audiences in mind. Professional jargon or terminology might not be understood by certain audiences. Typically, the style, tone, and specific terminology of a message intended for a fellow executive will be designed at a different level than that intended for lower level employees.

Box 7.3. Internal Communication Channels

Methods for communicating within organizations have greatly evolved in recent years. Whereas some traditional communication media, such as office memos and bulletins, have improved little (in many cases, they continue to be poorly written and lacking in conciseness), others, such as company newsletters and other in-house publications, have been enhanced greatly, with numerous items of personal interest to employees gradually replacing boring photos of company executives and the like (Cowling & James, 1994).

As Lengle and Daft (1988) noted, there is a close relationship between the medium through which messages are communicated and the effectiveness of the communication. In other words, certain media are more appropriate for communicating various kinds of messages. Along these lines, it is useful to think of internal channels of communication as varying along different dimensions. For example, one can consider the media choices as falling along a continuum of richness, ranging from lean to rich, where richness refers to the ability of a medium to allow for the simultaneous communication of multiple information cues (Richardson & Denton, 1996). Media ranging from standard, impersonal office notices, bulletins, memos, and personal letters are considered lean; by contrast, more interactive media, such as telephones, e-mailings, and face-to-face communications, are richer in nature.

Additionally, media can be considered as routine or nonroutine depending on their levels of complexity, novelty, and potential for ambiguity, misunderstanding, and emotional content. Nonroutine messages, which possess high levels of these attributes, are more effective when they are transmitted through rich communication channels, especially when little information is otherwise forthcoming (Richardson & Denton, 1996). Routine messages are more appropriately sent through lean channels, as when there is an overabundance of information. Accordingly, messages concerning impending large-scale changes or the implementation of a new corporate strategy are nonroutine and thus should be communicated through rich media, such as face-to-face team briefings. In change situations, when direct contact is not feasible, alternatives such as satellite hook-ups, closed-circuit television, teleconferences, and the like can be used. These latter channels tend to be frequently employed in companies with well-thought-out communication policies (Cowling & James, 1994).

---

7. Practice an open-door policy by encouraging employees to go directly to their supervisor or managers if they are confused about what is happening or want more information. The more employees trust management as being open and honest with them, the less likely they will turn to the grapevine as their sole or primary source of information.

8. Try to identify the most influential and active members of the grapevine (the liaisons) and then attempt to keep these individuals regularly supplied with current, factual information about the organization so that they can disseminate it to other grapevine participants. Attempt to solicit the participation of these influential persons as collaborators in formal efforts to improve workplace communication.

9. Take steps to reduce the opportunities for rumors to start. If an action is under consideration that could be threatening to employees or is likely to arouse anxiety or hostility, the facts should not be concealed or distorted to make them appear more acceptable. Rather, what is to be done and why should be explained, preferably through face-to-face meetings with those who could be affected. Trust and cooperation can be built by inviting the opinions or questions about the planned action from all parties concerned.

10. Should it become apparent that the grapevine is becoming uncommonly active and speculation is on the rise, efforts should be directed toward the identification and treatment of malicious rumors. This could involve the immediate establishment of a rumor control hotline or information center to track down misinformation, locate hotbeds of rumor activity, and relay the facts as quickly as possible.

It is important that each of these guidelines be followed without losing sight of the overall objectives—to reduce the psychological and situational conditions that are likely to promote rumor generation, to establish trust and confidence, and to enable the free flow of information throughout the organization. In working toward these objectives, employees will feel more confident that management is openly communicating the facts and giving them the information they need to know. This should serve to reduce anxieties and the need to turn to the grapevine for the "real" facts.

Responding to Organizational Rumors

Assuming that the grapevine management efforts discussed earlier will not be completely successful in preventing negative rumors, no matter how closely followed, attention then must shift to methods that can be implemented to put out the fire before any lasting damage can occur. The management of rumors in organizational settings presents some of the same challenges as attempts to control rumors in the consumer marketplace and many of the recommendations we offered for combatting marketplace rumors similarly apply to hearsay emanating from the grapevine. A key difference, however, is that within the context of an organization, management will tend to have more control over the dissemination of formal communications than when information must be transmitted to audiences in the external environment (Mishra, 1990).

Perhaps the most important recommendation that can be offered relative to responding to negative internal rumors is that attempts should be made to keep employees informed about what is going on and what may happen next. Information blackouts in the organization can have devastating effects because they will raise fears and can adversely affect productivity (e.g., people will be concentrating more on finding out what is going on than on their job-related tasks and responsibilities). As noted in the previous chapter, a "no comment" response (accompanied by an explanation about why matters cannot be discussed at the present time) may be required to deal with publics external to the company. By contrast, if this strategy is utilized internally among the firm's workforce it can seriously undermine credibility, trust, and cooperation.

A second recommendation for treating internal rumors requires that we re-iterate once again a point emphasized at various junctures in this book, which is that management should act promptly once the first signs appear that a rumor has begun to circulate. The longer a rumor remains in the grapevine, the more likely it will be believed and accepted as fact. Details will be altered to more readily conform to the needs, expectations, or fears of grapevine participants. A delayed response on the part of management likely will be perceived as a feeble effort at damage control and an attempt to save face.

Third, managers and supervisors should carefully attend to the content of what is being informally discussed among company personnel. Bearing in mind that about 80% of the information communicated through the grapevine is accurate, it is as important to focus on the part that is true as on the false content. This will be useful in developing a formal response and acknowledging that much of what people have heard informally is true will serve to reinforce the credibility of formal communications.

Another step that can be implemented to control internal rumors is to conduct periodic rumor training programs for representatives from all organizational levels. Beyond the obvious purpose of educating the workforce about the potentially harmful effects of false rumors, methods for identifying them, and means for their avoidance and treatment, the training sessions can provide an opportunity for management to learn whether rumors constitute a current problem for the firm.

One further recommendation is for managers to use the informal communication system to their advantage when attempting to counter false rumors. The grapevine can provide a fast and efficient means for distributing news and, when a "hot" rumor begins to circulate, people may choose to pay more attention to subsequent informal communications than to formal organizational messages. Each rumor situation, of course, will likely call for a different management strategy. In many cases, when emotions are running high, it may be imperative that managers meet directly with representatives of affected groups. For other situations, it may be less constructive to call a formal meeting, especially if insufficient details have not yet been assessed, including how active the rumor is, whether it is believable to those persons concerned, and so on. If the rumor has yet to catch fire and is not very credible, a more appropriate strategy would be to utilize a more low-key approach, such as sending a casual remark through the grapevine rather than calling attention to a falsehood that is likely to be impotent.

In addition to these general recommendations, some of the basic methods for controlling marketplace rumors described in the previous chapter can be adapted for dealing with internal rumors. For example, Mishra (1990) recommended a three-phase management program based on Esposito and Rosnow's (1983) information dissemination plan. The first phase constitutes the active gathering of information about the rumor, including the extent of its circulation, whether there is any degree of truth to its contents, and the sources underlying extant uncertainties and anxieties. Based on this information gathering process, a decision should be made about the probable life expectancy of the rumor: Is it likely to die a quick death or will it evolve into a potentially damaging force?

For problematic rumors, the next phase involves the preparation of a formal response. A decision will have to be made about whether the response will consist of accurate information that negates the premises of the rumor, a firm denial with accompanying explanation, or some combination of these approaches (see chap. 6 for more details about how the communication can best be formulated). Whatever information plan ultimately is put into action will likely be directed to audiences within the organization; however, the nature of the situation also may require a formal response directed externally through the mass media. Importantly, messages designed for internal or external dissemination must be consistent and mutually reinforcing. External communications will be necessary when there are information leaks or when it is believed that company personnel can be reached and influenced more effectively if they encounter the company's response on the evening televised news or on the front page of the local newspaper. Prior to proceeding to the third phase, it is important to reconsider whether the rumor is likely to continue to circulate or is apt to become irrelevant.

The final phase of the rumor management program is to implement the information plan. It is during this stage that Mishra (1990) argued that management should tap into the grapevine to identify and make use of key communicators. The antirumor messages designed during the preceding stage can be directed to grapevine liaisons, who then can be encouraged to actively transmit the information to others. Active managerial participation in the grapevine also can provide an opportunity to receive informal feedback from the workforce and monitor the impact that the information plan appears to be having over time. In fact, this is one way that a more formal message (e.g., one designed for the media) can be pretested prior to taking the risk that it could backfire and result in unintended effects. The message then can be re-designed to more effectively reduce uncertainties and help overcome tensions tied to the rumor.

The possibility that some messages can worsen the situation, no matter how much information gathering and preparation preceded their design, suggests the necessity for providing some sort of clearinghouse for personnel and the public to receive an immediate answer to lingering questions, clarifications, or further information. Thus, in addition to the information dissemination plan, many antirumor efforts would benefit from having a 24-hour rumor hotline or rumor control office in place during peak rumor periods. No matter how persuasive an office memo or explanatory Web site statement might be, people may not be totally reassured and convinced by the message until they speak directly to someone who is supposed to know the facts.

Enhancing Organizational Communication

In addition to effectively managing the grapevine, a variety of suggestions have been offered for improving communications in organizations to enhance efficiency and reduce the necessity for company personnel to turn to the grapevine for information that should be available through formal channels. Some of these suggestions are rather self-evident, especially when one imagines how a typical employee would ask to be treated by management. This is reflected in the following comments attributed to a senior vice president for human resources at Levi Strauss:

> [The challenges for managers are] to communicate with their employees, to give regular feedback, not just once-a-year appraisals, so there are no surprises. To give recognition, not just when merit increase time rolls around but to continually say thank you, and have some fun and make people feel appreciated. To allow diverse opinions and not to be so control-oriented as to deny you don't have all the answers. (Rawlinson, 1989, p. 53)

A multitude of specific factors have been found to facilitate or inhibit communication effectiveness, including characteristics of the participants (i.e., message sender and receivers), characteristics of the organization, the specific forms of communication utilized, and episodic (i.e., unique or temporary) characteristics surrounding the interaction (see Table 7.1). Although space does not permit a discussion of each of these influencing factors, a few do bear particular mention here because of their implications for rumor control. Our discussion of means for managing the grapevine to reduce the emergence of false rumors points to four individual characteristics as key facilitators of effective organizational communication: credibility, communication style, openness, and trust.

TABLE 7.1

Factors That Facilitate or Inhibit Communication Effectiveness

Factor	Examples	
Individual differences	Demographic characteristics Communication styles Trust	Source credibility Openness Anxiety
Organizational characteristics	Levels and status Communication roles Organizational links	Networks Complexity Reward systems
Forms of communication	Oral Nonverbal	Written Electronic
Episodic communication characteristics	Direction Overload and uncertainty	Message restraints Time restraints

Note. Adapted from Tosi, Rizzo, and Carroll (1994). Reprinted with permission of Blackwell Publishers Ltd.

Source Credibility. As is the case when firms attempt to communicate with their various publics to stem the flow of marketplace rumors, source credibility is critical in undermining falsehoods that travel through the grapevine. What this boils down to is whom to believe; for example, a grapevine confidant who casually passes on an unverified piece of news that could have a major impact on your employment status or a company official or superior who claims to know the true facts? Your decision will largely be based on your perception of the trustworthiness of the originators of the two conflicting messages, along with their expertise regarding the subject matter at hand, among other characteristics (see Fig. 7.2).

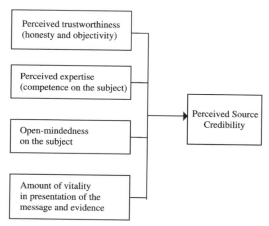

FIG. 7.2.   Factors related to source credibility. Adapted from Tosi, Rizzo, and Carroll (1994). Reprinted with permission of Blackwell Publishers Ltd.

The prevailing corporate culture will have an impact on perceptions of trustworthiness, which are influenced greatly by beliefs regarding whether or not the source has anything to gain if the message is accepted. If the culture is one marked by workers who put personal objectives ahead of corporate ones, suspicions could be high in exchanges one has with superiors or coworkers, depending on the situation and message subject. However, research has shown that when people argue for a position that is at odds with their own self-interest they tend to be perceived as more credible and thus more persuasive (e.g., Eagly, Wood, & Chaiken, 1978; Walster, Aronson, & Abraham, 1966). For example, assume that a manager drops a casual hint through the grapevine suggesting how a department can convince the company director to accept the purchase of an expensive new computer system. This advice might be perceived as more credible if it is presumed that the manager would stand to lose an anticipated salary increase if further major expenses are incurred by the company.

Communication Style.   People tend to adopt distinctive styles of communicating and this is especially evident in organizational settings. One may characteristically employ a subtle conciliatory approach to communication by attempting to convince another to accept a position while maintaining a respect for the other's opinions (Tosi et al., 1994). A more argumentative style of communicating is evident when a person strenuously declaims a specific position while bluntly rejecting any opposing views. Clearly, people can be expected to respond differently to such varying communication styles and may be expected to seek out (or actively avoid) consulting with others depending on the style of communication they expect to encounter. An employee may be averse to the possibility of an encounter with an argumentative supervisor, especially when the sought-after information can be obtained without hassle through the grapevine.

Effective managers are those who recognize that there are differences in communication styles and that frictions may ensue when there are sharp contrasts in the preferred style of the parties involved in an exchange. One approach to improving organizational communication has been developed and applied in the training of business personnel throughout North America by the management consulting group the Teren Company. Based on responses to the Teren test, a paper-and-pencil measure designed to identify an individual's characteristic communication style in one-to-one exchanges, people are classified according to where they fall on two dimensions: (a) tendency to express one's own feelings to others, and (b) tendency to actively seek out the feelings of others (see Fig. 7.3). For example, an individual who keeps feelings to oneself but tends to seek out and be sensitive to the feelings of others would be described by the communication style identified in the figure by quadrant D^1. According to the developers of the model, a D^1 person is apt to be perceived as

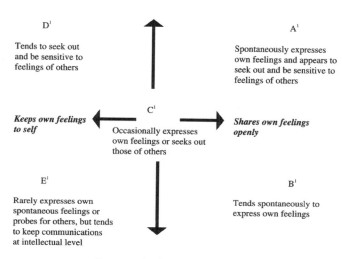

Seeks out the feelings of others

D¹

Tends to seek out
and be sensitive to
feelings of others

A¹

Spontaneously expresses
own feelings and appears to
seek out and be sensitive to
feelings of others

*Keeps own feelings
to self*

C¹

Occasionally expresses
own feelings or seeks out
those of others

*Shares own feelings
openly*

E¹

Rarely expresses own
spontaneous feelings or
probes for others, but tends
to keep communications
at intellectual level

B¹

Tends spontaneously to
express own feelings

Does not seek to know feelings of others

FIG. 7.3.   Communication styles. From The Teren Company (2002). Reprinted with permission of Richard J. Fortier, Teren Company, Inc.

sensitive and thoughtful (i.e., "warm"), and an excellent listener who encourages the free expression of feelings of others. This type of individual would be expected to be actively sought out to talk to and thus represents a good organizational barometer of employee morale.

By contrast, persons who fall into quadrant B¹ tend to be spontaneous with respect to their own feelings (which may be expressed without prompting), but appear to be disinterested in the feelings of others. This is the sort of person who is likely to be perceived as a poor listener and someone who is apt to dominate a conversation without being very sensitive to the reactions of others. With these and other such profiles in mind, a basic implication of the Teren model is that people can become more aware of differences between their own and others' characteristic communication styles and then make conscious adjustments in their interactions with others to obtain more positive outcomes. This idea is consistent with a well-known approach to interpersonal communication known as *accommodation theory*, which proposes that people tend to make adjustments in their speech, vocal patterns, and gestures to accommodate the persons they are interacting with (Giles & Smith, 1979).

Openness and Trust.   In organizational settings, openness and trust go hand-in-hand in facilitating the effectiveness of formal communications and countering the spread of rumors through the grapevine (see Box 7.4). This is especially true in situations involving interactions between members of the workforce who occupy different status levels. In terms of interpersonal relations, *openness* can be defined as "the willingness to listen, to accept 'bad' news, and to be tolerant of views divergent from one's own" (Tosi et al., 1994, p. 377).

Box 7.4. Rumor Management in French Consumer Goods Firms

That openness and trust can be effective mechanisms for rumor control in organizations was evident in my study of French consumer goods firms referred to at the start of Chapter 5. We obtained responses from 30 product or brand managers and communication specialists to a variety of questions pertaining to the kinds of internal and external rumors that come to their attention in their work and the strategies they use to deal with them (Kimmel & Audrain, 2002). When we asked our respondents to rate a list of 15 possible rumor effects, based on their overall experience with rumors, those listed most frequently as being moderate to severe in intensity were the following:

- Lowered employee morale.
- Loss of trust between management and staff.
- Increased employee stress.

As for the specific strategies used by our respondents for dealing with rumors, some strategies were identified as clearly more effective than others. In this case, respondents rated a list of 15 strategies in terms of how effective on average they were in preventing or neutralizing rumors. The following strategies were most frequently rated as being medium to high in effectiveness, in order of effectiveness:

- Attempt to increase trust.
- Provide people with requested information.
- Confirm or deny the rumor by a company official.
- Establish a task force to explore options.
- Establish a rumor hotline.

These results indicate that from the perspective of business professionals, being open and attempting to establish good relations with organizational personnel are approaches that go a long way to undermine some of the potential damage that can be wrought by false rumors in the workplace. This is likely accomplished through the reduction of uncertainties and anxieties linked to the rumor content. The least effective strategies? Not surprisingly, those most frequently identified by our respondents as being either never effective or low in effectiveness were those that are contrary to the spirit of openness and trust in the workplace:

- Ignore the rumor.
- Identify and punish people who spread the rumor.
- State "no comment."

When managers discourage the open expression of ideas and feelings from their subordinates, it is understandable that the latter ultimately would have little interest in approaching their superiors in times of uncertainty or have much confidence in the credibility of information they are receiving. Information is more apt to be considered credible when the source is trusted, and to the extent that members of the workforce lack trust in their superiors, the grapevine is more likely to be turned to and believed. However, it should be noted that perceptions of employee openness and credibility also influence how workers are treated by their superiors. In fact, there is evidence that superiors are more likely to communicate information to subordinates they highly trust (Roberts, 1984).

One approach to facilitating mutual trust and understanding among members of the workforce that has been applied in a number of organizations is known as *team briefing*. This refers to an interactive means of communication by which employers provide information to workers while ensuring that the information is both received and understood (Cowling & James, 1994). This method works as follows: Each level of management holds relatively short meetings (usually about 30 minutes in duration) with small groups of between 4 and 20 subordinates. During the meetings approximately 70% of the information transmitted concerns news of immediate relevance to the employees in attendance, with the rest devoted to general matters pertaining to developments in the organization as a whole. During each meeting, the employees are invited to openly respond to what they are hearing by asking questions and making comments. Team briefing is one example of a communication approach that adds the element of employee participation to the traditional process of transmitting information through formal communication means (e.g., memos, newsletters, and the like). Importantly, it assures that there is a two-way flow of information between employers and employees.

COMMUNICATING CHANGE

Perhaps in no other situations are all of the basic ingredients for the emergence and spread of rumors more evident than in those marked by organizational change. Changes affecting organizations may be signaled by economic, cultural, political, technical, or legal forces, such as when new markets and competitors emerge, new products are introduced or altered, new materials become available, and so on (Bennett, 1994). Developments in any of these areas can create enormous opportunities for a firm, but may also entail major difficulties that can have profound effects on the workforce. For example, certain technological innovations can render specific industries, job positions, or work skills obsolete. Thus, it is no wonder that both internal and external changes are accompanied by some degree of ambiguity, doubt, anxiety, fear, and, not surprisingly, rumors.

Organizational Change and Management Strategies

Some companies are more successful than others in implementing change and preparing the workforce for it. In Chapter 1, for example, I described Delta's exemplary Leadership 7.5 program, which was successfully implemented to facilitate the company's major restructuring during the mid-1990s. Communicating organizational change is a challenging and often daunting task that in most cases requires full disclosure and honest discussions with personnel at all organizational levels. As discussed in previous chapters, people tend to be averse to change in the marketplace and workplace. When workers or consumers are comfortable with the status quo, they do not have to worry about questions related to what will happen next and what the personal consequences will be on one's life. As Richardson and Denton (1996) noted with respect to human nature in change situations, "What we do not understand is always more frightening than what we know. It is always that way no matter how difficult the current situation. When times are tough, the appeal to return to old ways is almost irresistible" (p. 204).

Because change can be so emotionally unsettling for the workforce, many managers choose to say as little as possible to avoid worsening the situation by providing erroneous information or by causing people to feel that they have been misled. However, this approach is likely to fail because change periods are those during which people will be more in need of information about what is currently happening and what will happen next than at any other time. As discussed in previous chapters, when the details that people require to structure their thinking about what is going on in their world are not forthcoming, rumors will emerge in their stead to explain the unexplained. Consistent with these points, one CEO of a major American industrial firm noted that the key to changing companies is "consistent, persistent, and repetitive communications" (Richardson & Denton, 1996, p. 203).

Many corporate executives and managers who have gone through the experience of organizational change have reiterated that a major key to success is full disclosure and honest discussion regarding the various aspects of the change. In one large-scale survey of human resources and organizational development practitioners, more than 95% of 357 respondents identified (a) employee involvement in the planning and implementation of the change process, and (b) the articulation of the organization's future state by its leaders as two of the most important aspects of successful change efforts (Burke & Church, 1992). As noted in Chapter 1, one primary factor linked to failure during organizational change is employees learning about the change from outsiders (Semeltzer, 1991).

In a general sense, communications during organizational transition periods must satisfy the three criteria of quantity, quality, and credibility (Cowling & James, 1994). In short, this suggests that people must receive sufficient information about what is currently happening, what is planned, and what the likely outcomes of the change process will be. This information must be received from a trustworthy source and with available feedback channels in place. In fact, some of the same questions that must be considered by an organization during the planning of the change process can be used as a guide for identifying what specific information will have to be communicated to those in the organization who stand to be affected by the change. These include the following questions (Speers, 2000):

- For whom will the change likely have an impact?
- How will these persons be affected?
- Are they resistant to change? Why?
- Will their jobs change? How? What new skills do they need?
- What will the organization look like when the change is successfully completed?

It is clear from these sorts of questions that a successful change effort requires more than attention to the business process and technology changes, but also necessitates a clear focus on people-related changes. Unfortunately, there is sometimes the tendency for organizations to focus on the first two kinds of changes and neglect the third, due to an expectation that individuals who perform the tasks and other stakeholder groups will readily embrace and implement the change. To increase the likelihood that the company's personnel will respond positively to the change process, it is essential that they be given the opportunity to become involved early enough so that any barriers or resistance to change can be removed or minimized and to help ensure that the plans address their concerns. Otherwise, as soon as the first announcements about the planned change are communicated to the workforce, the grapevine will almost certainly quickly take over.

When preparing for organizational change, employer–employee planning sessions can be held during which ideas, reactions, and concerns are openly shared. For example, given that lower level employees are likely to be the ones who may be asked to perform their jobs differently, perhaps using new tools and equipment, it could be a useful exercise to invite them to identify more efficient ways of carrying out their job tasks in the new process (Speers, 2000). A summary listing of recommendations for change appears in Box 7.5.

Communication and the Change Process

Further insight into the effect of communication on the eventual acceptance of organizational change is provided by a longitudinal study conducted by Schweiger and Denisi (1991) involving a company undergoing a merger. The investigators assessed the relative effectiveness of an extensive communica-

---

Box 7.5. Guidelines for Communicating Change

1. Show wholehearted and visible support for the change from all of top management.
2. Give employees as much information as possible as early as possible.
3. Continue the communication effort throughout and even after the change, not just at the beginning.
4. Use "rich" communication media. The more face-to-face opportunities, the better.
5. Utilize supervisors and middle managers as key communication links. Encourage, train, and hold them accountable for keeping employees informed and providing a lot of interpersonal communication regarding the changes.
6. Recognize and be willing to deal with the emotional issues as well as the rational ones. Be prepared to deal with anxiety, fear, uncertainty, and mistrust. Openness, group meetings, toll-free telephone lines, and frequent newsletters can help.
7. Involve employees in the change process and in decisions about change as much as possible.
8. Use formal communication assessments to establish baselines, direct communication strategies, and monitor progress as the change unfolds.
9. Make sure that actions match words. The symbolic and behavioral communication of management is more important than its rhetoric. (Richardson & Denton, 1996, pp. 215–216). Communicating change, Richardson, P. & Denton, D. K., © 1996, Human Resource Management. Reprinted by permission of John Wiley and Sons, Inc.

---

tion approach implemented at one of the company's plants by comparing it to that of a control plant where typical announcements and memos were used to communicate the changes. Measurements were obtained at various times, including periods prior to anyone having knowledge of the change, during the change process, and several months following the change. The results revealed similar patterns of employee response during the early phase of the change process, with high levels of uncertainty, a decrease in job satisfaction, and a reduction of trust in management. However, 3 months after the announcement of the change, clear differences between employees at the two plants became evident, with the group that received extensive communications showing reduced uncertainty and higher levels of job satisfaction and trust, whereas the control group continued to decline on these factors.

The basic elements of the extensive communication approach leading to such positive long-term outcomes were similar to those implemented by Delta Airlines during its restructuring, including the following:

- A bimonthly merger newsletter to update employees on change developments.

- A telephone hotline to respond directly to employee questions.
- Weekly meetings involving the plant manager and the supervisor and employees of each unit to discuss issues and answer questions
- Individual meetings involving the plant manager and employees who were personally affected by a decision.

The positive results reported by Schweiger and Denisi (1991) and evidenced following Delta's Leadership 7.5 program highlight the important role that direct interactions between management representatives and employees can have during the change process, particularly in terms of promoting acceptance of the change throughout the workforce. Along these lines, employees at such companies as Chrysler and Hewlett-Packard have expressed their strong desire for receiving information during change periods through some direct form of interpersonal communication and have informed management that they would most like to receive information from their supervisors, as opposed to others in the organization (Richardson & Denton, 1996). The recognition that it may not be enough to obtain the trust and commitment of employees through the use of impersonal communication media, such as memos, newsletters, and bulletins alone was emphasized by a former CEO of an American firm, who claimed, "I've learned that just because you think it, write, it, or say it, doesn't mean employees hear it or believe it" (Rice, 1991, p. 112). These points also underline the importance of educating supervisors and middle managers in their communication role and training them to handle employee questions and concerns.

Change and the Grapevine

To this point, I have not said much about the role of the grapevine in the success or failure of organizational change, although its impact during transitional periods can be formidable. One of the most commonly cited reasons for the failure of change efforts happens to be the flow of inaccurate, negative rumors about what is going on (Semeltzer, 1991). Thus, it would hardly be in the interest of management to ignore the power of the grapevine during periods when the organization is undergoing some type of change, no matter how apparently minor in scope. The key, of course, is to attempt to minimize the risk of inaccurate information passing informally among the company's employees (see Box 7.6).

Some companies have successfully harnessed the potential negative power of the grapevine by supplementing the more formal communication approaches (such as newsletters, meetings, bulletins, etc.) with unexpected behaviors that are more likely to stimulate the grapevine than mere words. For example, Morrison (1993) described some of the actions of a Chrysler CEO that served to get people talking through the grapevine, such as visiting the com-

---

Box 7.6. Key Concerns When Communicating Internally

- *Communications must come from the top.* Visible senior management commitment is a must if you want communications to carry the necessary authority.
- *Devise a communications system.* Take into account formal and informal channels and try to incorporate the "grapevines" of your organization into the overall structure. Your system should be clear, concise, and speedy in dissemination. Do not give the gossips time to distort information.
- *Monitor and evaluate your system.* Continuous improvement is essential.
- *Be open and honest at all times.* In times of crisis or extreme change, do not try to smooth things over with half-truths and false reassurances. Be honest. Chances are that employees will find out the truth (secrets never stay under wraps for long in the corporate world) and you stand not only to lose face, but also the trust of all involved.
- *Combine written and face-to-face communications.* This mix provides the best results and demonstrates your commitment to employee awareness.
- *Be relevant.* Do not confuse employees with unnecessary facts and figures. Think what you would want to know if you were in their position, and if you're still unsure then ask—communication is a two-way process! (Kitchen & Daly, 2001, p. 48). Reprinted with permission of Emerald Publishing.

---

pany's customer relations department and taking the time to anonymously respond to questions and complaints from customers during 1 hour. The grapevine quickly got wind of this action and before long everyone was talking about how their CEO had taken the time to field complaints from customers. According to Richardson and Denton (1996), this is a good example of how "the grapevine only reports actions; it transmits what it sees and hears" (p. 213).

ORGANIZATIONAL COMMUNICATION: SOME SUCCESS STORIES

It should be clear from the preceding discussion that successful internal communications, transmitted credibly and completely through a system that allows for employee feedback, represents a key to successfully managing the grapevine so that the spread of inaccurate falsehoods can be kept to a minimum. As mentioned at the outset of this chapter, some companies are more successful at doing this than others. In this final section, we briefly consider some examples of companies that stand out in terms of managing internal communications better than others.

DuPont

One company that has a long, successful track record when it comes to managing both internal and external rumors is the chemical giant DuPont. To keep employees and consumers regularly informed, DuPont manages an interactive Internet site and utilizes an extensive multimedia mix, consisting of company magazines, newsletters, videotapes, and instant telephone and electronic newslines. These communication mechanisms are designed and regularly monitored through the hiring of outside consultants and pollsters. Because chemical companies stand the risk of a crisis linked to an explosion, oil spill, or some other disaster involving hazardous materials, DuPont has developed an extensive crisis management plan to anticipate and head off any rumors that might emerge. As early as the mid-1970s DuPont managed a hotline intended to report specific, up-to-the-minute details regarding any mishap or emergency as part of its Transportation Emergency Response Program (TERP; Rowan, 1979). The company now has in place an extensive corporate safety program that involves several procedures for educating and monitoring employees to reduce the risk of accidents and injuries.

DuPont also is one of a growing number of companies using a new approach to employee performance evaluation known as 360-degree evaluations. This procedure provides for performance feedback from a variety of contacts that employees might have in the performance of their jobs, ranging from mailroom personnel, secretaries, work teams, and peers to customers and mangers. Most organizations utilizing this process collect 5 to 10 evaluations per employee, although the number can reach as high as 25. As Robbins (1997) pointed out, this sort of evaluation approach fits well into organizations that actively make efforts to provide the entire workforce with a greater sense of participation in a range of company-related matters.

Other Top Performers

An analysis of the internal communications practices implemented by Fortune 500 firms was completed in 1999 by the Washington, DC-based Public Affairs Group, Inc. The analysis included an examination of each organization's performance along several dimensions, including employee focus on business objectives, engaging the employees, integrating staff functions, managing employee communications, and best use of technology, among others, to identify companies that stand out as the top internal communication leaders (Public Affairs Group, Inc., 1999). The complete list of "winners" that emerged from this study appears in Box 7.7.

According to the authors of the report, companies that place a strong focus on internal communications tend to rate high on *Fortune* magazine's list of best companies to work for. Other findings revealed that organizational change rep-

---

Box 7.7. Top Internal Communications Performers, 1999

- AT&TEmployee training
- AllstateEmployee engagement and viewing employees as an asset
- Southwest AirlinesEmployee innovation and involvement
- AvisEmployee involvement in customer service
- WalMartEmployee involvement and customer service
- SearsEmployee involvement in customer service; identification of the employee through special publications
- AdvanticaEmployee involvement with customers and a diversity initiative to drive employees on customer service
- MarriottEmployee involvement with customers and a diversity initiative to drive employees on customer service
- AIGGlobal Innovation and Employee Involvement to Return on Investment
- FedEx/UPSEmployee survey feedback systems
- General Electric360-degree feedback
- Ford Motor CompanyGlobal employee engagement and enthusiasm
- HallmarkEmployee involvement in creativity
- General ElectricEmployee involvement to understanding
- DisneyEmployee engagement and innovation
- Molson CanadaEmployee engagement and marketing

(Public Affairs Group, Inc., 1999). Reprinted with permission of Best Practices in Corporate Communications, an iVillage company, www.bpincc.com, tel.: 202.463.3780.

---

resents a core focus of the internal communications for 95% of the companies surveyed. Further, employee publications (both in hard copy and Internet formats) were found to have undergone a significant shift in recent years from simple deliverers of routine news announcements (such as birthdays, births, and special events) to central vehicles for supporting the business case. The internal communication approaches utilized at two of the top performing firms with respect to internal communication are briefly described next.

The Ford Motor Company.   Ford uses a variety of forums for sharing information with its employees and for obtaining feedback from them on a number of company, personal, and employment issues. The communication methods include "Let's Chat" e-mail notes from the company president, extensive use of the company's Intranet network, and publications and broadcasts from the Ford Communications Network. According to the Ford Web site page entitled "Creating a New Culture With Our Employees," the company holds a firm commitment for the development of effective two-way communications involving management and the Ford workforce (www.ford.com).

Recognizing the "essential and challenging" nature of effective internal communication, Ford uses a variation of the team briefing approach (a so-called cascade process) to communicate the company's strategies and tactics for achieving business objectives. This approach serves as a means for obtaining employee feedback and modifying specific plans for carrying out Ford's business strategies by having executives, union representatives, and employee resource groups discuss company plans through periodic, interactive meetings.

In response to concerns about growing stress and work–life balance issues among its workforce, Ford recently initiated a "Worklife Integration Week" at its facilities around the world to share information and provoke discussion about employee benefits, policies, and concerns. Employees responded very favorably to the Worklife Integration Week, which represented one aspect of a larger strategy to develop an employee-oriented culture at the firm. Further, Ford has taken steps to obtain and respond to additional employee feedback regarding the performance evaluation process. In fact, like DuPont, Ford also has adopted the 360-degree appraisal approach.

United Parcel Service (UPS).   Like the aforementioned companies, UPS also uses the performance review process as a primary forum for developing employee communication at the company. This is done primarily through an automated variation of the 360-degree feedback process ("Travelling Beyond," 1999). Prior to their participation in the performance review process, employees undergo a minitraining course about its purpose and how it is to be carried out. They also are provided with the opportunity to download additional information from the company's Intranet network. Once educated about the process, employees then initiate the peer-review process twice a year by asking peers, supervisors, and other company employees to evaluate them.

To provide education about both giving and receiving feedback from others in the organization, an in-house course was developed. The course uses role-playing exercises that, in part, are intended to assist managers in becoming more active listeners. Another mechanism for facilitating regular communication and feedback is the scheduling of informal "Talk, Listen, Act" meetings, during which managers, supervisors, and employees are encouraged to meet informally to discuss any issues. These meetings might be held during a coffee or lunch break and are expected to be scheduled at least a couple of times during the year, although they may be arranged impromptu at any time.

CONCLUSION

As this chapter makes evident, the organizational grapevine need not be feared. In addition to serving a useful role for an organization's employees, the informal communication network can be effectively managed to the benefit of the entire workforce. Managers not only can attempt to monitor the grapevine to tap into employee concerns and identify any misunderstandings flowing through the network in the form of false rumors; they also can become involved as active participants. Becoming active participants in grapevine discussions represents one strategy management can implement to enhance its image as a trustworthy and open source of information. By increasing the credibility of formal communications, employees should become more accepting of the information they receive from the top and less prone to accept unverified news through the grapevine relative to what is going on.

The enhancement of internal corporate communications promises to become an increasingly essential element of effective management as we progress further into the 21st century, where perhaps the only constant we can depend on is change. Internal communication no longer functions solely to sate the need to know, but also provides a mechanism for developing a corporate culture and set of values that are more in tune with the needs of the individual employee. In this day and age, the survival of a business depends on keeping both employees and consumers well informed.

References

Aaker, D. A. (1991). *Managing brand equity: Capitalizing on the value of a brand name.* New York: The Free Press.

AARP. (1994). *A report on the 1993 survey of older consumer behavior.* Washington, DC: Author.

Achrol, R. S. (1997). Changes in the theory of interorganizational relations in marketing: Toward a network paradigm. *Journal of the Academy of Marketing Science, 25,* 56–71.

Aditya, R. N. (2001). The psychology of deception in marketing: A conceptual framework for research and practice. *Psychology & Marketing, 18,* 735–761.

Ajzen, I. (1977). Intuitive theories of events and the effect of base-rate information on prediction. *Journal of Personality and Social Psychology, 35,* 303–314.

Allport, G. W., & Lepkin, M. (1945). Wartime rumors of waste and special privilege: Why some people believe them. *Journal of Abnormal and Social Psychology, 40,* 3–36.

Allport, G. W., & Postman, L. (1947). *The psychology of rumor.* New York: Holt, Rinehart & Winston.

Ambrosini, P. (1983). Clinical assessment of group and defensive aspects of rumor. *International Journal of Group Psychotherapy, 33,* 69–83.

American Marketing Association. (2001). *AMA code of ethics.* Chicago, IL: Author.

Anderson, E., & Weitz, B. (1989). Determinants of continuity in conventional industrial channel dyads. *Marketing Science, 8,* 310–323.

Anderson, P. H., & Sørensen, H. B. (1998). Reputational information: Its role in interorganizational collaboration. In P. Andersson (Ed.), *Track 1: Market relationships: Proceedings of the 27th EMAC conference: Research and practice* (pp. 13–29). Stockholm, Sweden: EMAC.

Anthony, S. (1973). Anxiety and rumor. *Journal of Social Psychology, 89,* 91–98.

Armour, S. (2002, February 5). *Year brings hard lessons, alters priorities for many.* Available: www.USATODAY.com

Armstrong, M. (1990). *How to be an even better manager* (3rd ed.). London: Kogan Page.

Arnold, V. D. (1983, July). Harvesting your employee grapevine: With insight, you can transform the rumor mill into a valuable communication network. *Management World, 12,* 28.

Bartlett, F. C. (1932). *Remembering.* Cambridge, England: Cambridge University Press.

Becton, N., & O'Harrow, R. O., Jr. (2000, September 2–3). Arrest in Emulex hoax shows Net's vulnerability. *The International Herald Tribune,* p. 11.

Belgion, M. (1939). The vogue of rumor. *Quarterly Review, 273,* 1–18.

Bennett, R. (1994). *Organisational behaviour* (2nd ed.). London: Pitman.

Berenson, A. (2000, September 5). Need for speed increases risk of costly errors at news wires. *International Herald Tribune,* p. 18.

Berge, J. (1991). Man's future. *The Northwest Technocrat, 53,* 1–3.

Bernstein, J. (2000, March 1). An ounce of prevention. *Crisis Manager: The Internet Newsletter About Crisis Management.* Available: www.bernsteincom.com

Berry, L. (1983). Relationship marketing. In L. Berry, G. Shostack, & G. Upah (Eds.), *Emerging perspectives on services marketing* (pp. 25–28). Chicago: American Marketing Association.

Bone, P. F. (1995). Word-of-mouth effects on short-term and long-term product judgments. *Journal of Business Research, 32,* 213–223.

Booth, S. (1993). *Crisis management strategy.* London: Routledge.

Brodin, O. (1995, January–April). Le contrôle des rumeurs [Rumor control]. *Décisions Marketing, 4,* 15–26.

Brodin, O., & Roux, E. (1995). *Food contamination rumors: Their effect on attitudes and individual reaction factors.* Paper presented at the 22nd International Research Seminar in Marketing Communications and Consumer Behavior, La Londe les Maures, France, June.

Brodin, O., & Roux, E. (1990). *Les recherches sur les rumeurs: Courants, méthodes, enjeux managériaux* [Research on rumors: Trends, methods, management stakes]. Working paper, Centre d'Etudes et de Recherche en Sciences Sociales, Economiques et Commerciales (CERESSEC), Cergy Pontoise, France.

Brunvand, J. H. (1981). *The vanishing hitchhiker: American urban legends and their meaning.* New York: Norton.

Brunvand, J. H. (1984). *The choking Doberman and other "new" urban legends.* New York: Norton.

Brunvand, J. H. (1986). *The Mexican pet: More "new" urban legends.* New York: Norton.

Brunvand, J. H. (1990). *Curses! Broiled again!: The hottest urban legends going.* New York: Norton.

Buckhout, R. (1974, December). Eyewitness testimony. *Scientific American,* pp. 23–31.

Buckner, H. T. (1965). A theory of rumor transmission. *Public Opinion Quarterly, 29,* 54–70.

Bulik, B. S. (2000, November 20). The brand police. Available: www.business2.com

Burke, W. W., & Church, A. H. (1992). Managing change, leadership style, and intolerance to ambiguity: A survey of organization development practitioners. *Human Resource Management, 31,* 301–318.

Chorus, A. (1953). The basic law of rumor. *Journal of Abnormal and Social Psychology, 48*, 313–314.

Cole, G. (1985, August). The office grapevine: What it can do for—and to—you. *MAT Scanner, 1*(8), 10–13.

Council for Marketing and Opinion Research. (1999). *Respondent bill of rights.* Available: www.cmor.org

Council of American Survey Research Organizations. (1995). *Code of standards for survey research.* Port Jefferson, NY: Author.

Cowell, A. (2001, March 30). Fading British retailer announces cutbacks. *The New York Times*, p. D1.

Cowling, A., & James, P. (1994). *The essence of personnel management and industrial relations.* New York: Prentice Hall.

Crampton, S. M., Hodge, J. W., & Mishra, J. M. (1998). The informal communication network: Factors influencing grapevine activity. *Public Personnel Management, 27*, 569–579.

Crawford, C. M. (1997). *New products management* (5th ed.). Chicago: Irwin.

Curran, J. M., Rosen, D. E., & Surprenant, C. F. (1998). The development of trust: An alternative conceptualization. In P. Andersson (Ed.), *Track 1: Market relationships: Proceedings of the 27th EMAC conference: Research and practice* (pp. 111–130). Stockholm, Sweden: EMAC.

CyberAlert. (2002). *Why monitor the Internet?* Available: www.cyberalert.com

Davis, K. (1953). Management communication and the grapevine. *Harvard Business Review, 31*, 43–49.

Davis, K. (1969). Grapevine communication among lower and middle managers. *Personnel Journal, 48*, 269–272.

Death of little Mikey. (2001, July 19). Available: www.snopes.com

Degh, L., & Vazsonyi, A. (1975). The hypothesis of multi-conduit transmission in folklore. In D. Ben-Amos & K. S. Goldstein (Eds.), *Folklore, performance and communication* (pp. 207–252). The Hague, The Netherlands: Mouton.

Delta Air Lines. (1994, May 6). Communications pose special challenge. *Delta Air Lines News Digest, 9*, 11.

Dery, M. (1999). *The pyrotechnic insanitarium: American culture on the brink.* New York: Grove.

de Vos, G. (1996). *Tales, rumors and gossip.* Englewood, CO: Libraries Unlimited.

DiFonzo, N., & Bordia, P. (1998). *How top PR professionals handle hearsay: Corporate rumors, their effects, and strategies to manage them.* Unpublished manuscript, Rochester Institute of Technology, Rochester, NY.

DiFonzo, N., Bordia, P., & Rosnow, R. L. (1994). Reining in rumors. *Organizational Dynamics, 23*, 47–62.

Donney, P. M., & Cannon, J. P. (1997). An examination of the nature of trust in buyer–seller relationships. *Journal of Marketing, 61*, 35–51.

Eagly, A. H., Wood, W., & Chaiken, S. (1978). Causal inferences about communicators and their effect on opinion change. *Journal of Personality and Social Psychology, 36*, 424–435.

Echoes of a hoax. (2000, August 30). *The International Herald Tribune*, p. 17.

Eisenberg, E. M., & Witten, M. G. (1987). Reconsidering openness in organizational communication. *Academy of Management Review, 12*, 418–426.

Ellis, W. (1991, June). African-American legends. *FOAFTale News*, pp. 10–11.

Engel, J. F., Blackwell, R. D., & Miniard, P. W. (1990). *Consumer behavior* (6th ed.). Chicago: Irwin.

Esposito, J. L. (1987). *Subjective factors and rumor transmission: A field investigation of the influence of anxiety, importance, and belief on rumormongering.* Unpublished doctoral dissertation, Temple University, Philadelphia.

Esposito, J. L., & Rosnow, R. L. (1983, April). Corporate rumors: How they start and how to stop them. *Management Review, 72*, 44–49.

European topics. (1994, June 2). *International Herald Tribune*, p. 4.

Evenson, B. (2001). Everything causes cancer—so relax. *National Post Online.* Available: www.nationalpost.com

Fearn-Banks, K. (1996). *Crisis communications: A casebook approach.* Mahwah, NJ: Lawrence Erlbaum Associates.

Fill, C. (1995). *Marketing communications: Frameworks, theories, and applications.* New York: Prentice-Hall.

Fine, G. A. (1979). Cokelore and Coke lore: Urban belief tales and the problem of multiple origins. *Journal of American Folklore, 92*, 478–479.

Fine, G. A. (1980). The Kentucky fried rat: Legends and modern society. *Journal of the Folklore Institute, 17*, 222–243.

Fine, G. A. (1986). Redemption rumors: Mercantile legends and corporate beneficence. *Journal of American Folklore, 99*, 208–222.

Fine, G. A. (1987). Welcome to the world of AIDS: Fantasies of female revenge. *Western Folklore, 46*, 192–197.

Fiske, S. T., & Taylor, S. E. (1991). *Social cognition* (2nd ed.). New York: McGraw-Hill.

Folkes, V. S. (1988). Recent attribution research in consumer behavior: A review and new directions. *Journal of Consumer Research, 14*, 548–565.

Fournier, S. (1998). Consumers and their brands: Developing relationship theory in consumer research. *The Journal of Consumer Research, 24*, 343–373.

Franklin, G. (1998). Snapple rumor. *The AFU and Urban Legend Archive.* Available: www.urbanlegends.com

Franks, J. (1999, May 4). *Procter & Gamble claims Amway spread Satan rumors about its trademark logo.* Available: www.foxnews.com

Freedman, A. M. (1991, May 10). Rumor turns fantasy into bad dream. *The Wall Street Journal*, p. B1.

Frémy, D., & Frémy, M. (Eds). (2002). *Quid 2003*. Malesherbes, France: Éditions Robert Laffont.

Friedman, M. (1999). *Consumer boycotts: Effecting change through the marketplace and the media.* New York: Routledge.

Friedrich, J., Fetherstonhaugh, D., Casey, S., & Gallagher, D. (1996). Argument integration and attitude change: Suppression effects in the integration of one-sided arguments that vary in persuasiveness. *Personality and Social Psychology Bulletin, 22,* 179–191.

Ganesan, S. (1994). Determinants of long-term orientation in buyer–seller relationships. *Journal of Marketing, 58,* 1–19.

Gayda, M. (1992, December). La rumeur. *Forensic,* pp. 45–48.

Geyskens, I., Steenkamp, J.-B., Scheer, L. K., & Kumar, N. (1996). The effects of trust and interdependence on relationship commitment: A trans-Atlantic study. *International Journal of Research in Marketing, 13,* 303–317.

Giles, H., & Smith, P. M. (1979). Accommodation theory: Optimal levels of convergence. In H. Giles & R. St. Clair (Eds.), *Language and social psychology* (pp. 45–65). Oxford, England: Blackwell.

Gladwell, M. (2000). *The tipping point: How little things can make a big difference.* London: Little, Brown.

Glazer, M. (2001, June). Microwaved water. *FoafTale News, 49,* pp. 3–4.

Goggins, S. M. (1978). *The wormburger scare.* Unpublished master's thesis, University of Georgia, Athens, GA.

Goldstein, M., & Carrel, L. (2000, August 25). *How a stock hoax happened.* Available: www.smartmoney.com

Gordon, I. (1997). *Relationship marketing.* Toronto, Canada: Wiley.

Gordon, M. (1999, August 27). *Psst! Tips, hot and otherwise.* Available: www.SmartMoney.com.

Greenberg, B. S. (1964). Diffusion of news of the Kennedy assassination. *Public Opinion Quarterly, 28,* 225–232.

Greenberg, J., & Baron, R. A. (1997). *Behavior in organizations* (6th ed.). London: Prentice-Hall International.

Griffin, T. (1994). *International marketing communications.* Oxford, England: Butterworth-Heinemann.

Hall, M. (1965). The great cabbage hoax: A case study. *Journal of Personality and Social Psychology, 2,* 563–569.

Hammonds, K. M. (1995, April 3). Hoop dreams. *Business Week.*

Hannerz, U. (1967). Gossip, networks, and culture in a Black American ghetto. *Ethnos, 32,* 35–60.

Hartley, R. F. (1998). *Marketing mistakes and successes* (7th ed.). New York: Wiley.

Hastings, G. B., & MacFadyen, L. (2000). A day in the life of an advertising man: Review of internal documents from the UK tobacco industry's principal advertising agencies. *British Medical Journal, 321,* 366–371.

Healey, P., & Glanvill, R. (1996). *Now! That's what I call urban myths.* London: Virgin Books.

Herr, P. M., Kardes, F. R., & Kim, J. (1991). Effects of word-of-mouth and product attribute information on persuasion: An accessibility-diagnosticity perspective. *Journal of Consumer Research, 17,* 454–462.

Hoax sends tech stock plunging. (2000, August 25). Available: www.USATODAY.com

Holak, S. L., Lehmann, D. R., & Sultan, F. (1987). The role of expectations in the adoption of innovative consumer durables: Some preliminary evidence. *Journal of Retailing, 63*, 243–259.

In Wake of Enron Scandal. (2002, May 21). *The New York Times Community*. Available: www.businesswire.com

Institute of Public Relations. (2003, April 3). *Careers in PR: What is public relations?* Available: www.ipr.org.uk

Jaeger, M. E., Anthony, S., & Rosnow, R. L. (1980). Who hears what from whom and with what effect: A study of rumor. *Personality and Social Psychology Bulletin, 6*, 473–478.

Jefkins, F., & Yadin, D. (1998). *Public relations* (5th ed.). London: Pitman.

Johnson & Johnson. (1982). *The Tylenol comeback*. New Brunswick, NJ: Johnson & Johnson Corporate Public Relations.

Jones, T. O., & Sasser, W. E. (1995, September–October). Why satisfied customers defect. *Harvard Business Review*, pp. 88–99.

Jung, C. G. (1917). A contribution to the psychology of rumor. In C. Jung (Ed.), *Collected papers on analytical psychology* (pp. 166–190). New York: Moffit Yard.

Jung, C. G. (1969). The concept of the collective unconscious. In *Collected works* (Vol. 9, Part 1, pp. 87–110). Princeton, NJ: Princeton University Press. (Original work published 1936)

Jung, C. G. (1959). A visionary rumor. *Journal of Analytical Psychology, 4*, 5–19.

Junk-bond rumors hit Deutsche Bank. (2000, October 12). *International Herald Tribune*, p. 13.

Kamins, M. A., Folkes, V. S., & Perner, L. (1997). Consumer responses to rumors: Good news, bad news. *Journal of Consumer Psychology, 6*, 165–187.

Kapferer, J.-N. (1989). A mass poisoning rumor in Europe. *The Public Opinion Quarterly, 53*, 467–481.

Kapferer, J.-N. (1990). *Rumors: Uses, interpretations, and images*. New Brunswick, NJ: Transaction.

Katona, G. (1975). *Psychological economics*. New York: Elsevier.

Kelley, H. H. (1973). The process of causal attribution. *American Psychologist, 28*, 107–128.

Kelly, J. W. (1985). Storytelling in high-tech organizations: A medium for sharing culture. *Journal of Applied Communication Research, 13*, 45–58.

Kimmel, A. J. (2003). Ethical issues in social psychology research. In C. Sansone, C. C. Morf, & A. T. Panter (Eds.), *Handbook of methods in social psychology*, Newbury Park, CA: Sage.

Kimmel, A. J., & Audrain, A.-F. (2002, August). *Rumor control strategies within French consumer goods firms*. Paper presented at the 110th American Psychological Association conference, Chicago.

Kimmel, A. J., & Keefer, R. (1991). Psychological correlates of the transmission and acceptance of rumors about AIDS. *Journal of Applied Social Psychology, 21*, 1608–1628.

Kimmel, A. J., Moore, D., Rind, B., & Rosnow, R. L. (1992). *Mass-mediated rumor and gossip.* Unpublished manuscript. Fitchburg State College, Fitchburg, MA.

Kirkpatrick, C. (1932). A tentative study in experimental social psychology. *American Journal of Sociology, 38,* 194–206.

Kitchen, P. J., & Daly, F. (2001). Internal communication during change management. *Corporate Communications: An International Journal, 7,* 46–53.

Klein, N. (1999). *No logo: Taking aim at the brand bullies.* New York: Picador.

Knapp, R. H. (1944). A psychology of rumor. *Public Opinion Quarterly, 8,* 22–27.

Knox, S. (1997). The death of brand deference: Can brand management stop the rot? *Journal of Product & Brand Management, 6,* 49–55.

Koenig, F. (1985). *Rumor in the marketplace: The social psychology of commercial hearsay.* Dover, MA: Auburn House.

Koller, M. (1992). Rumor rebuttal in the marketplace. *Journal of Economic Psychology, 13,* 167–186.

Koller, M. (1993). Rebutting accusations: When does it work, when does it fail? *European Journal of Social Psychology, 23,* 373–389.

Kotler, P., Armstrong, G., Saunders, J., & Wong, V. (1999). *Principles of marketing* (2nd European ed.). London: Prentice-Hall Europe.

Kozinets, R. V. (1998). On netnography: Initial reflections on consumer research investigations of cyberculture. *Association for Consumer Research, 25,* 366–371.

Kreitner, R. (1983). *Management.* Boston: Houghton Mifflin.

La Monica, P. R. (1999a, September 17). *On the wings of rumor.* Available: www.SmartMoney.com

La Monica, P. R. (1999b, July 23). *Rumor has it that ...* Available: www.SmartMoney.com

Langenderfer, J., & Shimp, T. A. (2001). Consumer vulnerability to scams, swindles, and fraud: A new theory of visceral influences on persuasion. *Psychology & Marketing, 18,* 763–783.

Lazarsfeld, P., Berelson, B., & Gaudet, H. (1944). *The people's choice.* New York: Columbia University Press.

Lecerf, Y., & Parker, E. (1987). *L'affaire Tchernobyl: La guerre des rumeurs* [The Chernobyl Affair: War of the rumors]. Paris: PUF Editions.

le Nagard, E., & Manceau, D. (1999). *Why are so many communication products preannounced? Simulating the market for preannounced products in the context of indirect network externalities.* Unpublished manuscript, ESSEC, Cergy-Pontoise, France.

Lengle, R. H., & Daft, R. L. (1988). The selection of communication media as an executive skill. *Academy of Management Executive, 2,* 225–232.

Lerbinger, O. (1997). *The crisis manager: Facing risk and responsibility.* Mahwah, NJ: Lawrence Erlbaum Associates.

Levin, J., & Arluke, A. (1987). *Gossip: The inside scoop.* New York: Plenum.

Levy, R. (1985). Foreward. In F. Koenig, *Rumor in the marketplace: The social psychology of commercial hearsay* (pp. v–vi). Dover, MA: Auburn House.

Lumley, F. E. (1925). *Means of social control.* New York: Century.

Magiera, M. (1993, June 21). Pepsi weathers tampering hoaxes. *Advertising Age,* pp. 1, 46.

Malheiro, A., Farhangmehr, M., & Soares, A. M. (2002, May). *Understanding consumers' ethical perceptions and their influence on purchase intention.* Paper presented at the 31st European Marketing Academy Conference, Braga, Portugal.

Mathur, L. K., Mathur, I., & Rangan, N. (1997). The wealth effects associated with a celebrity endorser: The Michael Jordan phenomenon. *Journal of Advertising Research, 37,* 67–73.

McFadden, R. D. (1986, February 18). Johnson is ending all capsules sold over the counter. *The New York Times,* pp. A1, B4.

McGregor, D. (1938). The major determinants of the prediction of social events. *Journal of Abnormal and Social Psychology, 33,* 179–204.

McGuire, W. (1965). Discussion of William N. Schoenfeld's paper. In O. Klineberg & R. Christie (Eds.), *Perspectives in social psychology* (pp. 131–152). New York: Holt, Rinehart & Winston.

Mexican Statement (1978, June). *The place of public relations in management education.* Public Relations Education Trust.

Mikkelson, B. (2001). *McSquirmies.* Available: www.snopes.com

Milgram, S. (1967). The small world problem. *Psychology Today, 1*(1), 60–67.

Miller, R. (1998). Locked in by loyalty. *Marketing, 2,* 157–163.

Mishra, J. (1990). Managing the grapevine. *Public Personnel Management, 19,* 213–225.

Misra, S. (1992). Is conventional debriefing adequate? An ethical issue in consumer research. *Journal of the Academy of Marketing Science, 20,* 269–273.

Mizerski, R. W. (1982). An attribution explanation of the disproportionate influence of unfavorable information. *Journal of Consumer Research, 9,* 301–310.

Moorman, C. G., Zaltman, G., & Deshpandé, R. (1992). Relationships between providers and users of marketing research: The dynamic of trust within and between organizations. *Journal of Marketing Research, 29,* 314–329.

Morgan, R. M., & Hunt, S. D. (1994). The commitment–trust theory of relationship marketing. *Journal of Marketing, 58,* 20–38.

Morin, E. (1971). *Rumor in Orléans.* New York: Pantheon.

Morrison, M. K. (1993, December 10). Communicating total quality: Solutions for operational effectiveness (pp. 1–5). *The Conference Board Communications Workshop.* Chicago.

Mowen, J. C. (1995). *Consumer behavior* (4th ed.). Englewood Cliffs, NJ: Prentice-Hall.

Myers, D. G. (1996). *Social psychology* (5th ed.). New York: McGraw-Hill.

Naughton, T. J. (1996). Relationship of personal and situational factors to managers' expectations of organizational change. *Psychological Reports, 78,* 313–314.

Nilson, T. H. (1998). *Competitive branding.* Chichester, England: Wiley.

Nkpa, N. K. U. (1975). Rumor mongering in wartime. *Journal of Social Psychology, 96,* 27–35.

Noble, B. P. (1993, January 19). Snapple escapes the grip of rumors. *The New York Times*, pp. D1, D7.

O'Connell, V. (2001, September 14–15). Companies use ads to show they are still in business. *The Wall Street Journal Europe*, p. 12.

O'Connor, J., & Galvin, E. (2001). *Marketing in the digital age* (2nd ed.). Harlow, England: Pearson Education.

Oracle Hit by Management Shakeup Rumors. (2000, November 2). Available: www.SmartMoney.com

P. & G. drops logo from its packages. (1985, April 25). *The New York Times*, pp. D1, D8.

Pearlstein, S. (2002, June 29). Outbreaks of scandal follow an old pattern. *International Herald Tribune*, p. 11.

Pearson, C. M., & Mitroff, I. (1993). From crisis prone to crisis prepared: A framework for crisis management. *Academy of Management Executive, 7*, 48–59.

Pearson, S. (1994). Relationship management: Generating business in the diverse markets of Europe. *European Business Journal, 6*, 28–38.

Perloff, R. M. (1993). *The dynamics of persuasion.* Mahwah, NJ: Lawrence Erlbaum Associates.

Peterson, W. A., & Gist, N. P. (1951). Rumor and public opinion. *American Journal of Sociology, 57*, 159–167.

Philip Morris becoming Altria (2001, November 16). Available: www.USATODAY.com

Ponting, J. (1973). Rumor control centers: Their emergence and operations. *American Behavioral Scientist, 16*, 391–401.

Porter, L. W., & Roberts, K. H. (1975). Communication in organizations. In M. D. Dunnette (Ed.), *Handbook of industrial and organizational psychology* (pp. 1553–1589). Chicago: Rand McNally.

Pound, J., & Zeckhauser, R. (1990). Clearly heard on the street: The effect of takeover rumors on stock prices. *Journal of Business, 63*, 291–308.

Prasad, J. (1935). The psychology of rumor: A study relating to the great Indian earthquake of 1934. *British Journal of Psychology, 26*, 1–15.

Procter & Gamble rumor blitz looks like a bomb. (1982, August 9). *Advertising Age*, p. 1.

Public Affairs Group, Inc. (1999). *Best practices in corporate communications: Internal communications.* Washington, DC: Author.

Rawlinson, H. (1989, August). Homegrown for HRM. *Personnel Administrator, 34*, 53.

Reeve, A. J. (1994). *Turn me on, dead man: The complete story of the Paul McCartney death hoax.* Ann Arbor, MI: Popular Culture, Inc.

Rehak, J. (2002, March 23). The recall that started them all. *International Herald Tribune*, p. 15.

Reichheld, F. F. (1996). *The loyalty effect: The hidden force behind growth, profits, and lasting value.* Boston: Harvard Business School Press.

Reichheld, F. F., & Sasser, W. E. (1990, September–October). Zero defections: Quality comes to services. *Harvard Business Review*, pp. 301–307.

Reid, T. R. (2002, May 21). Buying American? It's hard to know. *International Herald Tribune*, p. 2.

Reingen, P. H., & Kernan, J. B. (1986). Analysis of referral networks in marketing: Methods and illustration. *Journal of Marketing Research, 23*, 370–378.

Rice, F. (1991, June 3). Champions of communication. *Fortune*, pp. 111–120.

Richardson, P., & Denton, D. K. (1996). Communicating change. *Human Resource Management, 35*(2), 203–216.

Richardson, W., & Richardson, R. (1992). *Business planning: An approach to strategic management* (2nd ed.). London: Pitman.

Richins, M. L. (1983). Negative word-of-mouth by dissatisfied consumers: A pilot study. *Journal of Marketing, 47*, 68–78.

Richtel, M. (1999, March 8). Technology; Trolling for scuttlebutt on the Internet. *The New York Times*, p. C4.

The Right Moves, Baby. (1993, July 5). *Business Week*, p. 36.

Ring, P. S., & Van De Van, A. H. (1992). Structuring cooperative relationships between organizations. *Strategic Management Journal, 13*, 483–498.

Robbins, S. P. (1997). *Organizational behavior* (5th ed.). Upper Saddle River, NJ: Prentice-Hall.

Roberts, K. H. (1984). *Communicating in organizations*. Chicago: Science Research Associates.

Rogers, E., & Shoemaker, F. F. (1971). *Communication of innovations: A cross-cultural approach*. New York: The Free Press.

Rosen, E. (2000). *The anatomy of buzz: How to create word-of-mouth marketing*. New York: Doubleday / Currency.

Rosenberg, G. (1999, May 24). A universal water cooler for griping. *International Herald Tribune*, p. 9.

Rosenthal, E. (2000, December 15). MSG, scourge of Western palates, is the "King" of spices for Chinese. *International Herald Tribune*, p. 2.

Rosnow, R. L. (1991). Inside rumor: A personal journey. *American Psychologist, 46*, 484–496.

Rosnow, R. L. (2001). Rumor and gossip in interpersonal interaction and beyond: A social exchange perspective. In R. M. Kowalski (Ed.), *Behaving badly: Aversive behaviors in interpersonal relationships* (pp. 203–232). Washington, DC: American Psychological Association.

Rosnow, R. L., Esposito, J. L., & Gibney, L. (1988). Factors influencing rumor spreading: Replication and extension. *Language and Communication, 8*, 29–42.

Rosnow, R. L., & Fine, G. A. (1974). Inside rumors. *Human Behavior, 3*, 64–68.

Rosnow, R. L., & Fine, G. A. (1976). *Rumor and gossip: The social psychology of hearsay*. New York: Elsevier.

Rosnow, R. L., Yost, J. H., & Esposito, J. L. (1986). Belief in rumor and likelihood of rumor transmission. *Language and Communication, 6*, 189–194.

Rosnow, R. L. & Kimmel, A. J. (1979, June). Lives of a rumor. *Psychology Today*, 88–92.

Rosnow, R. L., & Kimmel, A. J. (2000). Rumors. In A. E. Kazdin (Ed.), *Encyclopedia of psychology* (Vol. 7, pp. 122–123). New York: Oxford University Press & American Psychological Association.

Ross, L., Lepper, M. R., & Hubbard, M. (1975). Perseverence in self-perception and social perception: Biased attributional processes in the debriefing paradigm. *Journal of Personality and Social Psychology, 32,* 880–892.

Rowan, R. (1979, August 13). Where did *that* rumor come from? *Fortune,* pp. 130–137.

Ryan, B., & Gross, N. (1943). The diffusion of hybrid seed corn in two Iowa communities. *Rural Sociology, 8,* 15–24.

Salmans, S. (1982, July 22). P.&G.'s battles with rumors. *The New York Times,* pp. D1, D4.

Schiffman, L. G., & Kanuk, L. L. (1994). *Consumer behavior* (5th ed.). Englewood Cliffs, NJ: Prentice-Hall.

Schlossberg, H. (1992, September 14). Latest image study finds mixed results for researchers. *Marketing News,* pp. 8–9.

Schlosser, E. (2001). *Fast food nation.* Boston: Houghton-Mifflin.

Schmeltzer, J. (1997, September 27). Gerber tries to control rumor rerun. *The News-Times.* Available: www.newstimes.com

Schumann, D. W., Hathcote, J. M., & West, S. (1991). Corporate advertising in America: A review of published studies on use, measurement, and effectiveness. *Journal of Advertising, 20,* 35–56.

Schweiger, D. M., & Denisi, A. S. (1991). Communicating with employees following a merger: A longitudinal field experiment. *Academy of Management Journal, 34,* 110–135.

Semeltzer, L. R. (1991). An analysis of strategies for announcing organization wide change. *Group and Organization Studies, 16,* 5–24.

Sharp, B., & Sharp, A. (1997). Loyalty programs and their impact on repeat-purchase loyalty patterns. *International Journal of Research in Marketing, 14,* 473–486.

Shavitt, S., Lowrey, P., & Haefner, J. (1998). Public attitudes toward advertising: More favorable than you might think. *Journal of Advertising Research, 38,* 7–22.

Shaw, D., & Duff, R. (2002, May). *Ethics and social responsibility in fashion and clothing choice.* Paper presented at the 31st European Marketing Association Conference, Braga, Portugal.

Sheatsley, P., & Feldman, J. (1964). The assassination of President Kennedy. *Public Opinion Quarterly, 28,* 189–215.

Shibutani, T. (1966). *Improvised news: A sociological study of rumor.* Indianapolis, IN: Bobbs-Merrill.

Simmons, D. B. (1985, November). The nature of the organizational grapevine. *Supervisory Management,* 39–42.

Smith, P. (1992). "Read all about it! Elvis eaten by drug-crazed giant alligators": Contemporary legend and the popular press. *Contemporary Legend, 2,* 41–70.

Smith, R. E., & Vogt, C. A. (1995). The effects of integrating advertising and negative word-of-mouth communications on message processing and response. *Journal of Consumer Psychology, 4*, 133–151.

Snapple Dragoon. (2000, June 25). Available: www.snopes.com

Snyder, M. (1974). The self-monitoring of expressive behavior. *Journal of Personality and Social Psychology, 30*, 526–537.

Solomon, M., Bamossy, G., & Askegaard, S. (1999). *Consumer behavior: A European perspective.* New York: Prentice-Hall Europe.

Speers, E. (2000, April). *A systematic process for managing change.* Paper presented at the International Association of Facilitation conference, Toronto, Canada.

Stern, B. B., & Gould, S. J. (1988). The consumer as financial opinion leader. *Journal of Retail Banking, 10*, 43–52.

A storm over Tropical Fantasy. (1991, April 22). *Newsweek*, p. 34.

Summers, J. O. (1970). The identity of women's clothing fashion opinion leaders. *Journal of Marketing Research, 7*, 178–185.

Sutton, H., & Porter, L. W. (1968). A study of the grapevine in a governmental organization. *Personnel Psychology, 21*, 223–230.

Swan, J. E., & Oliver, R. L. (1989). Postpurchase communications by consumers. *Journal of Retailing, 65*, 516–533.

Swartz, J. (2002, June 30). *Ebay faithful expect loyalty in return.* Available: www.USATODAY.com

TARP/Technical Assistance Research Program. (1981). *Measuring the grapevine: Consumer response and word-of-mouth.* The Coca-Cola Co., Atlanta, GA.

The right moves, baby. (1993, July 5). *Business Week*, p. 36.

Trademark of the devil. (2003, January 12). Available: www.snopes.com

Tosi, H. L., Rizzo, J. R., & Carroll, S. J. (1994). *Managing organizational behavior* (3rd ed.). Cambridge, MA: Blackwell.

Travelling beyond 360-degree evaluations. (1999, September). *HR Magazine, 44*.

Trout, J., & Rivkin, S. (1996). *The new positioning.* New York: McGraw-Hill.

Turner, P. (1993). *I heard it through the grapevine.* Berkeley: University of California Press.

Turner, P. A. (1992). Ambivalent patrons: The role of rumor and contemporary legends in African-American consumer decisions. *Journal of American Folklore, 105*, 424–441.

Tybout, A. M., Calder, B. J., & Sternthal, B. (1981). Using information processing theory to design marketing strategies. *Journal of Marketing Research, 18*, 73–79.

Unger, H. (1979, June). Psst—heard about Pop Rocks? Business rumors and how to counteract them. *Canadian Business*, p. 39.

Venkatraman, M. P. (1989). Opinion leaders, adopters, and communicative adopters: A role analysis. *Psychology & Marketing, 6*, 51–68.

Victor, J. S. (1993). The sociology of contemporary legends: A review of the use of the concept by sociologists. *Contemporary Legend, 3*, 63–83.

Walker, C. (1995, July). Word of mouth. *American Demographics*, pp. 38–44.

Walker, C. J., & Beckerle, C. A. (1987). The effect of anxiety on rumor transmission. *Journal of Social Behavior and Personality, 2,* 353–360.

Wallace, R. C., & Wallace, W. D. (1989). *Sociology* (2nd ed.). Boston: Allyn and Bacon.

Walster, E., Aronson, E., & Abraham, D. (1966). On increasing the persuasiveness of a low prestige communicator. *Journal of Experimental Psychology, 2,* 325–342.

Walton, E. (1961). How efficient is the grapevine? *Personnel, 28,* 45–59.

Weinberg, S. B., Regan, E. A., Weiman, L., Thon, L. J., Kuehn, B., Mond, C. J., Haegel, R., & Shorr, M. B. (1980). Anatomy of a rumor: A field study of rumor dissemination in a university setting. *Journal of Applied Communication Research,* 156–160.

Weinberger, M. G., Allen, C. T., & Dillon, W. R. (1981). The impact of negative marketing communications: The consumers union/Chrysler controversy. *Journal of Advertising, 10,* 20–28.

Weimann, G. (1982). On the importance of marginality: One more step into the two-step flow of communication. *American Sociological Review, 47,* 764–773.

Wells, G. L., & Loftus, E. F. (Eds.). (1984). *Eyewitness testimony: Psychological perspectives.* Cambridge, England: Cambridge University Press.

White, J., & Mazur, L. (1995). *Strategic communications management: Making public relations work.* Reading, MA: Addison-Wesley.

Whyte, W. H., Jr. (1954, November). The web of word-of-mouth. *Fortune,* pp. 140–143.

Wilcox, D. L., Ault, P. H., & Agee, W. K. (1989). *Public relations: Strategies and tactics.* New York: HarperCollins.

Wilson, J. R. (1994). *Word-of-mouth marketing.* New York: Wiley.

Wisenblit, J. (1989, Spring). Crisis management planning among U.S. corporations. *SAM Advanced Management Journal,* 31–41.

With euro on the way, this French shortage is no small change. (2001, April 3). *International Herald Tribune,* p. 8.

Wurman, R. S. (1989). *Information anxiety.* New York: Doubleday.

Yandell, B. (1979). Those who protest too much are seen as guilty. *Personality and Social Psychology Bulletin, 5,* 44–47.

Yeshin, T. (1998). *Integrated marketing communications: The holistic approach.* Oxford, England: Butterworth-Heinemann.

Zerner, E. H. (1946). Rumors in Paris newspapers. *Public Opinion Quarterly, 10,* 382–391.

Zivney, T. L., Bertin, W. J., & Torabzadeh, K. M. (1996). Overreaction to takeover speculation. *The Quarterly Review of Economics and Finance, 36,* 89–115.

Author Index

Subject Index